Virginia Woolf and Classical Music

Introduction

In 1918, Roger Fry decorated a small keyboard instrument made the previous year by the great instrument-maker and exponent of early music, Arnold Dolmetsch. The spinet, now in the Courtauld Gallery, London, embodies an eclectic mix of stylistic elements and wider social, political and aesthetic associations.[1] Its closed lid displays abstract shapes suggestive of the Salon Cubism of Gleizes and Metzinger (Fig. 1). Amid the rectilinear shapes a circle, resembling the soundhole of a stringed instrument, contains parallel lines that apparently represent the location of the spinet's strings – a motif familiar from innovative works including Picasso's *Guitar* and Braque's *Woman with a Guitar* (both 1913). Where a historical spinet's strings would be placed at c. 30° to the keyboard, however, the painted strings of this instrument are depicted at a larger angle and thus are a further anti-mimetic if not strictly abstract detail. Several of the geometric shapes are painted in the scumbled marbling characteristic of Fry's decorative work (and indeed that of Bloomsbury more widely); the technique evokes the modernity and spontaneity of Post-Impressionist aesthetics but also more traditional decorative styles, the latter connotation augmented by the soft colours of the decorative scheme as a whole.

When a player or viewer lifts the lid, however, the abstract but superficially innocuous design of the upper case is replaced with a startling figurative image of a female nude (Fig. 2).[2] The figure is awkwardly placed, her angular limbs butting against the edges of the lid, the muscularity of her legs and haunches contrasting with the delicate modelling of the relatively small head. She appears physically powerful, even monumental, yet also constrained by the space, her posture suggesting restriction or confinement within the instrument's case. Her face with its 'Oriental' eyes is turned away, as if eluding or resisting the viewer's gaze, and her braced left arm may suggest that she is about to rise, to move away, perhaps even to burst (out of) the frame. She appears both reticent, because

Figure 1   Spinet, 1917–18; Roger Eliot Fry (designer); Arnold Dolmetsch (manufacturer). Private Collection, on long term loan to The Courtauld Gallery, London. LF.1958.XX.254.

concealed by the closed lid, and bold, because of the theatricality of her unexpected entrance. Her nudity, and the pastoral or Arcadian landscape behind her, suggests that she is a muse rather than a specific model: she may be there to inspire the player or singers, but also perhaps to 'speak' herself. Certainly, the amplification of the sound that would result from the opening of the lid associates her with music and symbolically with female song or utterance. Is she, perhaps, a distant cousin of St Cecilia or one of the classical muses – Erato, Euterpe or Polyhymnia – associated with erotic poetry, elegiac poetry or hymns? As a naked muse, she evokes the classical world, yet her cropped hair and stylised physique are provocatively modern; the ambivalence of the figure's historical connotations is intensified by her placement in front of a plum coloured curtain reminiscent of sixteenth-century Italian mannerist painting.

This instrument, then, combines historical and avant-garde elements, most obviously encapsulated in the unexpected combination of an instrument popularised in the seventeenth century with contemporary decorative aesthetics. The contrast is not, however, simply between instrument and decoration, or between the revivalist intent of the French-Czech

Figure 2

instrument-maker and the avant-garde English art critic and decorator: both shared these modernising and historical sympathies (for all that Dolmetsch was appalled by Fry's decoration).[3] As we have seen, the spinet's decorative scheme evokes both contemporary and traditional aesthetics, and Dolmetsch's instrument itself embraces both elements – historical in design but made of modern, relatively inexpensive, materials such as plywood. This instrument has further nostalgic or revivalist elements: it is the same shape as the 'portable "jet" spinet', which Dolmetsch designed for transporting in London's hackney carriages, and it imitates the polygonal shape of its most popular predecessor among keyboard instruments, the virginals. The spinet may appear to recall a world of leisured affluence and of genteel, perhaps specifically feminine, domestic music making but its materials are typical of the relatively modest means of Arts and Crafts manufacturers and consumers (and indeed, historically, spinets were cheaper, space-saving alternatives to larger keyboard instruments). As Charlotte de Mille has noted, the spinet, which was superseded by the technically more advanced harpsichord, appears a strange choice of instrument for revival but Dolmetsch may have championed it precisely because it celebrated domesticity and music in the home.[4] Fry's and Dolmetsch's collaboration might appear at first glance an unequivocally insular – some would say escapist or self-indulgent – project in which to be engaged during the final stages of the First World War: the instrument's decorative scheme makes no overt allusion to its contemporary political context, and even the ravaged European landscape is forgotten or imaginatively restored in the depiction of an unspoiled pastoral scene. However, St Cecilia's brutal, protracted martyrdom has more resonance in these late-war and immediate post-war contexts than is first apparent, and the collaboration can itself be read as an instantiation of Fry's internationalist, pacifist politics more generally.

Virginia Woolf was certainly aware of Fry's interest in early music and keyboard instruments and (like the young Huxley)[5] saw this very instrument at Fry's home in Guildford.[6] In her 1940 biography of her friend, Woolf notes that in the late 1890s Fry's future wife Helen was decorating a Dolmetsch harpsichord that Fry greatly admired; his suggestions about the design 'sealed' their courtship.[7] *Roger Fry* also quotes his rapturous account of a visit from André Gide in 1918, who played the spinet just after Fry had acquired it:

> 'I feel almost as tho' I'd always known him. That I haven't is evident from the fact that I never suspected him of being a musician, but when I showed him my virginals he sat down and played all the old Italian things I have as no one ever played them before and exactly as I have always dreamt that they should be played. He's almost too ridiculously my counterpart in taste and feeling. It's like finding a twin.' (*RF*, 211)[8]

The instrument – and the personal, creative and aesthetic relationships associated with it – were '"real event[s]"' (*RF*, 211) to Fry at a time of despair caused by personal circumstances and the war. And Woolf's recognition of its importance was prompted, I would suggest, by the fact that music had a similarly vital part in her own emotional, social and creative lives.

The spinet introduces many of the topics that this study explores:

But one of the things I decided as I listen[ed] (its difficult not to think of other things) was that all descriptions of music are quite worthless, & rather unpleasant; they are apt to be hysterical, & to say things that people will be ashamed of having said afterwards. (D, I: 33)

'Impressions at Bayreuth' notes – and celebrates – the 'lack of tradition and of current standards' in music criticism and aesthetics ('the freest and happiest state that a critic can wish for'), yet observes that music criticism is often compromised by 'vague formulas, comparisons, and adjectives'; 'we are miserably aware how little words can do to render music' (E, I: 288, 291). Nevertheless, Woolf's own writing includes just such 'descriptions of music' and many of her formal innovations in narrative perspective, structure and form are indebted to musical techniques and genres: as Crapoulet asserts, music was 'undoubtedly the basis for some of her many literary innovations' although elaboration on this suggestive possibility is beyond the scope of her study.[40] In 1924, anticipating 'hours of solid pleasure' hearing the cellist Guilhermina Suggia, Woolf stated, 'its music I want; to stimulate & suggest' (D, II: 320) and in 1920 she attended a concert with the explicit aim of 'tak[ing] notes for my story' ('The String Quartet') (D, II: 24). In her diaries she repeatedly conceives of specific prose works, or sections thereof, in musical terms and in 1930 planned a 'broadsheet' that would include comment on 'Art, politics, Lit., music' (D, III: 292). Woolf's 'musicalization of fiction' (to use Huxley's famous phrase)[41] is more discreet, and her overt allusions fewer, than those of contemporaries including Lawrence, Forster, Richardson, Huxley, Joyce or Stein, yet as Crapoulet persuasively suggests,

[t]he concealed or covert aspect of her 'musicalization' is directly linked to her conception of the musicalization of fiction as a means of achieving both an impersonal and an expressive style of writing which draws the reader towards her artistic vision [. . .] unconscious of the craft which has brought the artist's vision before our minds.[42]

Given all this evidence of the scale and diversity of Woolf's 'musical life', I conclude by considering its place in Woolf's critical reception and the factors that have made recent attention to the 'musicalization' of her fiction possible.

Hearing Woolf

To many of Woolf's early reviewers, the parallels between (contemporary) music and her work were self-evident. In a 1932 article in the

Manchester Guardian, part of which Woolf copied into her diary, their principal music critic, Neville Cardus, friend of Beecham and Barbirolli, admiringly noted:

> nobody has so far commented upon the obvious fact that English music is at the present time following very closely a certain line of development of English fiction [. . .] A man might as well hang himself as look for a story, a plot, in 'To the Lighthouse' of Mrs Woolf, or in the Third Symphony of Arnold Bax [. . .] But there is more than headwork in the art of it all; there is muscle and nervous fibre, despite the lack of insinuating heart-throbbing tunes. (*D*, IV: 75, n)

V. S. Pritchett stated that reading *The Waves* had made a 'profound impression', 'as if a Bach fugue had built a cathedral in my head'; M. C. Bradbrook objected to its structure of 'futile counterpointing'; and in the preface to her 1937 French translation of the novel, Marguerite Yourcenar compared the 'individuals' to 'instruments', the 'design' to *The Art of the Fugue* and the 'musical narrative' as a whole to Mozart's symphonies.[43] Furthermore, Ines Verga's six-page pamphlet *Virginia Woolf's Novels and their Analogy to Music*, published in Buenos Aires in 1945, began with the proposal that her novels 'can always be compared to music' and continued, invoking Forster's description of *To the Lighthouse* as 'a novel in sonata form': 'it is not only in their form that her words are musical [. . .] but in the sensations they arouse'.[44] Observations such as Verga's that the distinctively modern aspects of Woolf's prose – resistance to causality and chronology, the use of repetition and the representation of memory – paralleled the innovations of composers such as Debussy now have renewed critical purchase, not only in relation to Woolf's writing but also to literary modernism more widely.[45] Brad Bucknell notes that the 'resistance to lexicality, and indeed, to syntactic, syntagmatic, and even narrative linearity and causality [. . .] appears in different forms in the "musical" experiments of the moderns'.[46] However, despite widespread contemporary perceptions of the 'musicality' of Woolf's writing (whatever diverse or imprecise meanings that term had), the significance of music to her life and work was quickly overlooked. Quentin Bell's biography (1972) is exemplary: music may have 'delighted' Woolf, but it formed merely a 'background to her musings'. 'She was not, in any strict sense, musical', he observed. 'She played no instrument; I do not think that she could follow a score with any deep comprehension.'[47] Perceptions of the incidental importance of music to Woolf's life and work have been persistent: to date, no academic monograph on Woolf and music exists, and most scholarly guides and popular introductions make little or no reference to music.[48]

Several studies on the literary influence of Wagner's operas, published from the 1960s, noted Woolf's explicit allusions to the composer and provided preliminary explorations of her formal debts to his music,[49] but, with rare exceptions (notably Jane Marcus), the insight that Woolf's prose was profoundly shaped by and engaged with music was not taken up by Woolf scholars. We have, as Marcus put it, collectively failed to 'hear' Woolf's work.[50] This was due, in part, to limitations in our critical practice: with the specialisation of much formalist music criticism and the loss of musical literacy as a standard element of formal education, critics have felt ill equipped to explore this intermedial subject. It has, too, been eclipsed by the extensive fine work on Woolf and the visual arts. Attention to Woolf's 'musical life' has also surely been hindered by the perception that her taste in music was considerably, even embarrassingly, more conservative than her knowledge of the visual arts, literature, philosophy and science. Certainly, throughout her life Woolf listened most frequently to the canonical Austro-German baroque, classical and Romantic repertoire, and her diegetic allusions to named works and composers in the fiction are most often to these figures. As Joyce E. Kelley puts it, she 'curiously avoids' alluding to musical modernists but instead uses the music of their predecessors in 'far from old-fashioned' ways.[51] Recent reconsiderations of Woolf's relations to the Victorians (pre-eminently, Steve Ellis' outstanding study) have emphasised the nuanced, dynamic part that the Victorian period played in constructions of modern(ist) writing. The nineteenth century was crucial, for instance, to expressions of masculinist modernist aesthetics differentiated from 'feminine', 'sentimental' Victorian writing and music, and such oppositions inform Woolf's uneasy relationship to figures including Vernon Lee – and to nineteenth-century music.[52] Consequently, although Woolf's knowledge of contemporary music was greater than has often been recognised,[53] this study concentrates on pre-twentieth-century repertoire, especially on Woolf's responses to nineteenth-century music: Wagner and Beethoven in particular loom large. Music, I will suggest, played a major role in Woolf's attitude towards her immediate predecessors.

As increased attention has been paid to Woolf's music education and to her activities as a performer, a listener and a reader of music criticism, we have gained an enhanced awareness of the precision and subtlety of her musical allusions and of the degree of her creative engagement with music. We have begun to attend to Woolf's autodidacticism in music as in other fields; her typically discreet allusions to music are now more frequently read as attentively as her intertextual allusions to fiction, poetry and drama. Statements such as her claim that she didn't listen like 'musical people' or that she was ill equipped to comment on music are no longer accepted at face value but recognised as responses to gendered contempt for female music education, dislike of academic music criticism, or reluctance to criticise friends' compositions.[54]

This critical shift has been aided by recent criticism exploring the influence of sound technologies and acoustic experience on Woolf's fiction and on modernist aesthetics more broadly. If not always directly about the musical aspects of Woolf's work – formal or diegetic – such criticism provides pertinent contextual material about Woolf's exposure to street noise, for instance, and to recorded sound, and has contributed to the increased attention to the aural qualities of Woolf's prose, its representations of sound and aural experience, and to the soundscapes of her life.[55] Melba Cuddy-Keane begins her account of the new sound technologies with the observation that '[w]e are, it would appear, at the beginning of writing a history of sound in the twentieth century and the task before us is vast.'[56] The 'aural turn' in criticism, exemplified in the work of theorists including Derrida, Kristeva, Cixous and Nancy, has also provided methodologies and critical vocabulary for exploring the aural qualities of Woolf's prose, and for considering her interest in and representation of non-verbal or non-semantic sounds – the wordless song of the beggar woman in *Mrs Dalloway*, the fractured sounds of the gramophone in *Between the Acts* and the 'slowed phonic pulse' of *The Waves*, for instance.[57] But this critical shift is due above all to the rise of interdisciplinary criticism, particularly the field of word-music studies, in the last twenty-five years. The proliferation of criticism on musical–literary relations has provided terminology and methodologies with which to analyse intermedial works,[58] creating a robust, congenial critical climate for this reappraisal of Woolf's work. The question of literality that troubled so much earlier criticism on literature and music has also been laid to rest and the metaphorical status of literature's claims to musicality embraced by scholars such as Eric Prieto: '[t]he question is not whether a metaphor is appropriate or not but where it can take us, how much it can teach us.'[59] Furthermore, in the last ten years much of this criticism has focused on the modernists, augmenting understanding of the shared aesthetic contexts, the intertextuality and the differences between Woolf's aesthetics and those of contemporaries including Joyce, Forster and Stein.[60] This study would have been impossible without this fine work, to which I am greatly indebted.

Prieto argues that the use of music in twentieth-century writing not only as a 'theme' but also as 'a model for the semiotic functioning of the narrative text' is 'unprecedented in literary history'. '[W]herever a musical model is present,' he continues, 'it always serves to further this inwardly directed mode of mimesis I call "listening in", where the primary object of representation is not the outside world but the subtly modulating interactions between consciousness and world.'[61] As his observations suggest, the majority of the criticism on literary modernism and music is formalist in approach, exploring music's influence on narrative techniques, textual structure and representations of interiority.[62] But, unusually among modernists, Woolf has also been the subject of criticism focused on the political significance of music. Despite Marcus' pioneering work, and the rise of Critical Musicology informed by Marxist, feminist, queer and cultural studies, however, the formative significance of music to Woolf's politics remains underexplored.[63] In part, this is due to the contested relationship between music and political discourses: despite Critical Musicology's attention to the socio-political work of music (on which my own readings draw), the (a)political status of music remains controversial, and to the 'musical idealists' music is absolutely separate and aloof from politics. Lawrence Kramer's observation about the late nineteenth century is still pertinent: 'esoteric conceptions of music based on its apparent transcendence of signification coexisted and contended with semantic conceptions that imbued music with poetic, narrative, or philosophical meaning and with socio-cultural agency'.[64] Further, as Linden Peach has argued, '[r]eading Woolf as a political novelist requires an approach posited on her oblique use of historical and contemporary events.' Her use of music typifies this obliqueness or 'cryptographic' approach;[65] we find fewer explicit references to music in her work than in the fiction of many contemporaries, and some of the musical allusions I discuss at length are brief, oblique and discreet. My readings place less emphasis on the theoretical implications of the mimesis Prieto describes than on the representation of 'the outside world' in Woolf's writing. I consider music's place in cultural history, attempting to recover some of the political discourses about music and ideas of music to which Woolf responded. Attending to the political significance of Woolf's uses of music concerns not only the diegetic representations of music in the fiction but also the politics of form itself. For this reason, this study adopts a two-fold focus, attending to the part that music plays in the socio-political vision of Woolf's writing – her understanding and representation of gender and sexuality, imperialism and pacifism, and national and ethnic politics – as well as in her aesthetics and formal experiments.

My analysis follows a broadly, but not rigidly, chronological sequence, discussing all the novels and selected essays and short fiction. The study begins with *The Voyage Out*, exploring Woolf's response to Wagner's *Tristan* and to the musical techniques of this and his other mature music dramas. It considers her critique of the *Gesamtkunstwerk* as a model of intermedial relations and teases out the ways in which Woolf's representations of interiority and use of narrative perspective were shaped by Wagner's work. Chapter 2 considers the way music shapes the sexual politics of this novel, concentrating on Woolf's representations of the Victorian period, the figure of the female pianist and the allusions to Beethoven. Chapter 3 extends the analysis to *Jacob's Room* and *Mrs Dalloway*, focusing on discourses about music, military aggression and the First World War. The following chapter continues the analysis of *Mrs Dalloway* by outlining the 'fugal' form of the novel. It places the novel in a matrix of medical, musical and military discourses about fugue before introducing two related questions: the association of music and homosexuality in *Mrs Dalloway*, *Jacob's Room* and *The Waves*, and the relationship between music and free association in *Mrs Dalloway*, *The Waves* and 'The String Quartet'. Chapter 5 returns to questions of national identity and nationalism, exploring music's role in the (de)construction of English identity in *Orlando*, *Between the Acts* and *The Years*. It takes as its focal points the early music and folk music revivals, and philo- and anti-Semitic narratives about music. The final chapter concentrates on *The Waves*, returning to Wagner and to Woolf's formal and political engagement with his work.

These readings spring from Woolf's diegetic references to named composers and works, most of which are part of the canonical repertoire – hence my use of the umbrella term 'classical music' as a synonym for art music, even if these allusions are as often to baroque and Romantic as to classical periods and styles. These readings are, inevitably, the product of my own training in literary criticism but I hope will be of interest to musicologists and historians as well as Woolf scholars; aiming for accessibility, I have kept the use of specialist musicological terms to a minimum. This study is suggestive rather than exhaustive: my principal focus is on Woolf's responses to art music, but there is much more to be said on this subject and also on the (formal) influence of folk music, jazz, recorded sound and ancient Greek music, for example, all of which are beyond the scope of my study. Subjects such as rhythm (so resonant a term in *To the Lighthouse* and *The Waves*), Bloomsbury's intermedial projects and popular music (prominent in *The Years* and *Between the Acts*) also cry out for extended consideration. This is far from a last word on Woolf and music, nor would I wish it to be. In 1927, Woolf wrote that the aim of future novels was to 'dramatise some of those influences which play so large a part in life, yet have so far escaped the novelist' – firstly, 'the power of music' (*E*, IV: 439). Her writing, as I hope will become clear, amply reflects this power.

Notes

1. Spinet, 1917–18; Roger Eliot Fry (designer); Arnold Dolmetsch (manu-facturer); Private Collection, on long term loan to the Courtauld Gallery, London. LF.1958.XX.254. The mechanism is not extant so it is difficult to know exactly what sort of instrument it was; I retain the Courtauld's clas-sification of 'spinet' throughout. For this detail I am indebted to Charlotte de Mille's Lecture at the Courtauld Gallery, London, May 2009 to the RMA Music and Visual Arts Group. I am grateful to Charlotte de Mille for making a copy available to me and for her account of this instrument, on which my own reading draws.
2. See Sutton (ed.), *Letters of Roger Fry*, II: 697 for a reproduction of Fry's sketch of the nude.
3. Spalding, *Roger Fry*, 221.
4. Lecture at the Courtauld Gallery, London, May 2009 to the RMA Music and Visual Arts Group. For an illuminating account of domesticity and Bloomsbury aesthetics, see Reed, *Bloomsbury Rooms*.
5. *Letters of Aldous Huxley* (Chatto and [*sic*] Windus, 1969), 169, cited in Spalding, *Roger Fry*, 221.
6. See *RF*, 275 in which Woolf notes that Fry replaced the 'virginals' with a gramophone in the 1920s.
7. *RF*, 101 and Spalding, *Roger Fry*, 58. For an account and reproduction of the 'green harpsichord', see Spalding, 58–9.
8. See also Sutton (ed.), *Letters of Roger Fry*, II: 433.
9. Despite errors in the biographical and historical material, Crapoulet's is a thoughtful study.
10. Details of performances throughout this study are from: Loewenberg, *Annals of Opera* and J. P. Wearing, *The London Stage*.
11. See Crapoulet, *Virginia Woolf*, 9–10 and Kelley, 'Virginia Woolf and Music', 418. I concur with Kelley's conclusion that her musical education was 'standard'.
12. See also *L*, I: 59, 62 and 88.
13. See Grand, *The Beth Book*, 163.
14. *New Statesman*, 16 October 1920, cited in *D*, II: 341.
15. Crapoulet reaches the same conclusion. *Virginia Woolf*, 11.
16. See, representatively, *D*, I: 142 and 206.
17. See Kelley, 'Virginia Woolf and Music', 425–6.
18. *D*, I: 83.
19. The Woolfs' attendance included: *Don Giovanni* twice in July 1913; *The Magic Flute* in June 1916; *Figaro* twice in 1917; *Die Entführung aus dem Serail* and *The Magic Flute* (*D*, I: 153–4) in 1918; *Don Giovanni* in 1920; *Cosi* in 1927; and *The Magic Flute* in 1925. See Leonard Woolf's Diary, University of Sussex, LWP II.R.3–29.
20. See, for example, *D*, I: 20 and II: 39; and *L*, II: 140.
21. See, for example, Entry dated 6 March 1913, Leonard Woolf's Diary, LWP II.R.5.
22. Entry dated 6 June 1909, Adrian Stephen's diary, University of Sussex, MHP. Ad. 13.
23. For details of their listening practice, see Leonard Woolf, 'Diary of Music

Listened To', University of Sussex, LWP IIR.64 and Leonard Woolf's 'Card Index of Gramophone Recordings', LWP Ad.28. The diary begins in 1939; it isn't possible to establish a complete record of their daily listening practice before that date although much detail is available from letters and diaries.

24. The cash accounts in Leonard Woolf's diary of 1925 confirm their subscription (entry dated 10 September 1925, 112 [LWP II.R.19]). Furthermore, correspondence in 1925 from Woolf to Robert Gathorne-Hardy, the society's secretary in 1925–6, enthusiastically expresses their intention to join and obtain records already issued by the society; they retrospectively acquired the first season's recordings, including the Schoenberg. (See the Robert Gathorne-Hardy collection, The Lilly Library, Indiana University.) It seems probable the Woolfs read *Gramophone*, as the NGS was advertised only there and in one insert in a concert programme at the Wigmore Hall, 9 February 1925. I am indebted to Nick Morgan, CHARM (AHRC Research Centre for the History and Analysis of Recorded Music) doctoral scholar under the University of Sheffield / British Library Concordat, for sharing his commanding knowledge of the NGS and for his unstinting help in interpreting this material.

25. For a list of NGS recordings, see www.pristineaudiodirect.com/LargeWorks/ NGS/NGS.html (accessed 18 September 2008).

26. This total includes erased entries on the verso of reused cards. See Leonard's 'Card Index of Gramophone Recordings'.

27. See Leonard Woolf's diaries of 1927 (LWP II.R.21) and 1930 (LWP II.R.24). I am grateful to Nick Morgan for drawing this to my attention.

28. Lee, *Virginia Woolf*, 239.

29. Crapoulet, *Virginia Woolf*, 21. Kelley similarly suggests that the 'idea of the [female] composer' was more influential than Smyth's music: 'Virginia Woolf and Music', 427–8.

30. *Virginia Woolf and the Languages of Patriarchy*, 51.

31. Garnett, *Deceived with Kindness*, 87.

32. See Reed, *Bloomsbury Rooms*, 268–72.

33. See Lee, *Virginia Woolf*, 215.

34. Crapoulet proposes that Woolf planned a 'book' on this subject as part of her 'Common History' project. (*Virginia Woolf*, 26).

35. The library included: Wakeling Dry's *Chopin: The Music of the Masters* (1926); *Studies and Caprices* (1926) by the composer and contributor to the *Musical Times*, Alexander Brent Smith; and Paul Bekker's *The Story of Music: An Historical Sketch of the Changes in Musical Form* (review copy, 1927). See http://www.wsulibs.wsu.edu/masc/specialcollections.html (accessed 11 October 2012).

36. Kelley suggests that the accounts of rhythm in this work may have influenced *The Waves*: 'Virginia Woolf and Music', 429.

37. Michael Tippett, *Those Twentieth Century [sic] Blues: An Autobiography* (London: Hutchinson, 1991), 126, cited in Southworth, 'Perfect Strangers?', 19. I am grateful to Helen Southworth for kindly making this essay available to me before publication.

38. See Sylvia McCurdy [née Stebbing], *Sylvia: A Victorian Childhood* (Lavenham: Eastland Press, 1973), 67, cited in Fewster, 'Bloomsbury

Books'. I am extremely grateful to Anna Fewster for her generosity in alerting me to and sharing her knowledge of Woolf's binding of sheet music.

39. See Fewster, 'Bloomsbury Books'.

40. Crapoulet, *Virginia Woolf*, 5.

41. Huxley, *Point Counter Point*, 384.

42. Crapoulet, *Virginia Woolf*, 9.

43. Pritchett, 'Fastidious and Anarchic', *Christian Science Monitor*, 21 November 1931, 10; Bradbrook, 'Notes on the Style of Mrs Woolf', *Scrutiny* I.1 (May 1932), 33–8 (35); and Marguerite Yourcenar, 'Virginia Woolf', in Woolf, *Les Vagues*, trans. Yourcenar (Paris: Stock, 1937), v, all cited in Herbert and Sellers (eds), *The Waves*, lxxxi-lxxxiv.

44. Verga, *Virginia Woolf's Novels*, 1. See Forster, 'Virginia Woolf' [1941], in *Two Cheers for Democracy*, 238–52 (243).

45. Verga, *Virginia Woolf's Novels*, 4–5.

46. *Literary Modernism and Musical Aesthetics*, 18. This is not to say, however, that these formal disruptions are in themselves necessarily musical: in some respects, they are contrary to usual modes of listening (18 and 139).

47. Bell, *Virginia Woolf*, I: 149.

48. *Virginia Woolf and Music*, ed. Adriana Varga, is forthcoming from Indiana University Press.

49. See, for example: Blissett, 'Wagnerian Fiction in English'; DiGaetani, *Richard Wagner*; and Furness, *Wagner and Literature*.

50. Marcus, *Virginia Woolf and the Languages of Patriarchy*, 51.

51. 'Virginia Woolf and Music', 417–18.

52. For Woolf on Lee, see, for example, 'Art and Life', *E*, I: 277–80, and for recent criticism on their relationship, see Denisoff, 'The Forest Beyond the Frame.'

53. Parallels between the late fiction, John Cage's work and serialism have, though, been proposed. See Cuddy-Keane, 'Virginia Woolf, Sound Technologies, and the New Aurality' and Kelley, 'Virginia Woolf and Music'.

54. Crapoulet, *Virginia Woolf*, 23.

55. See, for example: Cuddy-Keane, 'Virginia Woolf, Sound Technologies, and the New Aurality'; Zimring, 'Suggestions of Other Worlds'; Clements, 'A Different Hearing'; Frattarola, 'Listening for "Found Sound" Samples'; and Clements, 'Virginia Woolf, Ethel Smyth, and Music'.

56. 'Virginia Woolf, Sound Technologies, and the New Aurality', 69.

57. Stewart, *Reading Voices*, 261. See also McCluskey's early 'phonemic reading[s]' of sound patterns in the fiction (*Reverberations*, 3).

58. Werner Wolf in particular has proposed terms in which to distinguish between different types of intermediality. See *The Musicalization of Fiction*.

59. *Listening In*, 23.

60. See, for example: Wolf, *The Musicalization of Fiction*; Dayan, *Music Writing Literature*; Prieto, *Listening In*; Bucknell, *Literary Modernism and Musical Aesthetics*; and Fillion, *Difficult Rhythm*.

61. *Listening In*, ix-x.

62. Fillion's fine work on music and Forster's socio-political vision is a notable exception. Recent groundbreaking formalist analyses of Woolf's work

include: Clements, 'Transforming Musical Sounds into Words' and Slovak, 'Mrs Dalloway and Fugue'.
63. For a fine introduction to Critical Musicology and Victorian literature, see Weliver, 'A Score of Change'.
64. *Classical Music*, 4.
65. 'No Longer a View', 193.

Chapter 1

On Not Writing Opera

I went to Tristan the other night; but the love making bored me. When I was your age I thought it the most beautiful thing in the world – or was it only in deference to Saxon? (*L*, III: 56)

In his dazzling and provocative *Romantic Opera and Literary Form* (1977), Peter Conrad proposed:

> music and drama are dubious, even antagonistic, partners [. . .] opera's actual literary analogue is the novel. Drama is limited to the exterior life of action, and romanticism increasingly deprecates both the tedious willfulness of action and the limits of the form which transcribes it. The novel, in contrast, can explore the interior life of motive and desire and is naturally musical because mental. It traces the motions of thought, of which music is an image. Opera is more musical novel than musical drama.[1]

Conrad's argument springs from his analysis of Wagner's portmanteau term 'music-drama', and from his contention that this term succeeded as a slogan precisely because it elided consideration of 'the exact nature of [music and drama's] alliance': '[t]he equivalence between music and words which Wagner's theory of opera as drama assumes is a false compact. Actually the two are more like enemies. Music liquifies words, subduing them into notes; song infects language with an inspired unreason.'[2] His argument as it is outlined in these opening passages and developed through his study repeatedly associates opera with the formal characteristics of fictional narrative, with interiority, and with hostility to action, characteristics he identifies with the 'meditatively passive and self-exploratory' genre of the novel.[3]

Conrad's work encapsulates an argument the implications of which are increasingly being explored by musicologists, literary critics and narrative theorists. Recent studies of narrative form and voice, of interiority and of the representation of time in opera and the novel, are illuminating the parallels and the differences between these two superficially unlike genres.[4] Augmenting Carl Dahlhaus' argument that the 'story underlying an opera does not exist independently of the music; and the story in the libretto as such is not the story of the opera as a musical drama' Michael Halliwell, for example, observes:

> the orchestral music 'narrates' the action rather than having that action presented in an unmediated form, as is the primary mode in drama. This music 'tells' us about the characters as does the narrator in a novel [. . .] Opera's narrative mode can be seen more as diegetic (in the literary sense of 'telling') rather than mimetic ('showing' rather than 'telling'): the singer is not an autonomous character and does not 'speak' directly to the audience, but is part of a more complex narrative process.[5]

As Dalhaus, Halliwell, Carolyn Abbate and others have persuasively argued, the orchestra can be understood as a form of narrator; indeed, such analyses draw on a long history of writing about music, including some of Wagner's essays such as *Oper und Drama* (1851) in which he asserted that '[t]he orchestra indisputably possesses a *faculty of speech*'.[6]

These perceptions of the intermedial parallels between musical and literary narrative are particularly relevant to Woolf's first novel, *The Voyage Out* (1915). The central protagonist, Rachel Vinrace, is an accomplished amateur pianist and of all Woolf's novels this is the one in which music plays most conspicuous a part in the subject matter. Anonymous dance music, Bach's fugues and Beethoven's piano sonata Op. 111 are important intertexts in this novel, just as Woolf's later fiction alludes to a variety of composers, musical genres and national traditions, juxtaposing folk music and texts by other named composers with Wagner's work. Wagner's aesthetic theories and operatic practice have been central to critical explorations of intermedial relations and those between the novel and opera particularly; Woolf's work also turns to Wagner's example in order to tease out the relationship between these genres. *The Voyage Out* explores the partnership between words and music in opera, inevitably reflecting on the implications of this relationship for its own literary medium. Her novel also, I shall suggest, implicitly recognises the fundamental parallels between operatic and novelistic narration; it both critiques and adopts some of the narrative techniques of Wagner's work.

This chapter proposes that *The Voyage Out* is an extended critique of Wagner's *Tristan und Isolde* (1865) and that it is profoundly indebted to, if ambivalent towards, the music drama's libretto, aesthetics and music. Woolf's characters discuss Wagner's text; the plot reworks episodes from the action of the music drama; the protagonists and narrator echo

Wagner's libretto; and the prose repeatedly employs Wagnerian images. By exploring the novel's intertextuality with Wagner's drama I hope not only to suggest *Tristan*'s formative significance to Woolf's first novel, and thus to her aesthetic aims and techniques at the outset of her career as a novelist, but also to offer a case study of the ways in which one particular modernist writer drew on and critiqued two of the most important formal innovations of late nineteenth-century music – namely the leitmotiv (a melodic, harmonic or rhythmic unit commonly assigned to particular characters or ideas in the dramas) and the *Gesamtkunstwerk* (the union of music, words, dance and gesture into one 'total artwork'). Woolf's interest in the dramatic aspects of Wagner's *Gesamtkunstwerk* is apparent in the novel's allusions to Greek drama (an acknowledged influence on Wagner's model), the conversations about the idiosyncratic performance conditions at Bayreuth and the attention to dance and rhythm, but I concentrate here on the *Gesamtkunstwerk*'s combination of words and notes. As many have noted,[7] *The Voyage Out* overtly scrutinises the relationship between music, literature and language: Woolf problematises *Tristan*'s representation of language's limited communicative capacity and the opera's corresponding valorisation of musical expressivity. Probing the relevance of these ideas to fiction, *The Voyage Out* considers the interdependence of verbal inarticulateness and music; it anticipates the contrast between intensely articulate inner thought and the limited verbosity of spoken language characteristic of much of her later fiction. Wagner's works thus provided one model for Woolf's conception and realisation of the relationship between interiority and the spoken in her prose. Wagner's influence on the stream of consciousness novel has long been recognised:[8] as Prieto observes, 'music offers a set of formal, expressive, and referential principles that can be used in the attempt to better represent the inner space of consciousness'.[9] The first part of this discussion sets out the novel's affinities to *Tristan*, concentrating on its plot and libretto; the second explores the novel's representation of musical-literary relations and the influence of Wagner's musical techniques on Woolf's narrative strategies and prose style.

Wagner's music dramas are vital intertexts for several of Woolf's novels, which are suffused with explicit references and implicit debts to the composer's work. Some references – in *Jacob's Room* and *The Years*, for example – are overt, appearing in and propelling the events of the novels. Others are far more discreet, even covert. Woolf's work – like Mansfield's, Lawrence's, Forster's and Joyce's – illustrates the intense interplay between modernist fiction and nineteenth-century music. By the turn of the century, Wagner's works were part of the furniture of British musical life, familiar to the point of cliché; to some extent Woolf's familiarity with Wagner's works is representative of her age and social class. The operas had been staples of the concert and operatic repertoire in England since the 1870s, and by the 1890s British and Irish Wagnerism encompassed the political (from the Marxist, feminist and philanthropic, to the anti-Semitic and right-wing), the religious and spiritual (Christian, Theosophical, 'Eastern' and mystical), the anthropological (such as Jessie Weston's work on the dramas' mythology), the nationalist and the aesthetic (the drawings of Aubrey Beardsley and Arthur Rackham, as well as fiction, poetry and drama by Morris, Swinburne, Wilde, George Moore, Meredith, Henry James and numerous others).[10] Woolf's fiction records the variety of contemporary Wagnerian discourses, from the Society Wagnerism of Clarissa Dalloway and Kitty Lasswade to the religious Wagnerism of the Anglican vicar Edward Whittaker. Thus, if Wagner's work lacked the prescient modernity for Woolf that it had had for Nietzsche and his con-temporaries its cultural presence ensured its relevance both as a model and an antitype for modern art.[11] Wagner's significance for Woolf was augmented by reception conditions too: his works were among the first operas she encountered as a young woman in the 1890s, the decade in which full staged performances of the operas in Britain proliferated.

After hearing *Parsifal* (1882) for the second time at Bayreuth during the composition of *The Voyage Out*, Woolf wrote to Vanessa:

> We heard Parsifal yesterday; it was much better done, and I felt within a space of tears. I expect it is the most remarkable of the operas; it slides from music to words almost imperceptibly. However, I have been niggling at the effect all the morning, without much success. It is very hard to write in ones bedroom, without any books to look at, or my especial rabbit path, into the next room. (*L*, I: 406–7)

Despite the qualified terms of her praise, Woolf acknowledges that her attention has been arrested by the mature leitmotivic structure common to *Parsifal* and *Tristan*. It is Wagner's ability to 'slide from music to words' – and the 'imperceptibility' of this technique – that arouses Woolf's admiration (and in 'Impressions at Bayreuth' she developed her observation: 'the music is intimate in a sense that none other is; one is fired with emotion and yet possessed with tranquillity at the same time, for the words are continued by the music so that we hardly notice the transition' [*E*, I: 289]). Her observation may refer broadly to Wagner's reduction of conventional operatic distinctions between words and music, such as his abandonment of traditional clear boundaries between orchestral passages and vocal episodes such as arias. Or, more specifically, it may allude to his use of the leitmotiv, noting his ability to transfer thematic and harmonic motifs between the vocal parts and orchestra such that the orchestra anticipates, echoes and modifies the singers' music, appearing to 'comment on' the operatic protagonists. Her 'niggling at the effect' reminds us that Woolf was obliged to scrutinise this musical technique and to attempt to define it in critical language for 'Impressions at Bayreuth'. Her comments on *Parsifal* establish her interest in Wagner's mature leitmotivic technique and, I would suggest, hint at its relevance to her own formal experimentation.[12] If this letter anticipates the significance of Wagner's late dramas as models for Woolf's prose, the ambiguity of her portrayal of music in *The Voyage Out* hints at her difficulty in or ambivalence about adopting or revising Wagnerian techniques for prose; it is estimated that about nine 'drafts or fragments of drafts' of the novel were written[13] and the composition process was the most protracted in Woolf's oeuvre. Here, I explore the aesthetic rather than the biographical aspects of this painful composition process,[14] proposing that Woolf's formal innovations, specifically her desire to imitate Wagner's dramas, played a part in her numerous revisions to the text. As we shall see, *Tristan*'s role as an intertext grew as Woolf revised the novel.

Echoing Wagner

During the composition of *The Voyage Out* Woolf was immersed in Wagner's work,[15] attending the opera in London 'almost nightly' in May 1908 (*L*, I: 331), and visiting Bayreuth and publishing an essay on the festival in 1909. She heard *Tristan* twice at Covent Garden in May 1908, once in May 1910 and again in 1923 (*L*, I: 329–33 and 425 and III: 56), and most probably other performances too. Woolf appears to have written at least one incomplete 'draft' of the novel by October 1908, writing two longer 'drafts' between 1910 and 1912,[16] before the novel was sent to Duckworth for publication in March 1913;[17] thus, she heard *Tristan* several times during the writing, which had probably begun by early 1908.[18] Furthermore, she and Leonard owned a libretto of *Das Rheingold* in German, as well as epics and Romances based on the Arthurian, Nordic and Teutonic myths reworked by Wagner. Their library included, for example, William Morris' 1876 epic *The Story of Sigurd the Volsung and the Fall of the Niblungs* and two editions of Malory's *Morte d'Arthur*, another account, of course, of Tristan and Isolde's doomed love.[19] During the 1920s – after the publication of the novel – they also acquired three recordings of excerpts of *Tristan*.[20] As Wagner's essays had been available in English translation since the

1890s, it is also extremely probable that Woolf had read some of his theoretical or autobiographical writings.[21] *Tristan*'s subject matter of tortured erotic love and death is one with extensive affinities to *The Voyage Out*, her female *Bildungsroman* following the sheltered Rachel Vinrace on her voyage from London to a fictional South American resort where she meets and eventually becomes engaged to the young novelist, Terence Hewet.

Tristan's relevance is established at the start of the novel when the characters refer explicitly to Wagner's music and libretto. In the second chapter, Rachel reads the libretto on board ship and laughs out loud at the doggerel of the English translation; in the following chapter, the discovery of Rachel's copy of the score prompts discussions about *Tristan* and a Bayreuth performance of *Parsifal*. In the first of these examples, Rachel reads one of the standard late nineteenth-century English translations of Wagner's libretto by Henrietta and Frederick Corder. The novel quotes a passage from Act I, scene ii set on board ship as Tristan, whom Isolde has nursed following a battle injury, is transporting her to Cornwall so she can be married to his uncle King Marke. In this passage Isolde describes Tristan to her attendant Brangäne, denouncing his treatment of her and unwittingly acknowledging her mingled desire for and resentment toward him:

> [Rachel] had begun her meditations with a shout of laughter, caused by the following translation from *Tristan*:
>
>> In shrinking trepidation
>> His shame he seems to hide
>> While to the king his relation
>> He brings the corpse-like Bride.
>> Seems it so senseless what I say?
>
> She cried that it did, and threw down the book. (*VO*, 33)[22]

Here, Isolde associates erotic desire with shame and a desire for vengeance, and Rachel sees this passage as 'senseless' – she fails, in other words, to recognise or comprehend Isolde's emotions. The parallels between Rachel and the 'child' Isolde's sexual and emotional inexperience are emphasised,[23] the passage prefiguring the characteristics of Rachel's own erotic awakening. This brief incident also establishes, early in the novel, a contrast between Rachel's responses to written texts and music: whereas she is immediately and powerfully absorbed by music, the clunky translation of Wagner's libretto has little power to move her. (And in this Rachel departs from her nineteenth-century predecessors, many of whom were first influenced by written texts by and about Wagner.)

The implicit contrast between music and literature is echoed in the discussion of Bayreuth in Chapter 3, which follows a conversation about Shelley's poetry and Greek drama: Clarissa Dalloway's reminiscences characterise Wagner's music as exceptionally emotive (she recalls that she '"couldn't help sobbing"' at *Parsifal* [VO, 47]), again identifying music as a more emotive, even visceral, art than literature. There are no further explicit references to *Tristan* in *The Voyage Out* and Woolf never describes Rachel playing the work, but these early allusions alert readers to the significance of the music drama, introducing subjects common to the two texts: the relationship between music and words; the threat represented by erotic love (both operatic protagonists and Rachel die); and the blend of resentment and desire that characterises the lovers' relationships. These early allusions demonstrate the precision of Woolf's references to *Tristan*, but the significance of this intertext is not limited to the opening of the novel.

The plot of *The Voyage Out* is profoundly indebted to that of *Tristan*, which it mimics throughout the novel. Both texts begin with a sea voyage in which the female protagonist leaves her homeland to visit a foreign country. Like Isolde, the Irish princess taken to Cornwall to marry her future husband, Rachel's sea journey begins a literal and figurative voyage towards adult sexuality and engagement – her ship is described as 'a bride going forth to her husband, a virgin unknown of men' (VO, 30). During these voyages, both female protagonists experience threatening and disempowering sexual encounters: Isolde broods on Tristan's feelings toward her, while Rachel is disturbed by Richard Dalloway's unsolicited, unexpected kiss. Isolde perceives Tristan's treatment of her and her desire for him as humiliating and sinister, complaining to Brangäne that her 'shame' can only be atoned for by her own and Tristan's death.[24] Similarly, Richard's advances to Rachel, and her own ambivalent response, are associated with death: Rachel feels '[s]till and cold as death' (VO, 81) and is '"terrified"' by the encounter (VO, 85). In these episodes, Wagner and Woolf suggest that sexual desire threatens the autonomy of the female characters, for whom it has potentially fatal consequences. Additionally, Rachel's exhilaration at the violent storm (VO, 78–9) recalls Isolde's invocation of a storm in I, i,[25] and in both works the initial episodes onboard ship are followed by passages set in lush landscapes, providing apparently benign interludes in which the characters' erotic relationships flourish: Tristan and Isolde's adulterous meetings of Act II take place in the flower-filled garden of King Marke's court, while Rachel and Terence's relationship is set against the sensual and fragrant tropical landscape of South America. Woolf's uncharacteristically exotic setting, and the frequency with which she places her protagonists in the lush landscape, suggest *Tristan*'s widely observed hothouse qualities, by which they may be partly informed. Furthermore, in both plots a second voyage contrasts sharply with the first. In the drama, Isolde's second (off-stage) journey is made in order to return to and nurse the dying Tristan; his death immediately follows their reunion. In the novel, the second voyage is made to an indigenous South American village; it is the occasion on which Rachel and Terence declare their feelings, but is also widely blamed for the fever that Rachel contracts. In both cases, then, the first voyage is associated with the women's troubling initial experience of erotic desire,[26] and the second with the death of one or more of the lovers.

Terence and Rachel are, then, counterparts of Tristan and Isolde. Terence's name is itself a phonetic echo of 'Tristan', and Rachel's name may well be derived in part from *Rache* (*Ger.* 'vengeance'), a word declaimed several times by Isolde and fundamental to her relationship with Tristan.[27] As Woolf revised, she augmented and refined the novel's intertextuality with *Tristan*, making the parallels between Rachel and Isolde more extensive. In the extant lengthy typescript draft completed by July 1912,[28] for example, we are told that Rachel is a 'grudging student of the German tongue' and that she is reading the libretto partly because her father is pressing her to learn German; her reading is therefore a matter of obligation rather than, as in the published text, choice.[29] This draft quotes Isolde's reflections on her resentment towards Tristan in German and English, rather than only in English, the narrator describing it as 'that engaging passage'.[30] Thus, in the draft, Rachel's failure to understand the significance of Wagner's work is the result of linguistic rather than emotional inexperience. Her oversight of the drama's relevance is less pointed because of the narrator's ironic tone, and the absence of detail about Rachel's incomprehension and shout of laughter. Similarly, when Rachel tells Helen about Richard Dalloway's kiss, the draft emphasises her anger as well as her distress and she doesn't describe the experience in images of death; thus, the prefiguration of Rachel/Isolde's fate is absent.[31] In the published text, other characters also fulfil roles that parallel those of figures from Wagner's drama. Rachel's companion Helen Ambrose, for example, shares some of the characteristics of Isolde's nurse Brangäne. Brangäne accompanies Isolde on her voyage to King Marke as Helen accompanies Rachel; Brangäne is a maternal figure embodying the feminine occult knowledge of Isolde's mother whose 'subtle magic potions' and 'mother's arts' heal physical wounds and 'deepest grief', thus representing corporal knowledge and emotional intuition.[32] On the ship and subsequently Helen similarly acts as a protector and mentor for the motherless Rachel, educating Rachel in 'feminine' emotional matters – and Helen literally nurses Rachel when she becomes gravely ill with fever. Brangäne plays a pivotal role in the drama by supplanting the poison with the love potion and thus colluding in Isolde's illicit love for Tristan. Helen too (whose surname, Ambrose, itself recalls the ambrosial love potion)[33] encourages Rachel to experience adult sexual relations, with similarly tragic consequences.

In addition to the affinities between the plots of the two works, Woolf's syntax and lexical choices confirm her detailed knowledge of *Tristan*. The language of Wagner's poem is echoed precisely throughout *The Voyage Out* and Woolf's lovers frequently mimic the vocabulary of their Wagnerian counterparts at comparable episodes in the plot. A notable example is the passage in the tropical forest when Rachel and Terence declare their love. Here, they repeat each other's names and phrases, and question their separate identities: Rachel later asks, '"Am I Rachel, are you Terence?"' (*VO*, 316 and 336). Compare this with the vocabulary of Act II, scene ii, the operatic lovers' meeting in King Marke's garden, where Tristan and Isolde echo each other's words and sing: '"Is't I? – is't thou?"' before swapping names at the end of the scene, singing '"Tristan thou (Thou Isolda), / I Isolda (Tristan I), / no more Tristan. (no more Isolda)"'.[34] Such affinities are evident not only in the novel's dialogue but also in its imagery. *Tristan*'s association of the 'blissful realm' of night with erotic desire, illicit meetings and death is repeatedly echoed in the novel.[35] Although Rachel and Terence do not explicitly express a desire for death as Wagner's lovers do, they are persistently associated with the night and with images of death. Many of their moments of intimacy take place at night or in darkness: firstly, when Rachel and Helen watch Terence through the illuminated hotel window; then when Rachel and Terence first express their mutual desire in the darkness of the tropical forest; and again when they talk on the ship's deck returning from the indigenous village, and the 'darkness poured down profusely, and left them with scarcely any feeling of life' (*VO*, 337). Though Woolf's lovers find it hard to talk in daylight on the river trip, 'as the dark descended, the words of the others seemed to curl up and vanish as the ashes of burnt paper, and left them sitting perfectly silent at the bottom of the world. Occasional starts of exquisite joy ran through them, and then they were peaceful again' (*VO*, 322).

Furthermore, the novel's almost ubiquitous aquatic imagery may well be indebted not only to its setting on board ship and in a coastal resort but also to *Tristan*. Woolf's characters and narrator repeatedly employ aquatic images – especially images of drowning; these are particularly associated with Rachel and Terence's relationship, echoing the pervasive allusions to the sea and to drowning in *Tristan*. Their walk in the tropical forest is compared to a traveller 'walking at the bottom of the sea' (*VO*, 315); in chapter 21, Helen feels fearful for the lovers, imagining them drowning in an English river (*VO*, 333); and Terence reflects with resentment that Rachel is able to 'cut herself adrift from him' (*VO*, 352). When the lovers declare their desire in the forest, the narrator remarks: 'Voices crying behind them never reached through the waters in which they were now sunk' (*VO*, 330). The aquatic images augment the undercurrent of hatred and violence in Terence and Rachel's attraction, which is evident, more overtly, in Tristan and Isolde's. In the middle of a conversation about their marriage, for example, Terence exclaims that Rachel looks '"as if you'd blow my brains out. There are moments [. . .] when, if we stood on a rock together, you'd throw me into the sea"' (*VO*, 347). The aquatic images here and elsewhere frequently evoke the solipsistic, (self-)destructive qualities of Rachel and Terence's relationship – a familiar and often lurid staple of Wagnerian fiction.[36] Lawrence's Wagnerian novel *The Trespasser* of 1912 (originally titled *The Saga of Siegmund*), which Woolf read whilst on her honeymoon, may be a pertinent intertext: when Helena and Siegmund walk along the cliff tops she is 'thrilled' by his fear and described as 'psychically [. . .] an extremist, and a dangerous one'. The affinities to D'Annunzio's *Tristan*-inspired *Trionfo della Morte* (1894), which also includes clifftop scenes of imagined violence between the Wagnerian lovers, are also striking.[37] The Wagnerian parallels are consolidated when Rachel's death is described in aquatic imagery echoing that with which Isolde embraces death at the close of the drama.[38] Isolde sings of 'drown[ing]' in the 'balmy beauteous billows', imagining herself diving beneath and sipping the 'harmony' that 'flow[s] o'er [her]',[39] whilst Woolf describes the dying Rachel:

> s[eeing] nothing and hear[ing] nothing but a faint booming sound, which was the sound of the sea rolling over her head. While all her tormentors thought that she was dead, she was not dead, but curled up at the bottom of the sea. There she lay, sometimes seeing darkness, sometimes light, while every now and then someone turned her over at the bottom of the sea. (*VO*, 397–8)

Although Woolf's imagery is foetal rather than ecstatic this image of submarine death is one of comfort, security and homecoming for both female protagonists. Rachel's death from fever evokes the febrile qualities of the drama as a whole and of Isolde's 'Transfiguration' in particular – Isolde imagines herself drowning in Tristan's 'sweetest breath' as she sings her final aria over his body.[40] *The Voyage Out* is deeply indebted to *Tristan*'s aquatic imagery, and to Wagner's association of water with erotic desire and death.

In this context, we should reconsider the novel's notoriously problematic ending. Rachel's death of an unspecified fever deflates the narrative impetus of the *Bildungsroman*, which conventionally follows the protagonist through adolescent development to mature self-realisation, and gestures towards a symbolic significance that Rachel seems ill-suited to carry. The Wagnerian intertext, however, allows us to reconsider the novel's ending, suggesting why Rachel's death may have seemed the necessary or inevitable conclusion to Woolf. Firstly, Woolf invites us to recognise the similarities between Rachel's fate and that of Isolde, and thus to anticipate Rachel's death. As we saw, the passage that Rachel reads from *Tristan*'s libretto describes Isolde as the 'corpse-like Bride', a strong early hint of Rachel's inevitable death since she too is on board ship travelling towards adult sexuality and marriage (*VO*, 33). The narrator, the characters and even the novel's title repeatedly hint that Rachel is unlikely to survive her journey to South America and her experience of erotic love; the premonitions of Rachel's death remind us that Rachel is, so to speak, following a pre-determined Wagnerian role. When the travellers explore the indigenous village, Helen (like Brangäne in II, i and II, ii) has 'presentiments of disaster' and yearns to 'protect them from their fate' (*VO*, 333). The vocabulary in which Helen describes 'the lovers'' 'fate' stresses their symbolic quality, as if at this moment she half-perceives them as legendary or operatic figures rather than 'real' individuals. And when Rachel simply tells Terence that she has a headache (it then develops into the fatal fever), 'his sense of dismay and catastrophe were almost physically painful; all round him he seemed to hear the shiver of broken glass which, as it fell to earth, left him sitting in the open air' (*VO*, 381).[41] His is an ominously excessive response to Rachel's mundane statement. All of these examples suggest that the novel will, like the drama, end in death. Although Rachel's death is abrupt, lacking the explicit self-determination of Isolde's, Woolf seems to have intended a mix of haphazardness and symbolic inevitability: she famously wrote to Lytton Strachey that, 'What I wanted to do was to give the feeling of a vast tumult of life, as various and disorderly as possible, which should be cut short for a moment by the death, and go on again – and the whole was to have a sort of pattern, and be somehow controlled' (*L*, II: 82). A number of contemporary readers described the novel in similar terms: the anonymous review in the *Times Literary Supplement* spoke of the 'foreboding of some tragic ending' yet stated 'it *is* illogical, this sudden tragedy'.[42] Rachel's death seemed to many readers both abrupt and prefigured, to vacillate between realism and something more fictitious – or operatic.

The novel's debt to *Tristan* is nowhere more evident than in this conclusion. The most striking similarity between the two works is that the lovers experience in death the solipsistic union for which they have longed. In the celebrated duet of Act II, scene ii, the melodic motif of which exactly anticipates the *Liebestod* ('Love-Death') of Act III,[43] Wagner's lovers sing together:

> O might we then
> together die,
> each the other's
> own for aye!
> never fearing,
> never waking,
> blest delights
> of love partaking, –
> each to each be given,
> in love alone our heaven![44]

The language and tone in which Woolf describes Rachel's death and its aftermath are very similar. When Terence enters the room, Rachel recognises him for the first time in days, responding to his expressions of love and happiness with smiles. Their relationship thus ends on a note of intimacy and resolution, and the narrator comments, in a theatrical image: '[t]he curtain which had been drawn between them for so long vanished immediately' (*VO*, 411). After Terence realises that Rachel has died, he continues exultantly:

> this was death. It was nothing; it was to cease to breathe. It was happiness, it was perfect happiness. They had now what they had always wanted to have, the union which had been impossible while they lived. Unconscious whether he thought the words or spoke them aloud, he said, 'No two people have ever been so happy as we have been. No one has ever loved as we have loved.'
>   It seemed to him that their complete union and happiness filled the room with rings eddying more and more widely. He had no wish in the world left unfulfilled. They possessed what could never be taken from them. (*VO*, 412)

The absolute vocabulary, Schopenhauerian images of solipsistic unity, ecstatic anaphoras and mingled images of death and transcendence are shared by this passage and by *Tristan*.[45] The echoes of Wagner's lovers are clear: Rachel's death is Woolf's *Liebestod*.[46]

Dismantling the *Gesamtkunstwerk*

All these Wagnerian traces suggest that Woolf knew Wagner's drama intimately and that *Tristan*'s influence on Woolf's novel was profound. The remainder of the chapter turns to Woolf's representation of the relationship between words and music. Here, too, Woolf may have been influenced by specific details of Wagner's drama for, in addition to its formal innovations (such as the leitmotiv) that altered the conventional relationship between libretto and score, *Tristan* itself self-reflexively addresses this relationship: there are many points in the opera where the characters ask each other to listen or (over)hear singing. Wagner's protagonists comment too on the limits of language just as the orchestra 'comments' on them. The drama opens, for example, with Brangäne imploring Isolde to confide in her, to explain the 'secret' that she hides; in Act I Isolde complains of her 'despairing silence' that prevents her from publicly condemning Tristan; and later the lovers reflect on the 'little word' 'and' that 'bind[s]' them whilst syntactically reproducing their separation.[47] Both works contrast the limits of language with music's apparently greater potential for communication: the central protagonists not only repeatedly reflect on the limitations and difficulties of speech but are also (at least at points) conspicuously inarticulate. Like Wagner's protagonists, Rachel and Terence are frequently disappointed in their attempts to communicate; their speech is fractured and often incoherent. After one conversation, Terence reflects that words had 'drawn them so close together and flung them so far apart, and left him in the end unsatisfied, ignorant still of what she felt and of what she was like. What was the use of talking, talking, merely talking?' (*VO*, 254). Rachel herself is grotesquely inarticulate, and her vulnerability as a protagonist suggested by the fact that she cannot complete her sentences or frame questions that will give her the understanding she craves. The narrator describes her as having 'one enormous question, which she did not in the least know how to put into words' – she simply wants to be told '"everything"' (*VO*, 57). This absolute vocabulary suggests the immoderate nature of Rachel's wishes for social agency and communication, and the problematic disparity between her desires and her skills as a protagonist.

Woolf unequivocally links Rachel's frustration with language to her conception of music's expressive powers. She complains to Terence, for example:

> 'Novels,' she repeated. 'Why do you write novels? You ought to write music. Music, you see [. . .] music goes straight for things. It says all there is to say at once. With writing it seems to me there's so much [. . .] scratching on the match-box. Most of the time when I was reading Gibbon this afternoon I was horribly, oh infernally, damnably bored!' (*VO*, 239)

This statement is something of a manifesto for Rachel's faith in music's immediacy and totality of expression – a faith to which she adheres throughout the novel (with one brief exception).[48] And, as many have noted, Rachel's statement is echoed elsewhere by Woolf herself: when she advocates writing about 'things in themselves' in *A Room of One's Own*,[49] for example, or affirms in 'Sketch of the Past' 'we are the words; we are the music; we are the thing itself' (*MB*, 85). Brad Bucknell, following Alex Aaronson, notes that many moderns express a 'strange recuperation of a romantic belief in the expressive potential of music and in its capacity to go beyond the mere rationality of language'.[50] However, Woolf's attraction to the immediacy and totality of expression apparently offered by music was not unqualified. From the opening chapters of the novel it is clear that Rachel often turns to music when she has failed to understand literary texts or to make herself understood in conversation; Woolf implies that Rachel's perception of music is intrinsically linked to her social naivety and her inarticulacy. Early in the novel Rachel reflects on the difficulty of her relationships with her aunts, concluding: 'It was far better to play the piano and forget all the rest' (*VO*, 34).[51] The narrator too contrasts Rachel's interest in music with 'languages, science, or literature', observing that these other interests 'might have made her friends, or shown her the world' (*VO*, 32). At points, *The Voyage Out* suggests not only that music differs from language but also that it inhibits language. The *effect* of Wagner's music is, after all, to silence its listeners: Clarissa recalls being choked by *Parsifal* – '"It caught me here" (she touched her throat)' (*VO*, 47). Words and music, it seems, co-exist uneasily in Woolf's novel.

Again, the depiction of this relationship points back towards *Tristan*, which itself expresses a disjunction between words and music. For all Wagner's championing and development of poetic libretti, it is a commonplace of Wagner criticism that *Tristan*'s action and emotion are propelled by the music rather than the libretto.[52] The emotive, sensual score contrasts sharply with the static action and stilted dialogue (often, in fact, a series of monologues), and the music articulates emotions towards which the libretto can only gesture. Making this point, Conrad invokes Terence's plans to write '"a novel about Silence"', '"the things people don't say"' (*VO*, 249):

> Wagner's people are characterized by music, not drama [. . .] The consequences of this change from drama to music extend to this modern novel where, in part under Wagner's influence, people are characterized not through external action or conversation but through the silent, and hence musical, life of thought and feeling.[53]

In Wagner's drama, then, music appears to have a greater narrative and expressive capacity than words – and it is the referential quality of leitmotivs that is largely responsible for this perception.[54] Woolf herself raised the question of the relation between music and drama in 'The Opera' (1909). After acknowledging that Wagner's music 'excites the strongest sympathy in us', she continued:

> And yet, swept away as we are at some moments, there are others when we seem to be dropped again. Is it that there is some cleavage between the drama and the music? Music (it may be) raises associations in the mind which are incongruous with the associations raised by another art; the effort to resolve them into one clear conception is painful, and the mind is constantly woken and disillusioned. (*E*, I: 270)

These early reflections on the possible 'cleavage' between drama and music, informed by her reading about Gluck's theories of operatic reform, anticipate her response to *Tristan* in *The Voyage Out*.[55]

The language in which Woolf describes Rachel and Terence evokes the opera's exceptionally expressive music: as the lovers become closer, they remain inarticulate and socially awkward but appear to achieve an exalted state of communication resembling Rachel's description of music as 'go[ing] straight for things'. When they declare their love their combined voices are described as 'tones of strange unfamiliar sound which formed no words' (*VO*, 316). And when Rachel realises with astonishment that what she feels is that 'famous' thing 'happiness' the narrator remarks that '[s]o beautiful was the sound of their voices that by degrees they scarcely listened to the words they framed' (*VO*, 329–30). In a Wagnerian touch, the lovers' phrases imitate each other, and their movements too are synchronised at this point as in Act II, scene ii of the opera. Although this wordless communication might be read as an ideal union, it is also of course alarmingly non-intellectual and solipsistic – the musical imagery of 'sound' and 'tones' signals the characters' worrying indifference to the referents of the words. This communication is represented as outside everyday experience, as a marker of intense feelings and thus as individualistic or particular to their relationship; all these elements seem to endorse Terence and Rachel's relationship and this perception of musical expressivity. Yet their comments reveal the lovers' indifference not only to the wider world but also to each other: they 'scarcely listen' to each other or even, the phrasing may suggest, to themselves. 'Beauty' has supplanted dialogue and meaning. Here and elsewhere Woolf's emphasis on the problematic, even hostile, relationship between words and music suggests a critique of the *Gesamtkunstwerk*. Whereas in *Tristan* the role of music in conveying emotion and characterisation depends on and surely celebrates music's expressive capacity, in the novel the role and representation of music is much more ambiguous. Rachel's faith in music's expressive power is one the novel prompts us to view with caution.

Woolf's critique of the *Gesamtkunstwerk* continues as Rachel and Terence are contrasted as representatives of music and literature respectively; each defends their own medium to the other, reflecting on the similarities and differences between the arts. In a text populated with creative writers, translators and literary critics, Rachel is the solitary musician among the central protagonists; her history therefore invites interpretation as an exploration of the relations between words and music. And if we accept that Woolf's first novel is, among other things, a reworking of *Tristan*, the relationship between fiction and opera is inevitably central to this work. The *Gesamtkunstwerk* upholds the fusion of distinct arts and media as an aesthetic ideal even as it acknowledges differences between the arts; Woolf's characters, in contrast, more frequently emphasise the incompatibilities between the arts. When, for example, Terence proposes that '"What I want to do in writing novels is very much what you want to do when you play the piano, I expect,"' Rachel unequivocally replies, '"Music is different"' (*VO*, 252–3). Though Rachel can hardly be taken as an unproblematic authorial voice this is a suggestive resistance to Terence's assumption of aesthetic affinity. Her response is a flat rebuttal of Pater's famous aphorism: the novel thus critiques not only Wagner but also, more generally, Aesthetic uses of music in the late nineteenth century.[56] Like Pound, Joyce and Stein, Woolf is resistant to the 'notion of *total expressivity*' represented by the *Gesamtkunstwerk*.[57] Other characters also emphasise the differences between the arts, many trying to wean Rachel off music and turn her into a reader. Miss Allan, for example, unquestioningly assumes the incompatibility of musical and literary gifts: wondering if Rachel is interested in the English novel, she comments, '"Oh no, it's music with you, isn't it? [. . .] and I generally find that they don't go together"' (*VO*, 295). By making the differences between the arts an explicit subject of the published novel, Woolf questions the desirability of the Wagnerian ideal. In this respect, the published text differs considerably from Woolf's earlier versions: in the long extant draft, there is much less explicit attention to musical-literary relations. Neither Miss Allan's nor Terence's statements is present; indeed, Rachel herself appears confident that aesthetic sensibility transcends differences of media, responding to Terence's exclamation that she will '"love reading"' and '"go for the right things"' with the more Paterian explanation '"That's because I love music."'[58] The published novel's emphasis on the differences between the arts suggests Woolf's increasing engagement with and critique of the *Gesamtkunstwerk*, a critique that also informs the novel's ending.

If Rachel's death may have seemed the inescapable conclusion to Woolf, it is also true that the ending of the novel is deeply ironic and ambiguous. Far from being a homage to Wagner's work, Woolf's version undercuts some of *Tristan*'s most fundamental characteristics. In contrast to the Wagnerian source, in the novel it is only the female lover who dies; Terence, in defiance of his operatic role model Tristan, survives. In the ante-penultimate chapter, Woolf reverses the roles of Wagner's lovers: instead of the focus being on Isolde's celebrated lament for Tristan (her 'Transfiguration') Woolf centralises Terence's elegy for Rachel. Terence's lament is profoundly problematic, given that he is eulogising a silent – or silenced – Rachel. Having often resented Rachel's independence and dismissed her opinions, Terence is able to express unequivocal desire and contentment only, as Elisabeth Bronfen might say, over her dead body. These ambiguities illustrate the unresolved difficulties in the lovers' relationship, and in Woolf's depiction of the relationship between the two arts. It is tempting, perhaps, to conclude that Terence's survival indicates Woolf's endorsement of literature (represented by Terence) over music (represented by Rachel). This reading would see the conclusion of the novel as Woolf's assertion of the authority of her own literary medium over the originating operatic source, reversing the primacy of music over words in *Tristan*. Rachel's death could thus be read as a symbolic dismantling of the *Gesamtkunstwerk*, since in Woolf's narrative the lovers and the arts they represent are unequivocally severed. It might also be read as a critique of 'opera' more generally, exposing the gender politics of the many nineteenth-century operas that prescribed the death or domestication of their female protagonists.[59] Furthermore, the novel's conclusion might be read as an endorsement of literary proto-modernism over a nineteenth-century composer and over 'Victorian' aesthetics more generally, problematising Rachel's characteristically nineteenth-century, Paterian, faith in music's expressive powers. It conveys dis-ease about music as an 'epistemological and aesthetic ideal', a wariness about the 'disturbing plenitude or excess' towards which music may tend.[60]

However, Woolf's account of Rachel's death illustrates not only her critique of the *Gesamtkunstwerk* but also her profound debts to Wagner's formal techniques, his 'sliding from music to words'. If we compare the first typescript of the novel with the published text quoted above, several striking differences are apparent. The draft of Rachel's death reads:

He kissed her and said 'Rachel'. After a pause her eyes opened, first only the lower parts of the whites showed; then slowly the whole eye was revealed. She saw him for a moment distinctly; a large head above her; it became fringed with black and then became altogether black; she wished for a moment to fight for something, and then forgot, overwhelmed in the curves of blackness that were rising all round her. Sinking and sinking into them, she never heard him say 'Rachel' a second time; she did not know that her hand lay in his.

After Rachel had shut her eyes Terence sat perfectly still. He knew that she was dying. But the dazed unreal feeling that such a thing as this could not happen to them which had haunted him ever since she fell ill disappeared completely. He was possessed by an extraordinary feeling of triumph and calm happiness.

'It is only to us two in the world that this could have happened,' was the thought that filled him. 'Because we loved each other. Therefore we have this.'

He believed that Rachel shared his feeling and that her face reflected back his triumph and calm. When he saw that she was dead he was only conscious of great triumph and calm. This death was such a little thing. It seemed that they were now absolutely free, more free more entirely united than they had ever been before. They had received the most wonderful thing in the world. He heard himself saying as he sat with her hand in his, 'We have had what no people in the world have had. No one has ever loved as we love each other.'[61]

Here, in contrast to the published text, Rachel does not smile at Terence or speak to him and there are repeated hints that his perception of unity is mistaken: Rachel's last thoughts are of fighting; her lack of aware-ness of Terence is stressed; the repetition of Terence's 'triumph' begs the question of who or what he has defeated; and he imagines Rachel as a mirror 'reflecting' his own emotion. In this draft, the third person is used more extensively and there is more frequent alternation between Terence's and the narrator's perspective: phrases such as '[h]e believed' and '[i]t seemed' distance us from Terence's experience. In the published text, the shifts between third person narrative voice and free indirect discourse are less conspicuous and, as a result, Terence's emotions have more authority in that moment. Rather than 'it seemed that they were now absolutely free', for example, the published text reads 'They had now what they had always wanted to have, the union which had been impossible while they lived' (*VO*, 412). Furthermore, in the published text Woolf emphasises the immediacy and the sounds of Rachel's death: Terence listens to her breathing and the passage, with its repetition of 'breathe' and 'breath' (*VO*, 412), immerses readers in the moment and in the aurality of Terence's experience. Despite the broad similarities between these two versions, the published text reduces the difference between Terence's and the narrator's perspective, 'sliding' between these voices more discreetly. Arguably, Woolf is mimicking the almost 'imper-ceptible' shifts of voice and perspective that she had admired in *Parsifal*.[62] In her revisions to this passage, Woolf developed this Wagnerian technique that was to be honed in the later fiction (and in that of Proust, whose work she read with acute excitement and rivalry in the 1930s).[63] The published version of Rachel's death is – in its greater immersion in the characters' experience and their sense of unity – closer to the tone of *Tristan*; this affecting and much admired passage is informed by and even celebrates the drama's expressivity.[64] Yet it acknowledges, too, fiction's capacity to incorporate – and thus to temper or subsume – some of the most emotive aspects of Wagner's text. The novel does not, after all, conclude strictly with Rachel's death but with the panoramic account of the hotel guests on the following day. Following Woolf's '*Liebestod*', life continues in Rachel's absence and the emotional pitch drops; in the last two chapters, the focus moves from the grieving individual to the community, from intensely articulate but unspoken inner thoughts to clearly differentiated dialogue and third person narration. Rather than the narrator or orchestra amplifying the protagonists' final emotions, as happens in *Tristan*, Woolf's narrator sharply undercuts them. As the unsigned review in *Spectator* observed admiringly: 'how often [in real life] does an apparently intentional *crescendo* of interest collapse suddenly into pointlessness'.[65] The 'Wagnerian' account of Rachel's death thus becomes an interval in, rather than a replacement of, the predominant narrative tone of wry Meredithian satire. Woolf's published novel is more indebted – and more hostile – to the composer than the drafts, precisely because the disjunction between this scene and the hotel panorama that follows is greater. The death scene in the published text may be more 'Wagnerian' in its tone and its formal strategies than that of the draft, but it employs Wagner's own musical techniques to critique *Tristan*. And in this it anticipates the narrative and other formal experiments of her later fiction, which are both shaped by and resistant to Wagner's musical techniques.

Notes

1. *Romantic Opera*, 1.
2. Conrad, *Romantic Opera*, 1 and 4–5.
3. Conrad, *Romantic Opera*, 3.
4. Of this growing field, I have found the following particularly helpful: Cone's *The Composer's Voice*; Prieto's *Listening In*; Dayan's *Music Writing Literature*; Wolf's *The Musicalization of Fiction*; and Bucknell's *Literary Modernism*.
5. Dalhaus, 'What is a Musical Drama?', 101; and Halliwell, 'Intrusive Narrators', 222–3. See also Halliwell's fine study, *Opera and the Novel*.
6. Wagner, *Prose Works*, II: 316. Emphasis in original.
7. See, representatively, Hussey, *The Singing of the Real World*, 65–8.

8. See, for example, Furness, *Wagner and Literature*, 16–17.

9. Prieto, *Listening In*, x.

10. See Sutton, *Aubrey Beardsley* and Sutton, 'Wagner in the Visual Arts', in Vazsonyi (ed.), *The Cambridge Wagner Encyclopedia*, forthcoming.

11. In the preface to *The Case of Wagner*, Nietzsche observed: 'Through Wagner modernity speaks most intimately [. . .] "Wagner sums up modernity"': *'The Birth of Tragedy' and 'The Case of Wagner'*, 156. I have not been able to establish if Woolf had read this essay by the 1920s; direct allusions to Nietzsche in her work are scarce, but she appears to have known at least *Beyond Good and Evil* and *Zarathustra* by the late 1920s or early 1930s. See Woolf, *The Waves*, ed. Herbert and Sellers, 329, 392–3 and 395; and Christie, 'Willing Epigone'.

12. Cf. Prieto's argument that 'the leitmotiv is, at bottom, not a musical technique at all but, rather, a literary technique. Borrowed from drama [. . .] its usage is entirely determined by dramatic considerations [. . .] Use of such a musically inspired technique does not necessarily indicate any modification in the literary status of the text [. . .] techniques such as the leitmotiv can only be considered musical in a metaphorical sense.' *Listening In*, 16. Nonetheless, as Prieto acknowledges, the interest of such uses of music lies in what they can show us about Woolf's literary techniques.

13. Woolf, *Melymbrosia*, xiii. See also Heine, 'Virginia Woolf's Revisions of *The Voyage Out*', 399–452. Dating of early drafts remains a matter of debate.

14. For a biographical reading, see DeSalvo, *Virginia Woolf's First Voyage*.

15. Further detail is provided in Chapter 3, below.

16. Woolf, *Melymbrosia*, xviii–xxii.

17 Leonard Woolf, *Beginning Again*, 87.

18. DeSalvo, *Virginia Woolf's First Voyage*, 3.

19. Richard Wagner, *Das Rheingold: Vorspiel zu der Trilogie, Der Ring des Nibelungen* (Mainz: Schott's Söhne, [n.d.]); William Morris, *The Story of Sigurd the Volsung and the Fall of the Niblungs* (London: Ellis and White, 1877); Thomas Malory, *Le morte Darthur: Sir Thomas Malory's Book of King Arthur and of his Noble Knights of the Round Table*, ed. Edward Strachey (London: Macmillan, 1899) [Leonard Woolf's copy]; and Malory, *Le Morte d'Arthur* (London: Dent & New York: Dutton, 1906). See King and Miletic-Vejzovic (eds), *The Library of Leonard and Virginia Woolf*.

20. The excerpts were: the Preludes to Acts I and III, State Opera House, Berlin, conductor Moerike; the Prelude, State Opera House, Berlin, conductor Otto Klemperer and the 'Love Duet', Act II, with Frida Lewes and Lauritz Melchior; and the Prelude and *Liebestod*, State Opera House, Berlin, conductor Siegfried Wagner. Leonard Woolf, 'Card Index of Gramophone Recordings', Leonard Woolf Papers, LWP Ad.28, Sussex University.

21. William Ashton Ellis' eight-volume translation was published between 1893 and 1899. I have not found any 'proof' of Woolf's reading of the essays, but she would undoubtedly have been familiar with Wagner's principal aesthetic and political ideas.

22. The novel quotes a bilingual libretto: H. and F. Corder's *Tristan and Isolda*, 8. The punctuation and capitalisation are slightly altered and the

novel misquotes 'seeks' as 'seems'; this misquotation is absent in the earlier draft (*Melymbrosia*, 20).

23. Wagner, *Tristan and Isolda*, 5.
24. Wagner, *Tristan and Isolda*, 14.
25. Wagner, *Tristan and Isolda*, 6.
26. Although Isolde was betrothed to Morold before meeting Tristan, in Wagner's version of the legend Isolde's attraction to Tristan is represented as unprecedented. In the first typescript of the novel Rachel, too, has had a previous proposal of marriage. Woolf, *Melymbrosia*, 21.
27. Woolf's knowledge of German was sufficient for her to have known this word and to have noted its prominence in the libretto; by July 1908 she was able 'with some assistance' to review a German book and her study of German coincided with this period of frequent attendance at operas (*L*, I: 338 and Bishop, *A Virginia Woolf Chronology*, 14). Another play on 'Rachel'/'Rache' is used in Conan Doyle's first Sherlock Holmes story, 'A Study in Scarlet' (1887). The Stephens knew Conan Doyle; a photograph of him with Woolf's brother Thoby in 1896 is reproduced in Humm, *Snapshots of Bloomsbury*, 59.
28. This is the text ('Extant Draft B') on which DeSalvo based *Melymbrosia* and which I compare throughout with the first published text of *The Voyage Out*. See *Melymbrosia*, xix–xxi. Heine also dates the completion of this typescript draft to July 1912 in 'Virginia Woolf's Revisions', 400.
29. Cf. Leslie Stephen's letter to Thoby in 1901: 'I am trying to get a little German into Ginia. I guess you may have too': J. W. Bicknell (ed.), *Selected Letters of Leslie Stephen*, 2 vols (London: Macmillan, 1996), II: 517, cited in Koulouris, *Hellenism and Loss*, 38.
30. Woolf, *Melymbrosia*, 19–20.
31. Woolf, *Melymbrosia*, 62–4.
32. Wagner, *Tristan and Isolda*, 16, 19.
33. Isolde associates the love potion with her mother's 'balm' ('*den Balsam*'), and in II, ii Tristan eulogises the drink. Wagner, *Tristan and Isolda*, 16, 38.
34. Wagner, *Tristan and Isolda*, 34, 45. The repetition of each other's names and phrases is also evident elsewhere in the novel, as in the opera. See, for example, where the narrator mimetically draws attention to Terence's echo of Rachel's statement 'This is happiness' '[o]n the heels of her words': 'They began therefore to describe how this felt and that felt, how like it was and yet how different; for they were very different' (*VO*, 330).
35. See, notably, the duet of II, ii: Wagner, *Tristan and Isolda*, 39.
36. See Zuckerman, *The First Hundred Years of Wagner's 'Tristan'*.
37. *The Trespasser*, 77, and *L*, II: 6.
38. Terence also uses aquatic imagery for his farewell to Rachel: he imagines the room filled with 'eddying' 'rings' (*VO*, 412).
39. Wagner, *Tristan and Isolda*, 69–70.
40. Wagner, *Tristan and Isolda*, 69.
41. Woolf's image echoes the hothouse imagery of *Tristan*; in this moment, the glass-house literally shatters.
42. Unsigned review, *Times Literary Supplement*, 1 April 1915, 110, cited in Majumdar and McLaurin (eds), *The Critical Heritage*, 50; original

emphasis. Strachey, similarly, commented to Woolf that the novel had been 'almost accidentally – cut short by the death of Rachel'. Letter from Strachey to Woolf, 25 February 1916, cited in Majumdar and McLaurin, 65.

43. The motif reappears in A flat at the start of Isolde's Transfiguration.
44. Wagner, *Tristan and Isolda*, 43.
45. The passages also resemble Woolf's parting letters to Leonard. See Lee, *Virginia Woolf*, 756–7 and 759–60.
46. For another pertinent context, see Koulouris' account of Woolf's 'Greek notebook' of 1907–9: 'only "love" subjugated to death and "loss" was available to women in the Greek texts Woolf was reading.' Koulouris, *Hellenism and Loss*, 107.
47. Wagner, *Tristan and Isolda*, 6, 14, 43.
48. In chapter 10 Rachel is temporarily diverted by New Woman fiction and drama and 'for the moment music was deserted' (*VO*, 136).
49. Morag Shiach (ed.), *'A Room of One's Own' and 'Three Guineas'* (Oxford: World's Classics, 1992), 145, cited in Raitt, 'Virginia Woolf's Early Novels', 34.
50. Bucknell, *Literary Modernism*, 2–3.
51. A similar sentiment is expressed in Woolf's 1901 letter to Emma Vaughan (*L*, I: 41–2).
52. See, for instance, Carnegy, 'The Staging of *Tristan and Isolde*', 29.
53. Conrad, *Romantic Opera*, 27.
54. Here, of course, I simplify: for a commanding discussion of the relation between words, music and narrative in Wagner's work see Abbate, *Unsung Voices*. As Abbate notes of the *Ring*, Wagner 'undercuts security in the narrating voice even when that voice is musical, thus contradicting Wagner's own (Schopenhaurian) position on music as an untainted and transcendent discourse'; furthermore, at points, *Tristan* inverts the audience's 'usual privilege of hearing what the characters cannot' (xiv and 134).
55. The essay invokes Gluck as Wagner's opposite as a practitioner and theorist of musical-dramatic relations; Woolf's knowledge of these debates may have been shaped by Hadow, whose chapter 'Gluck and the Reform of the Opera' summarised Gluck's theories and practice. Hadow, *The Oxford History of Music*, 85–104.
56. For an outstanding account of Pater's significance to modernist conceptions of music, see Bucknell, *Literary Modernism*, chapter 2; and on Woolf's relations to Pater, see Meisel, *The Absent Father*. Angela Leighton also considers Pater and Woolf's 'continuing aestheticist yearning' in *On Form* (96).
57. Bucknell, *Literary Modernism*, 4. Emphasis in original.
58. Woolf, *Melymbrosia*, 221.
59. See Clément, *Opera*.
60. Bucknell, *Literary Modernism*, 20 and 24.
61. Woolf, *Melymbrosia*, 231–2.
62. Intriguingly, Conrad stops just short of making the same claim: in a passage about *Tristan*, he alludes to its 'technique of alternating points of view which the novel was to adopt' (*Romantic Opera*, 33).
63. See *L*, V: 296–7 and 304, and VI: 50, 112 and 282.

64. See for example Majumdar and McLaurin (eds), *The Critical Heritage*, 51, 56, 58, 59.
65. Unsigned review, *Spectator*, 10 July 1915, 54–5, cited in Majumdar and McLaurin (eds), *The Critical Heritage*, 63.

Chapter 2

Killing the Pianist in the House

The Voyage Out was, many contemporaries noted, an arrestingly modern work. In a letter to Woolf, Lytton Strachey observed that it was 'very, very unvictorian', and reviews variously described it as a novel of 'modern manners', the characters as 'contemporary people' and the protagonists as 'modern lovers'.[1] As the previous chapter proposed, *The Voyage Out* is profoundly shaped by Wagner's music dramas and by ideas about music. Written in a period when art music had, for at least a century, occupied a revered place in European culture and aesthetic theory, Woolf's novel registers music's exceptional cultural prestige and shifting attitudes towards responses to music and their representation in fiction. *The Voyage Out* can be placed in a long line of novels featuring musicians as protagonists or in which music is prominent in the action and dialogue: in this respect Woolf's first novel has a rather 'Victorian' subject.[2] Some of the characters, too, express responses to music that might have come straight from a *fin-de-siècle* novel: Clarissa Dalloway's arch remarks about the '"divine"' and '"thrilling"' *Tristan* are the most conspicuous examples. Clarissa's dismissal of '"the kind of attitudes people go into over Wagner"' (*VO*, 46–7) hardly dilutes the mannered emotionalism of her own recollections, and indeed Woolf's own writing about music occasionally employs similarly Aesthetic, perhaps specifically Paterian, language: referring, in a letter of 1906, to 'a debauch of music' she eulogised the 'pure simple notes – smooth from all passion and frailty, and flawless as gems' (*L*, I: 263–4).[3] Nonetheless, Clarissa's response is parodied and elsewhere Woolf also seems wary of the datedness of such forms of musical aestheticism. In 'The Opera', she follows her praise for an art which 'the minority' believe to be 'a serious artistic form' with the conclusion that opera is 'one of the oddest of all worlds – brilliant, beautiful, and absurd' (*E*, I: 271–2). Like many of her contemporaries, Woolf eschews the apparent subjectivity, solipsism and indifference to politics of some late-Victorian writing about music[4] but also looks to music as a means of creating distinctly modern – or modernist – writing. Her attitude towards nineteenth-century music exemplifies what Steve Ellis describes as Woolf's 'affiliation with and dissent from her Victorian past, which reciprocally and necessarily signifies affiliation with and dissent from her modern present'.[5] 'Street Music' (1905), for all the slipperiness of its tone, celebrates music's potential to revitalise contemporary literature: writing is 'chiefly degenerate because it has forgotten its allegiance' to music, she writes, exhorting poets and prose writers to 'invent – or rather remember – the innumerable metres which we have so long outraged' (*E*, I: 31). The earliest of her essays on music thus equates innovative modern writing with that influenced by music. *The Voyage Out*'s representation of the Victorian and modern periods (like that in *Night and Day*) is delineated partly through music, informing Woolf's conception of the modernity of her own writing. This chapter considers two aspects of this question: the way in which music shapes Woolf's gendered conception of the differences between Victorian writing and modern fiction, and the figure of the female pianist.

Music, mothers, modernism

The relationship between aesthetic tradition and modernity is a recurrent subject of *The Voyage Out*, delineated through the allusions to literature and visual art as well as music.[6] Between the iconoclasm of the eccentric painter Mrs Flushing, who maintains '"[n]othin' that's more than twenty years old interests me [. . .] Mouldy old pictures, dirty old books, they stick 'em in museums when they're only fit for burnin' [. . .]"' (*VO*, 222–3), and the uncompromising antiquarianism of the classicist Ridley Ambrose, who asks '"what's the use of reading if you don't read Greek? After all, if you read Greek, you need never read anything else, pure waste of time"' (*VO*, 192), the novel records a spectrum of attitudes towards aesthetic traditions and history. However, although the novel alludes to contemporary avant-garde writing and visual art (such as Terence's novel about 'Silence') there are no comparable references to music. *Parsifal* (1882) is the most recent musical work named in the novel and Rachel's interest in early music is made clear from the first account of her playing:

> Rachel was indignant with the prosperous matrons, who made her feel outside their world and motherless, and turning back, she left them abruptly. She slammed the door of her room, and pulled out her music. It was all old

music – Bach and Beethoven, Mozart and Purcell – the pages yellow, the engraving rough to the finger. In three minutes she was deep in a very difficult, very classical fugue in A, and over her face came a queer remote impersonal expression of complete absorption and anxious satisfaction. (*VO*, 58)

Rachel is clearly another child of the late nineteenth-century early music revival, and her historical tastes are emphasised as the novel unfolds. The explicit references to late Romantic repertoire (*Tristan* and *Parsifal*) occur early in the novel when '[h]er mind was in the state of an intelligent man's in the beginning of the reign of Queen Elizabeth' (*VO*, 31); by the twelfth chapter we are told that Bach 'was at this time the subject of her intense enthusiasm' (*VO*, 187). Later in the novel, the diegetic accounts of Rachel playing associate her with works by Bach, Beethoven and Mozart. Rachel's musical tastes thus move further away from contemporary music and they also shift from opera to absolute music – symbolically, they trace a move from music with a narrative or dramatic component to formal austerity, and from emotive, high Romantic music to classical and baroque moderation. (Chapter 4 considers the significance of Bach's formalism in more detail.) And, as the passage above suggests, Rachel's music making is often associated with escapism and a solipsistic withdrawal from the demands of contemporary life. This is certainly the perception of several of those who attempt to guide Rachel's education: her father complains that '"a little less [music] would do no harm"' (*VO*, 92) and Helen 'desired that Rachel should think, and for this reason offered books and discouraged too entire a dependence upon Bach and Beethoven and Wagner' (*VO*, 137). Music appears to them something that alienates Rachel from, and ill equips her for, life as an Edwardian young woman.

In contrast to these accounts of music, it seems at first glance that Rachel's enraptured response to the *fin-de-siècle* writing to which Helen introduces her will enhance Rachel's personal and artistic development. Rachel's introduction to New Woman fiction and Ibsen's feminist drama expands her understanding of 'women and life' (*VO*, 137), marking a new stage in Rachel's self-knowledge. Tellingly, '[m]usic was open on the piano, and books of music rose in two jagged pillars on the floor; but for the moment music was deserted' (*VO*, 136). Even the material appearance of these books contrasts with her aged, yellowed sheet music:

Rachel chose modern books, books in shiny yellow covers, books with a great deal of gilding on the back, which were tokens in her aunts' eyes of harsh wrangling and disputes about facts which had no such importance as the moderns claimed for them. (*VO*, 137–8)

Their bright colours (they are later described as 'red and yellow volumes' [*VO*, 340]) recall Mrs Flushing's vibrant paintings, augmenting the emphasis on their modernity. Music and literature are juxtaposed, and (in contrast to 'Street Music') music repeatedly associated with the past. In *The Voyage Out*, music's relationship with modernity and with feminism is ambiguous.

Nonetheless, during the composition of the novel Woolf repeatedly looked to music to develop her own aesthetic, distinct from that of her male literary predecessors. As many have noted, in the early stages of her career she identified her father Leslie Stephen as a figure against whom to define her own work: he was, in all the nuances of the term, a *Victorian* writer par excellence.[7] It is suggestive that during Woolf's visit to Bayreuth with Adrian and Saxon, when she was reflecting on the differences between music and writing and the significance of Wagnerian opera to her own fiction, she was also considering her father and his writing. This may have arisen, in part, from Saxon's resemblance to Stephen:

> Saxon is dormant all day, and rather peevish if you interrupt him. He hops along, before or behind, swinging his ugly stick, and humming, like a stridulous grasshopper. He reminds me a little of father. He clenches his fists, and scowls in the same way; and stops at once if you look at him. (*L*, I: 405)

Though her lifelong affection and admiration for Saxon are evident in her correspondence and unpublished writings,[8] Woolf was clearly frustrated by Saxon's pedantry, his zealous partisanship for Wagner's work and the intellectual bullying at the hands of her companions who 'make me read the libretto in German, which troubles me a good deal' (*L*, I: 407). ('The Opera' alludes tartly to 'scholarly Wagnerians' 'instructing humble female relatives in the intricacies of the score' [*E*, I: 271].) During this period of intense musical experience, then, the behaviour of her male companions reminded her of Leslie Stephen and echoed some of the dynamics of her relationship with her father. Only a few days after the letter quoted above, Woolf confided to Vanessa:

> I have been thinking a great deal about father too, and discussing him with Adrian. I believe he was really very modest; he was certainly not selfconscious in his work; nor was he an egoist, as I am. He had very few sympathies though; and practically no imagination. You might give your view; this is much at random. (*L*, I: 408)

Woolf differentiates herself from Stephen by her implicitly greater 'egoism', 'sympathies' and 'imagination', qualities that speak as much of her work as of her character. It is striking that at the very moment when

Woolf was prompted to experiment with 'Wagnerian' prose, she was acutely aware of her aesthetic divergence from Leslie Stephen. Despite Woolf's disclaimer that these observations are 'random', she acknowledges her sustained consideration of this subject. Woolf recognised, I would suggest, that an alternative to Stephen's literary aesthetics and to nineteenth-century writing more generally might lie in prose that drew its innovations partly from music. Here we might recall Jane Marcus' suggestion that Woolf not only associated music with her mother but also, more broadly, perceived music as a feminine art. Marcus notes Woolf's comparison of her parents and of music and literature in gendered terms in 'Sketch of the Past' (written 1939–40): 'Father himself was a typical Victorian', 'congenitally unaware of music' and 'had no ear whatsoever for music – when Joachim played at Little Holland House, he asked, when is it going to begin? – the Beethoven or the Mozart being to his ears only "tuning up"' (*MB*, 149 and 122). Her mother's praise for a story Woolf had written, on the other hand, confers intense pleasure, 'like being a violin and being played upon'. Recalling her mother, Woolf observes 'she could play the piano and was musical [. . .] [t]he sound of music also comes from those long low rooms' (*MB*, 105 and 97–8). Julia Stephen 'made life musical and whole', Marcus writes, terming Smyth her later musical 'mother'; Rachel, as we saw, finds music in at least one instance a solace for her 'motherless' condition. Marcus equates music with all that is nurturing, healing and positive, with 'the harmony and rhythm of daily life with her mother, before the interruptions of the aggressive male ego of her father'.[9] Woolf's attitude towards maternal music was, I shall argue, more ambivalent than Marcus suggests, but these letters from Bayreuth do suggest that Woolf's reflections on modern, 'musicalized' fiction went hand in hand with her desire to distinguish her work from that of her father and from paternal or patriarchal aesthetics more widely.

Marcus' reading of *Night and Day* (1919) proposes that music plays a similarly positive, liberating role in Woolf's second novel. Tracing the novel's thematic and structural debts to Mozart's work, particularly to *The Magic Flute*, Marcus identifies numerous instances of Woolf's reversal of the sexual (and class) politics of his opera. In her account, the web of explicit allusions and structural debts to *Don Giovanni* and *The Magic Flute* conveys Woolf's critique of patriarchy and her celebration of 'sisterhood' and female same-sex desire. More specifically, *Night and Day* targets male 'vanity and [. . .] pedantry' and 'the misogyny of Cambridge-Bloomsbury culture, which appropriated the classics and music as male property', celebrating 'the idea of the female utopia' as being 'domestic peace and freedom to work'.[10] Marcus persuasively suggests that the novel was shaped by a number of homosocial, élite contemporary versions of Mozart's opera, including Goldsworthy Lowes Dickinson's pamphlet *The Magic Flute: A Fantasia*, the 1911 Dent/Clive Carey production of the opera in Cambridge, and the 1916 and 1919 London performances. *Night and Day*, she proposes, celebrates a number of family matriarchs including Woolf's aunt, Lady Ritchie, who thought of literature '"as music"': the novel is a 'tribute to that [literal and literary] music created by the females in her family'.[11] 'Woolf attacks the fathers, as Mozart attacks the mothers,' Marcus writes; Woolf 'kill[s] the Angel in the House'.[12] Yet, even as music may offer Rachel and Woolf access to a liberating female art or aesthetic, Woolf's first two novels also reflect her acute awareness of music's role in nineteenth-century oppressions of women.

'Too much Beethoven'

As an amateur female pianist, Rachel Vinrace has a long line of historical and literary ancestors including Elizabeth Bennet in *Pride and Prejudice* (1813), Lady Audley in Braddon's 1862 novel and, more recently, Lucy Honeychurch in Forster's *A Room with a View* (1908). And as literary critics, musicologists and social historians have documented, this figure was the subject of extensive surveillance and commentary in fora from medical texts to conduct books to aesthetic theory and music history. The popularity of the instrument in nineteenth-century culture and domestic music making made the female pianist a focal point of discourses about femininity, the gendered nature of aesthetic consumption and artistic ability, propriety and the acquisition of 'culture'. Since it symbolised 'respectability', Cyril Ehrlich argues, 'the piano was at the centre of social change'.[13] Even as pianos became relatively less expensive and more popular during the nineteenth century – in 1871, it was estimated that 20,000 new pianos were produced by British manufacturers every year, and that a further 10,000 or so (mostly German) pianos were imported[14] – they continued to denote respectability, if not social distinction. The instrument's ubiquity was such that the penny weekly magazine *The Girl's Own Paper* ran a regular column between 1901 and 1908 offering pedagogical advice to young female pianists.[15]

The association of the female amateur keyboardist with women's role in the domestic sphere was pervasive in the nineteenth century. The piano 'served generations of nineteenth-century girls and their parents as a rite of passage into decently socialized womanhood'[16] and the social history of the piano is 'inextricably linked to issues of gender'.[17] Woolf's early novels reflect, and reflect on, discourses about female amateurism, social class and heteronormativity. As Rachel's example illustrates, music is a ladylike 'accomplishment' – a marker, as it was for many in the eighteenth and nineteenth centuries, of her family's wealth and social aspirations. Indeed, Mr Vinrace reminds Rachel 'rather sharply' that '"music depends upon goats"' (upon, in other words, the goods transported by his ships [*VO*, 19]). The cost of non-utilitarian music lessons proclaims Mr Vinrace's wealth and his desire to protect Rachel by restricting her to the domestic sphere: these desires evidently override his reservations about how much, and what, she plays. Cassandra Otway in *Night and Day* exemplifies the conventional expectation that women's playing was primarily intended to provide pleasure in the home – ultimately, for the patriarchs. She does 'her best to create an atmosphere of unmixed beauty' and her playing spirits Mrs Hilbery 'into a perfectly congenial mood', winning the 'approval' of Mr Hilbery (*ND*, 438). Terence's response to Rachel's playing in chapter 22 expresses the same assumptions through his objections to her choice of repertoire. Unabashedly admitting his desire to 'interrupt' her, he explains:

> 'I've no objection to nice simple tunes – indeed, I find them very helpful to my literary composition, but that kind of thing is merely like an unfortunate old dog going round on its hind legs in the rain.' (*VO*, 340)

His remarks unequivocally portray this performance as unwelcome, unattractive and (via Johnson's famous dictum about women preaching) unnatural.[18] Rachel's awareness of, but indifference to, the opportunities for social advancement and genteel displays of femininity afforded by musical 'accomplishment' are apparent in her dismissal of Aunt Bessie's concern that she will '"spoil her arms"' by too much practice and '"then one won't marry"' (*VO*, 15).[19] Cassandra, on the other hand, shows an astute awareness of the potential for social performance offered by domestic music making and on her first night at the Hilberys' compares 'the buzz of voices inside the drawing-room' to 'the tuning up of the instruments of the orchestra' (*ND*, 363). She is a skilled social performer: her flirtation with William Rodney is played out through performances and discussions of music, and the social cachet of musical accomplishment confirmed when Mrs Hilbery reluctantly accepts their attraction with the consoling reflection that, '"after all, she plays the piano so beautifully"' (*ND*, 505). William's pompous reflections reveal the central part that music, displays of femininity and gentility play in his desire. She:

> had a very fine taste in music, and he had charming recollections of her in a light fantastic attitude, playing the flute in the morning-room at Stogdon

House [. . .] The enthusiasms of a young girl of distinguished upbringing appealed to William, and suggested a thousand ways in which, with his training and accomplishments, he could be of service to her. (*ND*, 293)

Rachel and Cassandra are antithetical examples in Woolf's reflections on the social and gender politics of female amateur music.

The piano's part in enforcing women's domestic gender roles and the status quo is exemplified in the Revd. H. R. Haweis' enormously popular *Music and Morals* of 1871. Equating the piano's significance in girls' education with that of Latin for boys, he suggested that music be used therapeutically as a 'healthy outlet for emotion': 'A good play on the piano has not unfrequently [*sic*] taken the place of a good cry up-stairs, and a cloud of ill-temper has often been dispersed by a timely practice.'[20] Here, of course, it is not just any emotions but irritation, resentment and distress that are muted by the piano: for young women it is, as Mi Zhou pithily puts it, 'an instrument of pacification, not change'.[21] Rachel's playing has a similar outcome early in the novel: '[a]bsorbed by her music she accepted her lot very complacently, blazing into indignation perhaps once a fortnight, and subsiding as she subsided now' (*VO*, 35). Woolf's representations of female pianists thus critique these discourses: the piano serves as a paradigm of Victorian attitudes towards women, even as Woolf uses the figure of Rachel to challenge and subvert these ideologies.

Throughout her fiction – perhaps most overtly in *Orlando* (1928) – Woolf equates the piano with the nineteenth century.[22] In the passage introducing the Victorian period, Woolf's narrator writes:

mantelpieces [led] to pianofortes, and pianofortes to drawing-room ballads, and drawing-room ballads (skipping a stage or two) to innumerable little dogs, mats, and china ornaments, the home – which had become extremely important – was completely altered. (*O*, 158)

The percussion, woodwind and brass instruments that had provided often raucous soundscapes in the earlier sections of the novel are supplanted when Orlando reaches the nineteenth century with allusions to the piano and (Aeolian) harp, instruments that Woolf unequivocally associates with women, with domesticity and with the cult of marriage. The instruments of the earlier periods had evoked group performance (orchestras and marching bands), peripatetic minstrels, humble figures and picaresque lifestyles; they are replaced by those associated with solitary, genteel, feminine domestic music. Orlando's realisation of her desire for a wedding ring is conveyed in a composite image of stringed instruments, most obviously the (Aeolian) harp: 'she became conscious,

as she stood at the window, of an extraordinary tingling and vibra-
tion all over her, as if she were made of a thousand wires upon which
some breeze or errant fingers were playing scales.' (*O*, 165). (And
here Woolf's image may be informed by her dinner in 1909 with 'a
chocolate box young woman', the eminent harpist and beauty Miriam
Timothy, the only woman in Queen Victoria's private band.)[23] After
noting that 'the spirit of the nineteenth century was antipathetic to her
in the extreme', the narrator describes Orlando's urgent wish to marry
in an image that fuses allusions to religion, matrimony, the harp and a
musical-emotional fall:

> Thus did the spirit work upon her, for all her past pride, and as she came
> sloping down the scale of emotion to this lowly and unaccustomed lodging-
> place, those twanglings and tinglings which had been so captious and so
> interrogative modulated into the sweetest melodies, till it seemed as if angels
> were plucking harp-strings with white fingers and her whole being was per-
> vaded by a seraphic harmony. (*O*, 168)

Orlando's humiliating collapse down the 'scale of emotion' suggests
that such images are more than incidental details 'documenting' historical changes in musical taste and instrument making: the piano, like the
wedding ring with which it is associated, is emblematic of women's
oppression and heteronormative sexuality. And the novel registers too
the way in which access to, and the exclusion of, music and sound had
become markers of financial, social and, typically, masculine privilege
by the nineteenth century: immediately after visiting Carlyle's sound-
proof room (a synecdoche of the 'coddl[ed]' male 'genius'), and with-
holding her 'conclusion upon Victorian literature', Orlando welcomes
the 'humble' sound of a 'gasp[ing]', 'groan[ing]' barrel organ as the
'music of the spheres' (*O*, 201–2). The intervention symbolically disrupts the sheltered seclusion of Carlyle's Chelsea study, heralding and
aurally evoking the birth of Orlando's son. As Jacques Attali observes,
to listen – or not listen – to 'music' or 'noise' is to realise 'that its
appropriation and control is a reflection of power, that it is essentially
political'.[24]

Seen in this context, Woolf's famous simile about Mr Ramsay in *To
the Lighthouse* (1927) takes on a different emphasis:

> It was a splendid mind. For if thought is like the keyboard of a piano, divided
> into so many notes, or like the alphabet is ranged in twenty-six letters all in
> order, then his splendid mind had no sort of difficulty in running over those
> letters one by one, firmly and accurately, until it had reached, say, the letter
> Q. (*TL*, 47)

The association of Mr Ramsay/Leslie Stephen with the piano is an unexpected – and barbed – one given Woolf's perception of her father's hostility to the pianola acquired by his children and his lack of musical sensibility *in toto*. Woolf employs an intriguingly and conspicuously provisional double simile, the first part of which appears to be qualified or abandoned as the comparison unfolds. Yet the musical simile is sustained longer through the sentence than might first be apparent: the words 'running over these letters one by one, firmly and accurately' surely more immediately suggest the touch of assured fingers on a piano keyboard rather than their ostensible subject, the letters of the alphabet. Of course, Woolf's ambiguous simile that acknowledges the 'splendid' reach of Mr Ramsay's mind at the same moment as bathetically registering its limit only works with the second image: unlike an alphabet, there is no single starting point on a piano keyboard – a scale on an even tempered instrument will sound the same from whichever note it begins – and consequently there is no absolute end point that would denote incompletion in a comparable way to that of the letter 'Q'. The simile thus relies on its second part, the alphabet, to work and Woolf's critique is further sharpened by deploying a literary or at least linguistic simile against Ramsay when recalling her father and male literary tradition more broadly. Yet here she has her cake and eats it, for the point may be that the black and white of the piano keyboard is also a metonym for the patriarch's dichotomised, simplistic, inflexible thought. The piano keyboard and the alphabet are both images of abstract schema, of classification and rigid order, and contrast with the representation of Mrs Ramsay's mind and, symbolically, 'the feminine'.[25] An instrument associated with domesticity, female performers and the feminine thus informs Woolf's critique of the patriarch.

Woolf's allusions to the piano in her earlier fiction also reflect a further aspect of contemporary discourses about female musicians: the trivialising of women's playing. The preservation of existing gender hierarchies depended absolutely on the distinction of male from female performance. Thus, women were not expected to play 'difficult', 'advanced' music (as Terence's request for 'nice simple tunes' reveals), nor were they expected to become exceptionally proficient as performers – such behaviour would denote 'unfeminine' ambition and skill, destabilising a woman's position in her family home and altering her symbolic and actual dependence on her male protectors. Amateurism became a feminine virtue, marking the divergence between male professional 'virtuosity' and female amateur 'accomplishment'.[26] Recall Katharine Hilbery's irritation with her mother's 'musical sentences' and Mrs Hilbery's performance of 'a famous lyric of her father's which had been set to an absurdly and charmingly sentimental air by some early Victorian composer' (*ND*, 116 and 119). The amateur music of these Victorian mothers may be, as Marcus suggests, nurturing but it is also dangerously trivialised and uncongenial to a New Woman like Katharine.[27] In this context, the question of *what* women played was a crucial one. Attention to Rachel's repertoire in *The Voyage Out* invites a very different reading of her character and aesthetic authority than that available without the musical context. Like Lucy Honeychurch, with whom she shares a number of similarities, Rachel is a devotee of Beethoven's late piano sonatas and particularly the last, Op. 111. Woolf reviewed Forster's novel in 1908 as she was writing *The Voyage Out* and it is a pertinent intertext for her own work. The protagonists of these female *Bildungsromans* share many characteristics and Lucy and Rachel are the only central protagonists in each novelist's oeuvre who are practising musicians.[28] As recent outstanding studies by Michelle Fillion and Mi Zhou have established,[29] Lucy's choice of piano repertoire is inextricable from Forster's representation of her exceptional musical accomplishment, and of her aesthetic and emotional promise. Yet the fact that Rachel plays the same Beethoven sonata has not been considered in detail in readings of Woolf's novel.[30]

Woolf's review of *A Room* was lukewarm but she praised Forster's evocation of Lucy's latent potential – a quality she shares with Rachel:

> We care very much that Lucy should give up trying to feel what other people feel, and we long for the moment when, inspired by Italy and the Emersons, she shall burst out in all the splendour of her own beliefs. (*E*, I: 221)

Though her review makes no mention of music, Woolf was well placed to recognise the aesthetic and socio-political associations of Forster's musical allusions. Both knew their Beethoven well: Forster's knowledge of the piano sonatas was thorough (Britten praised it), and based on his experiences as a performer as well as a listener – indeed, the sonatas were the subject of his only (incomplete) attempt at musicological analysis.[31] Woolf's detailed knowledge of Beethoven's work was surely informed in part by *The Oxford History of Music*, as his instrumental work (including, briefly, Op. 111) was the subject of chapter 10 of the fifth volume that she reviewed in 1905. Praising Hadow's 'sane', 'well balanced' criticism and his 'scholarly', 'epigrammatic' style, Woolf nonetheless regrets that 'the history of music is still so largely a history of form'. This leads her to offer an assured summary of the composer's development:

It may be his attention to the formal side of music which makes Mr Hadow, as it seems to us, understate the immense advance made by Beethoven in musical expression. When once he was out of leading-strings he never repeated himself, but was ever going forward. The earlier masters seem to reach a certain stage of maturity and then to vary but little from the level, high though it may be, to which they have attained. But with Beethoven each fresh composition reflects a fresh emotional mood, and the mood in itself gives a new kind of unity to each composition. Especially is this true of the nine great symphonies. (*E*, I: 374)

Woolf's account is certainly not advanced musicology and indeed endorses the position of the 'common listener',[32] but her willingness to take issue with an eminent music critic, and to do so in language that confidently implies her own knowledge of these works, is striking.[33] This knowledge informs her response to Forster's work and to the crucial role of Beethoven in it and shapes too her own allusions to Beethoven in *The Voyage Out*.

Lucy's performance of the first movement of sonata Op. 111 occurs at a provincial English parish concert; the performance is recalled by Mr Beebe in the third chapter, set in Florence. As Fillion and Zhou explain, the Beethoven sonata is perceived as an inappropriate, even transgressive, choice, selfishly disregarding the tastes of the audience and displaying troubling aesthetic ambition. The vicar reflects:

'I do not consider her choice of a piece happy. Beethoven is usually so simple and direct in his appeal that it is sheer perversity to choose a thing like that, which, if anything, disturbs.'[34]

His language (echoed, as Rachel also plays a late Beethoven sonata, in Terence's longing for 'nice simple tunes'?) registers Lucy's intractability and even suggests, through 'perversity', moral corruption. And it evokes, too, the challenging qualities of this work for listeners as well as pianist: to the vicar, it fails to qualify as music, eludes critical language and can only be described as a 'thing'. Published in 1823 when Beethoven was completely deaf, Op. 111 is a work of notorious technical and interpretative difficulty. The first movement includes a startlingly disjointed opening melodic line, played on doubled octaves in the bass register of the piano; a deferred announcement of the tonic ('home') key at the start of the work; a leap of five and a half octaves; and a harmonic structure organised on diminished-seventh chords making the movement as a whole highly chromatic and harmonically ambiguous.[35] The agility required from the performer is hardly compatible with the physical modesty expected of the female pianist, whose body (as many instruction manuals insisted) was to be maintained in a position of restrained, self-effacing decorum as she played. Nor is this the restful soothing repertoire likely to meet the taste of the audience at an amateur provincial concert: the sonata lacks a poetic subtitle to aid audience comprehension,[36] and critics have termed Op. 111 'stormy', violent and 'vehemently' gripping – in 'The C Minor of that Life' (1941) Forster himself described the sonata's opening as a 'dive into the abyss'.[37] Furthermore, as Fillion explains, the 1909 edition of Wilhelm von Lenz's monograph on Beethoven describes Op. 111 as 'very rarely performed', so Rachel and Lucy's choice of repertoire is even more unexpected and startling than it might now seem.[38]

It is this sonata of which Rachel is 'thinking' in chapter 2 during the first long account of her education and character:

> Inextricably mixed in dreamy confusion, her mind seemed to enter into communion, to be delightfully expanded and combined with the spirit of the whitish boards on deck, with the spirit of the sea, with the spirit of Beethoven Op. 112 [*sic*], even with the spirit of poor William Cowper there at Olney. (*VO*, 35)

And in chapter 22, Rachel plays as Terence tries to write despite the distracting effects of the music:

> Up and up the steep spiral of a very late Beethoven sonata she climbed, like a person ascending a ruined staircase, energetically at first, then more laboriously advancing her feet with effort until she could go no higher and returned with a run to begin at the very bottom again. (*VO*, 339–40)

Here, Woolf doesn't specify the work being played but indicates that, if not Op. 111, it is one of the other 'very late' piano sonatas that shared many characteristics of the last. (And when writing to Saxon Sydney-Turner to clarify the Opus number, printed incorrectly in the first edition, Woolf described Op. 111 as the sonata Rachel '*plays*' [*L*, II: 418; emphasis added], suggesting that Woolf had this sonata in mind for the latter passage as well as that in chapter 2).[39] The significance of these allusions to Beethoven at the two ends of the novel lies partly in the late sonatas' technical and aesthetic difficulty: they add considerable weight to Rachel's assertions (to St John Hirst) that she '"play[s] the piano very well [. . .] better, I expect, than anyone in this room"' and (to Terence) that she is '"the best musician in South America, not to speak of Europe and Asia"' (*VO*, 171 and 340). Yes, her remarks are driven by irritation at the men's unthinking dismissal of female amateur musicianship, but the specificity of Woolf's references to Rachel's playing and musical knowledge tells us that they are not hyperbolic. Furthermore, they are significant because they discreetly augment the matrix of allusions to Rachel's growing feminism, associating her with repertoire that was unequivocally perceived as 'masculine'.

The expectation that men and women should play different repertoire had existed at least since the nineteenth century and was institutionalised through phenomena such as the annual competitions at the Paris Conservatoire, for which different works were set for men and women. As Katharine Ellis demonstrates, the difference was marked through Beethoven's work, which appeared intermittently on the men's list between 1863 and the end of the century but not once on the women's.[40] A similar pattern is evident in the exams at England's Royal College of Music where the late sonatas were restricted to the most advanced, mostly male, students. Op. 111 appears not to have been perceived as repertoire for amateurs at all: although other late sonatas appear frequently, the last sonata was on the repertoire list for Associateship Examination for Piano Solo in 1918, but then not until 1929–30, and then not until 1944.[41] And as Zhou documents, in pedagogical essays on Beethoven's sonatas published in *The Girl's Own Paper* in the 1880s and between 1901 and 1907, aimed at female amateurs like Lucy and Rachel, Op. 111 and other late sonatas were invariably omitted – described, in fact, as 'quite unattainable'.[42] Forster's and Woolf's protagonists play repertoire that was, in effect, prohibited for women.

The perception that this was 'masculine' music was the result not only of the technical and interpretative complexity of this late repertoire, but also of gendered discourses about Beethoven and his music more generally. From Wagner's novella *Eine Pilgerfahrt zu Beethoven* (*A Pilgrimage to Beethoven*, 1840), to Beethoven's position as the focal subject of the Vienna Secession in 1902, to innumerable biographies, philosophical works and musicological studies, Beethoven was characterised as the exemplary Romantic 'genius' and 'hero'. Piano sonatas including Op. 57 the 'Appassionata', Op. 31, no. 2 the 'Tempest', Op. 13 the 'Sonata Pathétique' and Op. 53 the 'Waldstein' had been 'heroic icons' since the nineteenth century.[43] Furthermore, the long critical tradition identifying Beethoven's music as 'sounding philosophy' associates Lucy and Rachel with a male intellectual world.[44] And the masculinity of these discourses was emphatic, stressing Beethoven's formidable energy, his originality that appeared independent of models or influence, his defiance of 'fate', his fortitude in the face of personal and aesthetic difficulties, and his isolation and uniqueness. Hadow judged that his work 'has all the attributes of a vigorous, well-rounded manhood' and in *Beethoven: Les grandes époques créatrice* (1928, translated in 1929 as *Beethoven the Creator*), Romain Rolland famously described him as 'the most virile of musicians': 'there is nothing [. . .] of the feminine about him [. . .] He is the masculine sculptor who dominates his matter and bends it to his hand; the master builder, with Nature for his yard'.[45]

The mature Beethoven may be physically 'ruined' like the sonata Rachel plays but his authority is unwavering; as Lawrence Kramer notes, he is the paradigmatic musical 'Father', 'one who feminizes others but who can never himself be feminized'.[46] Woolf could not have known Rolland's essay when writing the novel but she would certainly have been aware of the hyper-virile perceptions of Beethoven and it is very likely she knew (of) Rolland's ten-volume novel *Jean-Christophe* (1904–12). As Forster noted, the early volumes suggest Beethoven's childhood and he recalled: '[t]he theme of it is the hero as musician [. . .] I can remember our excitement at the beginning of the century when [the volumes] were coming out'.[47] This trope of the musician as masculine hero lingers in the account of Mr Ramsay and James travelling towards the lighthouse in the boat: 'But his father did not rouse himself. He only raised his right hand mysteriously high in the air, and let it fall upon his knee again as if he were conducting some secret symphony' (*TL*, 253). Here, the image of conducting is one of control and domination, the allusion to the symphony suggesting a large-scale classical or Romantic work, such as Beethoven's ground-breaking examples. In Woolf's image, the symphony is conducted not by one of the participating players (whether violinist or keyboardist), but by a separate musician, symbolically masculinised and occupying a unique position responsible for the performance as a whole. The mystification of the conductor as the imperious pre-eminent artist is suggested too in the words 'mysteriously high'. As Chapters 5 and 6 consider further, Woolf would return to the relationship between heroism and music in her late fiction but in the early novels her explicit attention is primarily to women and music.

By the later nineteenth century, the piano had become associated with feminism and women's educational aspirations, linked to debates about women's independence and the possibility that a 'woman's music could be a disruptive rather than a harmonising force in the home'.[48] Mrs Honeychurch complains that music 'always left her daughter peevish, unpractical and touchy', and other characters attribute Lucy's periodic rebellions to just this cause – 'too much Beethoven'.[49] Yet Forster portrays the effects of playing more sympathetically: it makes Lucy more confident, more discriminating, and more self-aware – she 'never knew her desires so clearly as after music'.[50] Similarly, after Terence complains about the disruptive effects of Beethoven's 'late sonata', invoking conventional expectations about the repertoire and ameliorative function of women's playing, Rachel responds unhesitatingly: '"Think of words compared with sounds! [. . .] Think of novels and plays and histories –" Perched on the edge of the table, she stirred the red and yellow volumes contemptuously' (*VO*, 340). Woolf emphasises that far from accepting Terence's view, Rachel's confidence has grown as a result of her playing (perhaps specifically her playing of Beethoven), enabling her to assert her own authority and that of her chosen art in uncompromising terms. The narrator notes the increased frankness and equality between the lovers at this stage: '[t]hey were no longer embarrassed, or half-choked with meaning which could not express itself; they were not afraid of each other' (*VO*, 338). Such confidence suggests a means through which Rachel may be able to question or resist the 'status quo' that, early in the novel, it was easier to accept.

As Rachel's comment implies, her playing, like Lucy's, is characterised as primarily self-directed rather than serving an obliging social function or being intended for social and matrimonial display. Lucy's preference for her '"own playing"' rather '"than anyone's"'[51] is echoed in Rachel, whose self-absorption and relative indifference to her audience are emphasised.[52] As Zhou argues, the physicality of piano playing can generate a sense of 'autointoxication' and a greater awareness of one's own body and senses.[53] Roland Barthes proposes that music that is performed, rather than listened to, 'comes from an activity that is very little auditory, being above all manual', and he suggests that this is particularly true of Beethoven's music. Further, Barthes links this tangibility to the composer's deafness, suggesting that Beethoven's music contains 'something *inaudible* (something for which hearing is not the *exact* locality)' – it is 'not abstract or inward, but [. . .] endowed [. . .] with a tangible intelligibility, with the intelligible as tangible'.[54] In Barthes' account, as in more recent works by Kristeva, Nancy and others, music that is played is a corporeal rather than only the sonic experience traditional musical phenomenology would suggest. And for all the intangibility of sound, piano playing allows these women to perceive their worlds as more orderly and more solid. Lucy, 'who found daily life rather chaotic, entered a more solid world when she opened the piano'.[55] Similarly, Rachel's playing conjures a world of concrete, architectural images (the stone staircases and the 'building with spaces and columns' perceived by the listeners at the dance [*VO*, 187])[56] which contrast sharply with her early sense that other people are 'symbols' like 'people upon the stage' (*VO*, 35), or her suggestion to Terence after playing the 'late sonata' that '"we're nothing but patches of light"' (*VO*, 341). Playing allows these women immersion in their own experiences, pleasure and corporeality, and thus offers a means of recuperating the value of amateur domestic playing. Woolf's depiction of Rachel is, however, more ambiguous, even cautious, on this point than is Forster's of Lucy. As Suzanne Raitt suggests in her subtle account of Rachel's playing, music empowers Rachel, allowing her to perform her own 'voice' and to protect her autonomy from the demands of others, but it also exposes the fragility of her own selfhood and sense of her body.[57] The (al)lure of music in this novel is, as the previous chapter proposed, one the female protagonist must approach with caution – and she must be especially wary of unguarded musical responses.

Woolf's choice of the Beethoven intertext, though, is both musically astute and bold. Lucy and Rachel's playing offends conventional gender expectations on several fronts: their aesthetic and personal ambition, their disregard for their audiences, their technical and interpretative skill and their choice of hyper-masculine repertoire all defy the behaviour expected of the female amateur. Their performances of the late sonatas and of Op. 111 specifically give them an auditory force, an aesthetic authority, which has the potential to resonate far beyond these brief diegetic descriptions. They confirm, too, the exceptional qualities of these women, even as they are often 'commonplace' and conventional in other aspects of their lives.[58] Why, then, has attention to the details of their repertoire been so belated? It may be simply that we have not taken Woolf's musical knowledge sufficiently seriously, or have felt ill equipped to venture into music history or musicology, but Lucy's case suggests that there may also be a more specific explanation. In neither the Merchant–Ivory film (1985) nor Andrew Davies' TV adaptation (2007) of Forster's novel does Lucy play Op. 111.[59] It seems that this work still retains a difficulty, a shock value, an inaccessibility for the 'common listener' that is incompatible with the filmmakers' representations of Forster's heroine, or their estimations of public musical taste and feminist sympathies. Perhaps it is only now that readers and film audiences are ready to hear these women, and to hear the full force of the music they play.

Notes

1. Lytton Strachey, Letter to Woolf, 25 February 1916; Allan Monkhouse [review], *Manchester Guardian*, 15 April 1915, 4; and [Mr James, review], *Spectator*, 10 July 1915, 54–5, cited in Majumdar and McLaurin (eds), *The Critical Heritage*, 64, 62 and 58.
2. See, for example: Weliver, *Women Musicians in Victorian Fiction*; Solie, *Music in Other Words*, 85–117; and Fuller and Losseff (eds), *The Idea of Music in Victorian Fiction*.

3. The image surely echoes the 'hard, gem-like flame' of *The Renaissance*'s 'Conclusion'.
4. For more on Edwardian and modern constructions of late-Victorian writing on music as apolitical, see Sutton, *Aubrey Beardsley and British Wagnerism in the 1890s*, particularly the 'Epilogue'.
5. Ellis, *Virginia Woolf and the Victorians*, 2.
6. *Pace* Ellis' observation that 'any explicit discussion of the relation between the Victorian past and the present' is limited. *Virginia Woolf and the Victorians*, 34.
7. Nonetheless, as Ellis notes, Woolf elsewhere frequently embodies 'the Victorian period' in maternal images. *Virginia Woolf and the Victorians*, 5.
8. See, representatively, 'One of Our Great Men', in Woolf, *The Platform of Time*, 184–7.
9. Marcus, 'Thinking Back through Our Mothers', 19. See also Marcus, *Virginia Woolf and the Languages of Patriarchy*, 96–114.
10. Marcus, *Virginia Woolf and the Languages of Patriarchy*, 35, 33, 21 and 27.
11. Marcus, *Virginia Woolf and the Languages of Patriarchy*, 23 and 29.
12. Marcus, *Virginia Woolf and the Languages of Patriarchy*, 30.
13. *The Piano*, 10.
14. H. R. Haweis, *Music and Morals*, 3rd edn (London: Strahan and Co, 1873), 514–15, cited in Zhou, 'Sublime Noise', 86.
15. See Zhou, 'Sublime Noise', 86.
16. Fillion, *Difficult Rhythm*, 57.
17. Zhou, 'Sublime Noise', 84.
18. Grammatically, his objections are targeted at the composition but the allusion to Johnson, noted by Raitt and others, also vilifies Rachel as a female performer. Raitt, 'Virginia Woolf's Early Novels', 35.
19. Zhou provides a fine account of Victorian and Edwardian writing on piano techniques and of attention to the body of the female pianist. See Zhou, 'Sublime Noise', Part II, especially 89–101.
20. *Music and Morals*, 3rd edn (London: Strahan and Co, 1873), 516, cited in Zhou, 'Sublime Noise', 84.
21. Zhou, 'Sublime Noise', 84.
22. See also, for example, the conversation about selling a piano that '"blocks up the hall"' in *The Waves* (W, 69); the instrument is obstructive litter from an earlier era. In contrast, the arrival of 'the present moment' in *Orlando* is imaged as aural and mental overload, 'as if a piano tuner had put his key in her back and stretched the nerves very taut' (O, 206) – an example of Woolf's ambivalence towards modernity and nostalgia for some aspects of nineteenth-century life.
23. Their meeting is described in the sketch 'Jews'. See 'Jews', in Woolf, ed. Bradshaw, *'Carlyle's House'*, 14–15 (14) and 22–3. The harp was one of the few instruments considered genteel for women in the nineteenth century. See Ehrlich, *The Music Profession in Britain*, 156–61.
24. *Noise*, 6.
25. Compare Mrs Ramsay who more frequently perceives sounds in visual terms, perhaps specifically those of a musical score: 'the story of the Fisherman and his Wife was like the bass gently accompanying

a tune, which now and then ran up unexpectedly into the melody' (*TL*, 48).

26. See, for example: Pendle (ed.), *Women and Music*; Hyde, *New-Found Voices*; Loesser, *Men, Women and Pianos*; and Gillett, *Musical Women in England*.

27. See also chapter 7 in which Mrs Hilbery recalls her own mother '"and the old days in Russell Square! I can see the chandeliers, and the green silk of the piano, and Mamma sitting in her cashmere shawl by the window, singing"' (*ND*, 101). Domestic music making again evokes social privilege, femininity and a historical period for which both affection and ridicule are expressed.

28. Louise A. DeSalvo discusses *A Room*'s importance as an intertext; although her discussion does not consider the relation between the two pianists she quotes Woolf's account, in her diary kept during her 1906 visit to Greece, of a young woman who loves music '"for itself and its own sake"' but who also uses it for '"her little triumph"' of social display and flirtation. The diary and Forster's novel shaped the final text of *The Voyage Out*. *Melymbrosia*, xxxiii–xxxvi (xxxv).

29. Fillion, 'Edwardian Perspectives', Zhou, 'Sublime Noise' and Fillion, *Difficult Rhythm*.

30. For brief accounts see: DeSalvo, 'A Textual Variant'; Hafley, 'Another Note on Rachel and Beethoven'; DeSalvo, '*The Voyage Out*: Two More Notes'; and Rosenbaum, '*Voyage Out* Variant No. 2'.

31. Between 1939 and 1940 Forster kept a notebook intending to annotate all the piano sonatas; his comments were 'unabashedly programmatic' (Fillion, *Difficult Rhythm*, 113). See *Difficult Rhythm*, 108–22 for Fillion's analysis and the first publication of 'Beethoven's Piano Sonatas' (i.e. the notebook). For information on Woolf's knowledge of Beethoven see Clements, 'Transforming Musical Sounds into Words'.

32. The phrase is Peter Jacobs': '"The Second Violin Tuning in the Ante-Room"', 239.

33. William Henry Hadow was a prominent educationalist as well as a composer, a writer on music and advisor to the 'Tudor Church Music' series; his publications include *Studies in Modern Music* (1893–5), *Beethoven's Op. 18 Quartets* (1926) and *English Music* (1931).

34 Forster, *A Room with a View*, 51.

35. Zhou, 'Sublime Noise', 103–6.

36. Fillion, 'Edwardian Perspectives', 275.

37. Eric Blom, *Romance of the Piano* (London: Foulis, 1928), 237, and Wilfred Mellers, *Beethoven and the Voice of God* (London: Faber & Faber, 1983), 243, cited in Zhou, 'Sublime Noise', 103, and Forster, 'The C Minor of that Life', in *Two Cheers for Democracy*, 121. Even the sonata's tonality, which it shares with works including the Fifth Symphony, augments the heroic myth of Beethoven's 'defiant opposition to fate'. See Fillion, 'Edwardian Perspectives', 276.

38. 'Edwardian Perspectives', 275.

39. I concur with Heine who concludes that Woolf did not intend an allusion to Op. 112, the cantata set to Goethe's poems about sea voyages. For more detail and a summary of critical debate on this point, see 'Virginia Woolf's Revisions of *The Voyage Out*', 405–8 and 452.

40. Katherine Ellis, 'Female Pianists and their Male Critics in Nineteenth-Century Paris', *Journal of the American Musicological Society* 50.2/3 (1997), 353–85, cited in Zhou, 'Sublime Noise', 106–7.

41. Zhou, 'Sublime Noise', 107.

42. Lady Benedict, 'How to Play Beethoven's Sonatas (In Four Parts)', *The Girl's Own Paper*, 7 January 1882, 106, cited in Zhou, 'Sublime Noise', 108–9.

43. Fillion, 'Edwardian Perspectives', 271. For a useful summary of the construction of Beethoven's heroism, Forster's reading in this literature and the critical material on it see Fillion's essay, 274–5.

44. Fillion, 'Edwardian Perspectives', 275 and see *Difficult Rhythm*, 63. Summarising Lucy's diverse musical tastes as they are delineated in the novel as a whole, however, Fillion makes the intriguing suggestion that they imply 'a transgendered musical orientation' that would have been appealing to Lucy's homosexual male observers/narrators and to Forster himself ('Edwardian Perspectives', 294). Is there a trace of this in Rachel's taste for Beethoven, amplifying the hints of female same-sex desire intimated in episodes such as the embrace with Helen in chapter 21?

45. Hadow, *The Oxford History of Music*, 283, and Rolland, *Beethoven the Creator*, trans. Ernest Newman (London: Victor Gollancz, 1929), 27, cited in Zhou, 'Sublime Noise', 106.

46. *After the Lovedeath: Sexual Violence and the Making of Culture* (Berkeley and Los Angeles: University of California Press, 1997), 5, cited in Fillion, 'Edwardian Perspectives', 276.

47. 'Romain Rolland and the Hero' [1945], in Forster, *Two Cheers for Democracy*, 226–9 (228 and 226). Forster links Rolland's 'rather Teutonic cult for the great man' with Nazism (226).

48. Mary Burgan, 'Heroines at the Piano: Women and Music in Nineteenth-Century Fiction', *Victorian Studies* 30 (1986), 51–76 [52], cited in Zhou, 'Sublime Noise', 84.

49. Forster, *A Room with a View*, 61 and 59.

50. Forster, *A Room with a View*, 60.

51. Forster, *A Room with a View*, 52.

52. Rachel's playing at the dance is exceptional; more usually, she avoids an audience.

53. See Zhou, 'Sublime Noise', 110–14.

54. *Image-Music-Text*, trans. Stephen Heath (London: Fontana, 1977), 149 and 152–3, Barthes' emphasis, cited in Zhou, 'Sublime Noise', 129–30.

55. Forster, *A Room with a View*, 50.

56. Woolf's images derive from a long tradition in aesthetics and literature, most notably, perhaps, Goethe's famous description of architecture as 'frozen music'. As Bucknell suggests, 'both music and architecture can be considered non-representational, and hence, dependent on structural relationships to achieve coherence' (*Literary Modernism*, 33). This view, as he notes, is opposed to Wagner's emphasis on emotion and might loosely be termed formalist. For more on spatial metaphors about music, see Bucknell, chapter 1.

57. Raitt, 'Virginia Woolf's Early Novels', 34–7.

58. Fillion, 'Edwardian Perspectives,' 268. As Fillion notes, critics who ignore the novel's musical allusions tend to see Lucy as a 'flat' character.

59. Nonetheless, the choice of sonatas for the Pension scene in the Merchant–Ivory film was astute: they 'virtually replicate the unfolding of Forster's description of op. 111': Fillion, 'Edwardian Perspectives', 271.

Chapter 3

Death in Effigy

In May 1913, the Woolfs heard Wagner's *Ring* at Covent Garden. It was at least the fifth cycle Woolf had attended since her first in 1898 and it was to be her last. She wrote to Ka Cox:

> We came up here 10 days ago to attend the Ring – and I hereby state that I will never go again, and you must help us both to keep to that. My eyes are bruised, my ears dulled, my brain a mere pudding of pulp – O the noise and the heat, and the bawling sentimentality, which used once to carry me away, and now leaves me sitting perfectly still. Everyone seems to have come to this opinion, though some pretend to believe still. (*L*, II: 26)

Woolf's disenchantment appears unequivocal. Characterising the *Ring* as bellicose, domineering and debilitating, her wearied account is unsurprising in the context of rising nationalist and patriotic rhetoric during the advent of the First World War: in this period, Wagner was central to debates about the relationship between music and what Kramer calls 'socio-cultural agency', as he is for many still.[1] Yet Woolf's enduring engagement with Wagner was far more unresolved than this 'break' suggests – though it is suggestive that she sets the long Wagner scene in *The Years* in 1910, the year when 'human character changed' (*E*, III: 421). Even after the war, her correspondence, essays and fiction demonstrate her indebtedness to – as well as her wariness of – Wagner's work, from which she needs 'help' to keep away. Her allusions to his work become increasingly satirical but she is unable, ultimately, to expel Wagner from her fiction or to put him aside. Far from having resolved her attitude towards Wagner in 1913, she found his work persistently provocative and troubling and it was, I will suggest, formative to her conception of musical-political relations around the war. This chapter traces the ways in which *The Voyage Out*, *Jacob's Room* and *Mrs Dalloway* explore the relationship between nationalism, politics and music, reflecting the disputed status of Wagner's work. The novels suggest that Woolf increasingly perceived music as constitutive of contemporary discourses about national identity, empire and militarism, anticipating her unequivocal critique of Wagner in *The Years* (1937) (discussed further in Chapter 5). All three explore the approach or aftermath of the First World War, and all are shaped by Woolf's ambivalent attitude towards and intimate knowledge of his dramas. Her discreet musical allusions flesh out the novels' pacifism and their socio-political vision more broadly, as they amplified the sexual politics of *The Voyage Out*.

The scale of Woolf's engagement with Wagner's work before the war is striking. She attended: the four parts of the *Ring* at Covent Garden in 1898 (*L*, I: 17); a second cycle in 1900 (*MB*, 156); *Meistersinger*, *Götterdämmerung* and *Das Rheingold*, and probably the complete *Ring*, at Covent Garden in May 1907 (*L*, I: 293–4);[2] and *Götterdämmerung* again in May 1908 (*L*, I: 329). For two weeks in 1908, when attending the opera almost every night, Wagner's works comprised more than half of the repertoire: there were performances of *Götterdämmerung*, *Tannhäuser*, *Die Walküre*, *Meistersinger* and *Tristan*, and Woolf almost certainly saw all of these works at least once during this fortnight (*L*, I: 329–33). She saw *Meistersinger* twice within a week at Covent Garden in February 1909 (*L*, I: 382 and 384); *Parsifal* twice and *Lohengrin* once at Bayreuth in August 1909 (*L*, I: 404, 406–7 and 409); and in 1911 the complete *Ring* again and an additional performance of *Siegfried* at Covent Garden (*L*, I: 478–9). She missed the British premiere of *Parsifal* in February 1914 because she was ill, but Leonard attended.[3] Her attendance continued after the war, albeit less frequently: she saw *Tristan* in 1923 (*L*, III: 56); *Tannhäuser* in 1924;[4] *Die Walküre* in 1925 (*L*, III: 186); *Götterdämmerung* in June 1926;[5] and *Parsifal* with Leonard in 1930.[6] The war may have marked a break for Woolf and the 'graveyard' of a certain kind of literary Wagnerism,[7] but the composer's protean, contested influence was not so easily discarded, as the works of Joyce, Lawrence, Forster, Eliot and Woolf herself amply attest.

'A little world of one's own': *The Voyage Out* and *Mrs Dalloway*

Woolf's first novel, set in an unspecified pre-war period of escalating political tension,[8] includes, as Chapter 1 noted, a small number of overt allusions to Wagner's work. And, in spite of the opinions expressed by the Dalloways, it persistently suggests the inextricability of music and politics; the couple assert the absolute separation of politics and art, yet repeatedly espouse the most jingoistic sentiments in the novel. Clarissa observes, in her first conversation with the ship's passengers:

> 'When I'm with artists I feel so intensely the delights of shutting oneself up in a little world of one's own, with pictures and music and everything beautiful, and then I go out into the streets and the first child I meet with its poor, hungry, dirty little face makes me turn round and say, "No, I *can't* shut myself up – I *won't* live in a world of my own. I should like to stop all the painting and writing and music until this kind of thing exists no longer."'
> (*VO*, 44)

Her perception of music as solipsistic and transcendent resurfaces in her reminiscences about Bayreuth: the operas are '"divine"', '"thrilling"' and '"like nothing else in the world"' – clearly the terms of a card-carrying musical idealist (*VO*, 46–7). Similarly, Richard characterises art as apolitical and politics as a separate and superior domain: '"On [their] own lines"', he judges, poets and artists '"can't be beaten"', but they '"evad[e] [their] responsibilities"' by producing '"visions"' but '"*leav*[ing] things in a mess"' (*VO*, 43, emphasis in original). His idealist conception of art is inextricable, Woolf suggests, from his belief in the separate spheres of the sexes: he excuses Rachel's ignorance of factory conditions with the comment that, '"You play very nicely, I'm told, and I've no doubt you've read heaps of learned books"' (*VO*, 67) and continues:

> 'I never allow my wife to talk politics [. . .] It is impossible for human beings, constituted as they are, both to fight and to have ideals. If I have preserved mine [. . .] it is due to the fact that I have been able to come home to my wife in the evening and to find that she has spent her day in calling, *music*, play with the children, domestic duties – what you will; her illusions have not been destroyed.' (*VO*, 68, emphasis added)

These early conversations establish the novel's attention to the relation between gender, class and racial prejudices and an apolitical conception of music. And later in the novel Rachel observes that the vote will make no difference to her because '"I play the piano"' (*VO*, 240) – this conception of music, the novel stresses, is dangerous, even self-destructive.

The Voyage Out hints not only that musical idealism is to be viewed with caution but also that Wagner's music amplifies pre-war nationalism: it's these Society Wagnerites who champion nationalist and imperialist values. Richard commends Britain's imperial activities to Rachel with the words '"the English seem, on the whole, whiter than most men, their records cleaner"' (*VO*, 67), and when they sight two warships from the Mediterranean fleet Clarissa squeezes Rachel's hand 'convulsively', exclaiming '"Aren't you glad to be English!"' (*VO*, 72). In conversation with her husband, too, Clarissa considers '"what it really means to be English"':

> 'One thinks of all we've done, and our navies, and the people in India and Africa, and how we've gone on century after century, sending out boys from little country villages – and of men like you, Dick, and it makes one feel as if one couldn't bear *not* to be English!' (*VO*, 51, emphasis in original)

Woolf's critique of their naïve patriotism, imperialism and solipsistic conception of art invites us to reconsider Clarissa's enthusiasm for Wagner, and it is striking that the very first simile in which the Dalloways are described is as orchestral instruments: when they make vapid small talk after arriving on the ship Richard's 'boom[ing]' 'bass' voice is compared to his wife's, 'like the bassoon to the flourish of his wife's violin' (*VO*, 41).[9] Woolf's point is perhaps simply that their collective social performance is orchestrated and glib, but in light of their later association with music and militarism the simile takes on an added resonance. Certainly, Woolf hints at an affinity between the emotionalism of Clarissa's experience at Bayreuth and her knee-jerk patriotism at the sight of the warships, between the glib fluency of the Dalloways' political sentiments and Wagner's affective music – but it is only a hint: the novel is ultimately inexplicit about Wagner's politics and those of his operas. As we shall see of *Jacob's Room* too, Woolf seems as interested in the effect of the performance conditions as the operas themselves on the experience, and the ideology, of listeners. The darkened opera house (one of Wagner's innovations), the formality of the etiquette and the social composition of the Bayreuth audience all play their part in the (political) experience of the listeners, allowing us to conclude either that the performance conditions augment the operas' bellicose politics, or that they obscure Wagner's more subtle and ambiguous representations of war. Suggestively, though, Woolf responded rapturously to Mozart's work during the war: recall her description of *Figaro* in December 1917 as 'the perfection of music, & vindication of opera' and after hearing *Don Giovanni* in June 1918 she wrote, '[I] thought rather better of humanity for having that in them' (*L*, I: 83 and 153–4). Her comments suggest revulsion from nationalist music and appropriations of music, and here Woolf (like many of her contemporaries)[10] may be invoking the eighteenth century as an antidote to Wagnerian aesthetics.

As nationalist rhetoric flourished in the early stages of the war, Woolf was disgusted by the jingoism of public concerts: in 1915, she found the 'patriotic sentiment [at the Queen's Hall] so revolting that I was nearly sick' (*L*, II: 57). She observed with concern the increasing nationalism of

British performance practice and of academic writing on music evident, representatively, in Stanford's 1916 *History of Music*. The composer was a figurehead of the English Musical Renaissance, the musical education movement and group of composers who championed British (principally English) music in the late nineteenth and twentieth centuries. Despite the spectrum of political sympathies held by its exponents, nationalism was arguably the English Musical Renaissance's unifying ideology, whether in the form of jingoistic patriotism (often directly in response to the stereotype of England as *Das Land ohne Musik*), resistance to non-British musical idioms, the recovery and promotion of national composers, works and genres, or celebration of national subject matter such as English literary, historical and pastoral topics.[11] Haweis' *Music and Morals* was one of the movement's founding texts: 'We must not be content with foreign models', he wrote, 'we must aim at forming a real national school, with a tone and temper as expressive of, and as appropriate to, England, as French music is to France, Italian to Italy, and German to Germany.'[12] Stanford's *History* assessed the state of English music at the start of the war and, in particular, its indebtedness to Germanic traditions and influences. In contrast to numerous late nineteenth-century accounts of shared Northern European culture, some of which had claimed composers including Wagner for a lineage of British music,[13] Stanford's *History* was a call to patriotism. '[T]he artistic health and productivity of any community increases exactly with its proportion of nationalists', he wrote, describing the relations between the 'nationalists' and the 'denationalists' as 'a quarrel of [. . .] the man who loves his country and the man who loves someone else's'.[14] Despite Stanford's bellicose language, individual composers unsurprisingly differed in their attitudes towards the war; nonetheless, Hughes and Stradling suggest that overtly patriotic projects and commissions were those most popular with individual sponsors, interest groups and charities in the absence of a government 'policy' to promote patriotic music.[15] These sentiments were mirrored in performance practice: at the start of the war, public performances of German music were banned in Britain (though this was not upheld) and German musicians interned as 'enemy aliens'.[16] Composers and performers whose music had dominated Edwardian and Georgian concert and operatic repertoire became persona non grata once war had broken out. (In Forster's 'Postscript' to *A Room with a View* Lucy Honeychurch expresses her conscientious objections by playing Beethoven, and is reported to the police for playing 'Hun Music'.)[17] Even instruments were targeted: schools, showrooms, performers and newspapers were attacked, literally and figuratively, for using or advertising German pianos.[18] The increasingly fraught relationship between music, bellicose politics and nationalism is apparent in the Wagnerian allusions in *Jacob's Room* (to which we will return) and *Mrs Dalloway*; both novels extend and emphasise the conjunction of opera and militarism of the pre-war *The Voyage Out*.

Mrs Dalloway develops Woolf's exploration of the relationship between Wagner's music and military aggression by contrasting pre- and post-war musical practice in England. Diegetic musical allusions are, however, more discreet in the 1925 text than in the two earlier novels: indeed, there are only two explicit references to Wagner in *Mrs Dalloway*, both in connection with Peter Walsh, the man Clarissa rejected to marry Richard. These two allusions suggest the intersection of music with national and gender politics, the conjunction of the intimately personal and the civic. Shortly after Peter first appears in Clarissa's recollections we are told that, 'It was the state of the world that interested him; Wagner, Pope's poetry, people's characters eternally, and the defects of her own soul' (*MD*, 6). Clarissa is recalling her youth at Bourton, so Peter's Wagnerism can be dated to the early 1890s,[19] the decade when Woolf herself first attended Wagner's operas. Peter's interest in 'the state of the world' and his curiosity about party politics in middle age suggest that he is aware of the political controversies surrounding Wagner, or that he is attracted by Wagner's own politics; we are told that Peter and Clarissa frequently argued about politics and that both were 'Socialists' in their youth,[20] so it is likely that Peter's interest in Wagner sprang in part from Wagner's youthful revolutionary activities and the proto-socialism of works such as *Die Kunst und die Revolution* (*Art and Revolution*) and *Das Kunstwerk der Zukunft* (*The Art-Work of the Future*) (both 1849).[21] *Mrs Dalloway* doesn't make explicit whether Clarissa shares Peter's interest, but in *The Voyage Out* her Wagnerism is unequivocal and her youthful 'first *Parsifal*' must also date from the *fin de siècle*. Their interest in Wagner's politics and music takes on a retrospective irony in *Mrs Dalloway*'s 1923 setting now that art music has been overtly appropriated for propagandist purposes in Britain; in the aftermath of the war, the notion of 'pure' music has become much more problematic, and Woolf stresses the interdependence of music and politics in the novel's post-war passages. The strident nationalism of many members of the London public is emphasised in the novel's early pages, for example, and contemporary patriotism associated with the formality of opera performances: Buckingham Palace appears to Richard Dalloway 'an old prima donna facing the audience all in white' (*MD*, 99). Furthermore, there are two references to 'military music' when Elizabeth is near St Paul's Cathedral (*MD*,

117) – a neat association of music with the church and the state, like the references to Big Ben's 'musical' 'warning' before it strikes (*MD*, 4 and 99).

Furthermore, the xenophobia of the post-war London public is contrasted with Clarissa's youthful relationships with Germans:[22] as a child, Clarissa has a German governess, Fräulein Daniels (*MD*, 7),[23] and when Clarissa is a young woman, Joseph Breitkopf comes annually to Bourton 'for weeks and weeks' where he 'pretended to read German with her, but really played the piano and sang Brahms' (*MD*, 30). Joseph Breitkopf's singing and playing of Brahms at Bourton is recalled three times in the novel; he is a 'poor old man' at whom Clarissa and Peter laugh because he sings 'without any voice' (*MD*, 30, 131 and 154). Breitkopf, whose name recalls the leading German music publishers Breitkopf und Härtel, publishers of Brahms' and Wagner's work,[24] is one of two (Anglo-) Germans in the novel who are associated with music. The other is Miss Kilman (originally Khielman) who plays the violin badly and converts to Anglicanism, we are told, partly because of the music:

> She had heard the Rev. Edward Whittaker preach; the boys sing; had seen the solemn lights descend, and whether it was the music, or the voices (she herself when alone in the evening found comfort in a violin; but the sound was excruciating; she had no ear), the hot and turbulent feelings which boiled and surged in her had been assuaged as she sat there, and she had wept copiously. (*MD*, 105)

Miss Kilman lost her teaching position at Miss Dolby's when 'the war came' because she refused to 'pretend that the Germans were all villains' (*MD*, 105); Breitkopf's voicelessness thus prefigures the silencing of many Germans in Britain during and after the war. The allusions to Breitkopf performing 'Hun music' and specifically Brahms – the composer of patriotic works including *Lieder* (Op. 41, 1861) and the *Triumphlied* (Op. 55, 1871) celebrating German victory in the Franco-Prussian war[25] – in England in the 1890s discreetly indicate the extent to which Anglo-German relations have shifted in Clarissa's lifetime. Since Breitkopf is presumably singing *Lieder*, of which Brahms composed thirty-one volumes, Woolf may also be implying that intimate genres such as the song have been displaced by public taste for overtly political, grandiose genres such as opera (another jibe at Wagner, perhaps, whose rivalry with Brahms was notorious?). Woolf's allusions to Brahms – who she described as an 'old brute' in a 1933 letter to Smyth (*L*, V: 168) – may also have been informed by her attendance, in 1924, at a Brahms recital by the great German soprano Elena Gerhardt whose career exemplified the breakdown of Anglo-German relations during the war: following her British debut in 1906, Gerhardt had become one of the most popular German singers with London audiences but her British performances were halted for the duration of the war.[26] As Gerhardt found, the Anglo-German intimacies of Clarissa's youth have become strained in the aftermath of war and although Clarissa's hatred of Miss Kilman is not explicitly linked to her nationality it is a suggestive hint of the post-war political climate in Britain, especially as Clarissa repeatedly employs military imagery when she thinks of Miss Kilman, imagining her, for example, as 'some prehistoric monster armoured for primeval warfare' (*MD*, 106). It is suggestive too that the adult Clarissa no longer visits Bourton (*MD*, 36), that venue of pre-war cosmopolitan music making; the house is now owned by Herbert Parry, whose name surely recalls another figurehead of the English Musical Renaissance, Hubert Parry (the Stephens' neighbour in Kensington). At Bourton, the English nationalist Parry has symbolically displaced the German nationalist Brahms. *Mrs Dalloway*'s discreet allusions to British and German composers thus indicate the increasingly nationalist climate in Britain and the intolerance of Anglo-German aesthetic and personal relations among prominent British composers and educationalists. They suggest the difficulties of sustaining that cherished nineteenth-century belief in a shared Northern European musical, aesthetic and ethnic identity in the aftermath of war.

Having no country: *Jacob's Room* and *Mrs Dalloway*

Woolf's scrutiny of the relationship between Wagner's operas, national identity and military aggression becomes overt in the extended account of a performance of *Tristan* in chapter 5 of *Jacob's Room*. The Durrants, Mr Wortley and Jacob attend Wagner's representation of doomed adulterous love, dynastic rivalry and the female disempowerment that results from it. Isolde, the Irish princess transported to Cornwall by Tristan to become a bride for his uncle, King Marke, is a pawn in the political liaisons between Ireland and Cornwall, a condition she bitterly acknowledges during the voyage, terming herself a 'prize' and the marriage 'an insult'.[27] Her entrapment and thwarted autonomy are stressed in Wagner's version of the medieval legend; the interdependence of marital relations, dynastic power and warfare shapes the plot, characterisation and themes of the opera. As we shall see, *Tristan*'s dynastic plot informs Woolf's characterisation and the representation of contemporary politics in *Jacob's Room*.

Clara Durrant's relationship with Jacob is, for example, ironically contrasted to that of Wagner's lovers. Clara and Jacob meet immediately after Jacob's sea voyage to Cornwall, and their relationship unfolds to some extent to music: they attend the opera together, and we see them conversing during the music at the Durrants' party. Though a super-ficially unlikely Isolde, Clara imagines herself as Wagner's heroine as she watches the opera unfold: she 'said farewell to Jacob Flanders, and tasted the sweetness of death in effigy' (*JR*, 57), parting from her lover in imagination as Isolde does 'in reality' in the third Act of the opera, when she sings her great lament over Tristan's body. Other characters hint at Clara's capacity for Romantic love: 'to very observant eyes' she 'displayed deeps of feeling which were positively alarming; and would certainly throw herself away upon some one unworthy of her [. . .] unless [. . .] she had a spark of her mother's spirit in her – was somehow heroic' (*JR*, 135). Like Isolde, who is depicted during the first Act prin-cipally in the company of her nurse Brangäne, Clara is repeatedly shown in relation to a maternal figure. Suffocated by her mother's influence, Clara, like Isolde, struggles to find a voice for self-expression and is taunted by unspoken desires. Isolde is adept at hiding her desires from herself and others – Tristan calls her '[c]oncealment's mistress'[28] – and Clara similarly frustrates Mr Bowley by leaving a complaint about her mother unfinished: 'Clara never confided in any one,' the narrator tells us (*JR*, 146). The parallels with Wagner's lovers are ironic. The point is, of course, that despite Clara's hopes Romantic love will not blossom; although Jacob will go on to have an adulterous affair under the nose of his patron and on foreign soil, as Tristan does, it will be with Sandra Wentworth Williams rather than with Clara. Wagner's emotional regis-ter is undercut, and the romantic plot of the medieval lovers one of the many narratives unfulfilled in the novel. Like the harmonic and melodic deferment of the opera's music, exemplified by the '*Tristan* chord', the novel privileges irresolution and incompletion.

Nonetheless, *Tristan*'s Schopenhaurian association of erotic desire and death is repeatedly evoked in the novel's descriptions of Cornwall. In the opera, Cornwall is the setting for Tristan and Isolde's affair: the operatic lovers first acknowledge their mutual desire on the sea voyage to Cornwall, and it is in Cornwall that they meet illicitly at King Marke's court, celebrating their love in the *Liebestod*. It is here too that the lovers are caught together, and Tristan betrayed and stabbed during the hunt. In *Jacob's Room* – as in the opera – Cornwall is associated with erotic desire and with imminent death. Its landscape evokes sorrow and deliri-ous joy: the scene appears to '[rise] to heaven in a kind of ecstasy' yet the cottage smoke 'has the look of a mourning emblem, a flag floating its caress over a grave' (*JR*, 39).[29] The narrator observes that 'loveliness is infernally sad. Yes, the chimneys and the coast-guard stations and the little bays with the waves breaking unseen by any one make one remember the overpowering sorrow. And what can this sorrow be?' (*JR*, 40). The sorrow is, perhaps, not only a product of Woolf's loss of the idyllic site of childhood but also the result of national displacement or exile. Woolf's narrative returns Wagner's tale to its English setting, to its British textual roots (and Woolf undoubtedly knew several English predecessors of Wagner's version of the tale).[30] One could thus argue that the novel's echoes of *Tristan* are a repatriation of Wagner's text, a reclaiming of the widely known nineteenth-century German account. (Though such a simplification would have to overlook the legend's French sources, the fact that the opera is, stylistically, a very 'French' work, and Woolf's familiarity with works including *The Waste Land*, an Anglo-American response to the legend mediated via Verlaine.)[31] But although Woolf's allusions to *Tristan* arguably domesticate and provincialise the operatic text that would more usually be encountered in metropolitan, cosmopolitan opera houses, there is little sense of secure homecoming for the characters or the narrator of this novel. It is, on the contrary, the failure of literary representation provoked by the opera that prompts the first and one of the most conspicuous of the first-person narrative interventions in the novel: after noting the impossibility of recording the diversity of experience at the opera house, the narrator remarks 'no – we must choose. Never was there a harsher necessity! or one which entails greater pain, more certain disaster; for wherever I seat myself, I die in exile' (*JR*, 57). This interruption is, perhaps, an unexpected moment of narrative empathy with Isolde. It is, after all, Isolde who dies in exile at Brittany by Tristan's neglected castle Kareol. In Wagner's opera, she imagines her love for Tristan as supplying a homeland for her: caught *in flagrante*, she sings to Tristan, '"Thy kingdom now art showing, [...] / why should I shun that land / by which the world is spann'd?"'[32] But Isolde pointedly does die in exile from her Irish homeland, alone but for the body of her dead lover – as a (married) woman Isolde has no country. Whether we read the opera as celebrating the lovers' transcendence of and ultimate indifference to national ties or as a critique of patriarchal dynastic and imperial relations, *Tristan* unquestionably elicits a sense of exile from Woolf's narrator. Whereas the musical allusions in *Mrs Dalloway* convey the rise of popular patriotism after the war, these passages in *Jacob's Room* explicitly record the narrator's national dislocation, the impossibility of national affiliation for this authorial figure. In their different ways, both post-war novels resist and critique the nationalism that had dominated so much recent discourse about music.

Given the prominence of this narrative fissure, the Covent Garden
episode in chapter 5 invites detailed attention:

> The autumn season was in full swing. Tristan was twitching his rug up under
> his armpits twice a week; Isolde waved her scarf in miraculous sympathy
> with the conductor's baton. In all parts of the house were to be found pink
> faces and glittering breasts. When a Royal hand attached to an invisible body
> slipped out and withdrew the red and white bouquet reposing on the scarlet
> ledge, the Queen of England seemed a name worth dying for. Beauty, in its
> hothouse variety (which is none of the worst), flowered in box after box; and
> though nothing was said of profound importance, and though it is generally
> agreed that wit deserted beautiful lips about the time that Walpole died – at
> any rate when Victoria in her nightgown descended to meet her ministers, the
> lips (through an opera glass) remained red, adorable. Bald distinguished men
> with gold-headed canes strolled down the crimson avenues between the stalls,
> and only broke from intercourse with the boxes when the lights went down,
> and the conductor, first bowing to the Queen, next to the bald-headed men,
> swept round on his feet and raised his wand.
>   Then two thousand hearts in the semi-darkness remembered, anticipated,
> travelled dark labyrinths; and Clara Durrant said farewell to Jacob Flanders,
> and tasted the sweetness of death in effigy; and Mrs Durrant, sitting behind
> her in the dark of the box, sighed her sharp sigh; and Mr Wortley, shifting
> his position behind the Italian Ambassador's wife, thought that Brangäne
> was a trifle hoarse; and suspended in the gallery many feet above their heads,
> Edward Whittaker surreptitiously held a torch to his miniature score; and . . .
> and . . .
>   In short, the observer is choked with observations. Only to prevent us from
> being submerged by chaos, nature and society between them have arranged a
> system of classification which is simplicity itself; stalls, boxes, amphitheatre,
> gallery. The moulds are filled nightly. There is no need to distinguish details.
> But the difficulty remains – one has to choose. For though I have no wish to
> be Queen of England – or only for a moment – I would willingly sit beside
> her; I would hear the Prime Minister's gossip; the countess whisper, and
> share her memories of halls and gardens; the massive fronts of the respect-
> able conceal after all their secret code; or why so impermeable? And then,
> doffing one's own headpiece, how strange to assume for a moment some
> one's – any one's – to be a man of valour who has ruled the Empire; to refer
> while Brangäne sings to the fragments of Sophocles, or see in a flash, as the
> shepherd pipes his tune, bridges and aqueducts. But no – we must choose.
> Never was there a harsher necessity! or one which entails greater pain, more
> certain disaster; for wherever I seat myself, I die in exile. Whittaker in his
> lodging-house; Lady Charles at the Manor. (*JR*, 56–7)

The scene is one of conservatism and patriarchy: the women with
'glittering breasts', the bald men with 'gold-headed canes', and the
platitudes about Walpole and Queen Victoria characterise opera as a
privileged, staid cultural institution. Though the audience comment
on the decline of wit and conversation, this scene is predominantly an

image of endurance – of the persistence of social habits, of class hierarchies and even of conversational gambits. (And in this the novel differs from 'The Opera', in which Woolf emphasises the class diversity of the opera house audience, from the 'elderly old-fashioned gentlemen' to the '[s]trange men and women [. . .] in the cheap seats' [*E*, I: 271]).[33] The 'bald distinguished men' sitting in the stalls represent one possible future for Jacob, with whom the adjective 'distinguished' is repeatedly associated in the novel. Yet, as Woolf reminds us, these social lineages will be shattered by the war: Jacob will indeed die as Clara imagines, he will not develop into one of these suave patriarchs whose social routine includes regular attendance at the opera. It is precisely the apparent archaism of opera that evokes the looming cultural shift. When the Durrants and Mr Wortley attend Covent Garden for the second time in the penultimate chapter of the novel, war has just been declared. Jacob is not with them and the faces of the audience, which were 'pink' in the first account, now 'all alike were red in the sunset'. Clara imagines that she glimpses Jacob in the 'blazing windows' (*JR*, 153): this scene just two pages from the end of the novel is one of individual and national destruction, succinctly anticipating the red and gold imagery of *The Years*, which Marcus terms Woolf's *Götterdämmerung*.[34] Whereas the first performance left Lady Charles sleepless, 'tunnelling into the complexity of things' (*JR*, 56), the second is followed by the sound of the gun ships in Piraeus, 'tunnelling its way with fitful explosions among the channels of the islands' (*JR*, 154).[35]

In the first operatic episode, Woolf leaves us in no doubt of the affinities between militarism and the performance practice of opera. The audience at the London opera house share a sentiment of uniform nationalism: 'When a Royal hand attached to an invisible body slipped out and withdrew the red and white bouquet reposing on the scarlet ledge, the Queen of England seemed a name worth dying for.' This is a neat synecdoche of imperialism: the hand of imperialism invisibly but tangibly attached to the head of state. (Here, too, Woolf anticipates *The Years*: at the performance of *Siegfried* the audience 'instinctively' watch the royal box and speculate on the king's imminent death [*Y*, 174] – the power of the monarch and patriarch, augmented by the architectural space of the opera house, is emphasised.) Many in the audience, including Jacob, will indeed die for this name in the war and the colours of the bouquet evoke not only the English flag but also the colours of the Red Cross – they are 'omens of death'.[36] This passage suggests opera's role in articulating and maintaining royalist national identity, the event's jingoistic effect perhaps explaining the narrator's queasy sense of exile. The scene also evokes, through the presence of the Italian ambassador's wife, the crucial role of diplomatic negotiations in the years preceding the declaration of war. And the relationship between this operatic performance and imperialism is stressed in the narrator's speculations about the interior lives of the audience: the narrator imagines the possibility of 'assum[ing] for a moment some one's – any one's' headpiece. After the narrator has imagined overhearing the queen's conversation, they imagine being 'a man of valour who has ruled the Empire'; the fictitious audience members whose lives are briefly sketched are a monarch and an imperialist. Despite the potential scope of the narrator's speculations, these are the only minds to which we are allowed access, augmenting the association between metropolitan opera, nationalism and imperialistic aggression. Again, this anticipates the imperialism associated with Wagnerian performances in *The Years*: at *Siegfried*, Kitty meets a young man who is 'something in the Foreign Office; with a handsome Roman head' and 'exalted' by the music she reflects, 'I've three boys. I've been in Australia, I've been in India [. . .]' (*Y*, 174–5).

The patriotism of this scene, Woolf suggests, is a product both of the social practice of opera at this date – the royal patronage, class stratification and formality of performance conditions – and of the opera itself. The scene considers, in other words, not only the politics of Wagner's work but also of performance practice more generally. The narrator highlights the uncomfortable parallels between the nationalism of the episode's pre-war setting and the text being performed, allowing the possibility that *Tristan* itself plays a part in the audience's effusion of patriotism. In the three paragraphs describing the operatic scene, Woolf shifts between generic allusions to opera and precise allusions to episodes in Wagner's work. The passage thus starts with allusions to multiple performances: '[t]he autumn season was in full swing. Tristan was twitching his rug up under his armpits twice a week; Isolde waved her scarf in miraculous sympathy with the conductor's baton' (*JR*, 56). The artifice of opera is exposed, the tone sceptical. It is in this paragraph that the narrator notes the affluence, age and respectability of the audience, and emphasises too the totemic presence of the monarch at the performance. The references to Tristan's 'rug' and Isolde's 'scarf' indicate that the narrator is recalling the third Act of the opera, when the dying Tristan turns restlessly on his couch, awaiting Isolde who waves to the waiting Tristan and his attendant as her ship approaches. This moment in the opera immediately precedes the lovers' reunion and their deaths – an ominous omen for Jacob and Clara sitting in the audience. The first paragraph thus begins by alluding to the final section of the opera and to 'the season' in general; the narrative only turns to this specific performance with the description of the audience chattering before the curtain goes up – 'In all parts of the house were to be found pink faces and glittering breasts.' After the description of the conductor bowing to the audience and raising his baton, the narrator describes the start of the Prelude: 'Then two thousand hearts in the semi-darkness remembered, anticipated, travelled dark labyrinths; and Clara Durrant said farewell to Jacob Flanders, and tasted the sweetness of death in effigy [. . .]' (*JR*, 57).

This second paragraph marks the start of the unfolding of the music, and the effect of the performance on the listeners. The audience is described remembering and anticipating – a description that could stand equally well as a description of the experience of Wagner's characters, hinting that the audience share the characters' experience as the opera unfolds. With its mature leitmotivic structure, *Tristan* functions through the repetition, recollection and reworking of musical themes, but the characters too are themselves preoccupied with their memories and anticipations. This is particularly true of the first Act, when Isolde broods at length on Tristan's treatment of her and reports many of the events that precede those unfolding on stage. The first four scenes of Act I are dominated by Isolde's reflections to Brangäne; the opera opens with this long interaction between the two women, exploring Isolde's relationship with her substitute mother and her humiliation and entrapment between Tristan and King Marke. This is the part of the opera in which Brangäne plays the most prominent part, and Mr Wortley notes that the soprano seems 'hoarse'. Thus Woolf discreetly indicates that this second paragraph is describing the first Act of the opera, and suggests the parallels between Clara and Isolde: Clara is placed in close proximity to her mother in the box, and the 'sweetness of death' she imagines may even be Brangäne's poison/love potion that Isolde challenges Tristan to drink in atonement for his treatment of her.

With the third paragraph, though, the narrator turns from following the unfolding performance and reflects instead on the array of observations that 'choke' them. After the narrator's observations on the 'difficulty' of choosing between viewpoints, the references to the action of the opera tell us that the first two Acts have passed: the 'shepherd [who] pipes his tune' appears at the start of the third Act of the opera – he pipes to soothe the dying Tristan and to tell him when Isolde's ship has been sighted. We have returned, that is, to the third Act at which the allusions to the 'autumn season' started. Woolf suggests, though, that the subject and significance of the opera (which has unfolded unrecorded between the second and third paragraphs) have been incomprehensible to the 'man of valour' she imagines listening. Instead of recognising the links between militarism, dynastic alliances and romantic love that Wagner's opera depicts, he is inattentive to the details of the opera, thinking instead of 'fragments of Sophocles', 'bridges and aqueducts' while the final scenes of the lovers' reunion unfold. The lessons of Wagner's tragic plot have been ignored by this listener and by society as a whole, moving unthinkingly towards mass warfare. More alarmingly, the very phrase 'man of valour' indicates the perpetuation of patriarchal views of romantic love and war. The chivalric vocabulary suggests the continuity between the world of Wagner's medieval lovers, and the bellicose, imperialist sentiments of this pre-war audience member. The allusions to Wagner's *Tristan* form part of a web of references to dynastic rivalries intertwined with romantic love: the Trojan wars are evoked in the final pages of the novel, for example, as Clara walks the terrier Troy through Hyde Park.[37] Wagner's narrative, for all the self-evident 'pompous ceremony' (*JR*, 153) of opera, depicts a painfully contemporary tale. Whether we conclude that Woolf was indicting Wagner's glorification of dynastic warfare and patriarchal sexual politics, or (in a reading more sympathetic to Wagner) that she was drawing attention to *Tristan*'s exploration of this sinister ideological symbiosis, *Jacob's Room* suggests this is a symbiosis society overlooks at its peril.

Mrs Dalloway also evokes, and critiques, Wagner's celebration of Romantic love and *Tristan* particularly through its second explicit reference to Wagner. Just before Clarissa recalls the momentous moment when she and Sally Seton kissed at Bourton, she notes that 'Peter Walsh and Joseph Breitkopf went on about Wagner'. Both men then turn and face the women, shattering their intimacy with a violence Clarissa compares to 'running one's face against a granite wall in the darkness' (*MD*, 30); this allusion associates Wagner with insistent heteronormative sexuality.[38] The representation of Clarissa and Peter's love takes on a new resonance when we recall that Peter's desire is described as 'excessively' intimate and self-destructive – as *Tristan*-like? Clarissa reflects:

> For in marriage a little licence, a little independence there must be between people living together day in day out in the same house; which Richard gave her, and she him [. . .] But with Peter everything had to be shared; everything gone into. And it was intolerable, and when it came to that scene in the little garden by the fountain, she had to break with him or they would have been destroyed, both of them ruined, she was convinced; though she had borne about her for years like an arrow sticking in her heart the grief, the anguish: and then the horror of the moment when someone told her at a concert that he had married a woman met on the boat going to India! (*MD*, 6–7)

Clarissa's rejection of Peter seems to arise as much from resistance to unconstrained intimacy, to a Wagnerian (specifically *Tristan*-like) model of heterosexual love, as from resistance to Peter himself. Peter's model

of romantic love recalls Tristan and Isolde's 'immoderate' desire for intimacy and it was just this aspect of the opera from which Woolf turned
during the composition of the novel, writing that the 'love making bored
me' (*L*, III: 56). Given that Peter is a persistent romantic ('always in
love with the wrong woman' [*MD*, 103]), and an admirer of Wagner's
music, Woolf is surely implying an affinity between Wagner's work
and possessive patriarchal heterosexuality. Though Peter seems not
to have got over his Wagnerian conception of romantic love, Clarissa
has consciously renounced it: she says of 'love and religion' that they
destroy 'the privacy of the soul' (*MD*, 107).[39] The novel's echoes of
Tristan continue as both scenes of romantic rejection – when the lovers
choose the 'wrong' partner – are associated with music: the musician
Joseph Breitkopf interrupts the scene by the fountain when Clarissa tells
Peter ' "[t]his is the end" ' (*MD*, 55), and Clarissa hears of Peter's marriage at a concert. Furthermore, Peter has married a woman met on a
boat, perhaps an unconscious, parodic, re-enactment of the *Tristan* plot.
Woolf's allusions to *Tristan* are far from schematic, but Peter's presence
on the boat echoes Isolde's disempowerment, and the 'arrow sticking in
[Clarissa's] heart' may recall Tristan's fatal wound; certainly, the erotic
triangles between Peter, Richard, Sally and Clarissa are repeatedly characterised in the vocabulary of medieval chivalry, as appropriate to the
Tristan legend. After Sally's kiss, for example, Clarissa imagines Peter
and Sally as rivals for her hand, and describes Sally 'gallantly taking
her way unvanquished' (*MD*, 31). The parallels to *Tristan* suggest that
Clarissa, like Isolde, has made a strategic rather than a romantic match,
and that the true lovers have been divided. This implication is most
apparent immediately after Peter has told Clarissa of his love for Daisy:

> Take me with you, Clarissa thought impulsively, as if he were starting
> directly upon some great voyage; and then, next moment, it was as if the five
> acts of a play that had been very exciting and moving were now over and she
> had lived a lifetime in them and had run away, had lived with Peter, and it
> was now over.
>   Now it was time to move, and, as a woman gathers her things together, her
> cloak, her gloves, her opera-glasses, and gets up to go out of the theatre into
> the street, she rose from the sofa and went to Peter. (*MD*, 40)

Here, Clarissa immediately associates the unfulfilled relationship with
Peter with a sea journey, with emotional excess, and with opera; again,
she retreats from the 'Wagnerian' emotional pitch.[40] As in *Jacob's
Room*, Woolf uses discreet allusions to *Tristan* to stress the enduring
allure – and the dangers – of chivalric models of heterosexual relations
for men and women.

In addition to elucidating the romantic relations of Clarissa, Peter and Sally, musical allusions link *Mrs Dalloway*'s parallel narratives, reinforcing the interdependence of what might be cursorily labelled the 'romantic' and the 'war' plots. Woolf uses music and the spatial movement of sound to link the domestic and the civic, to suggest the interdependence of national and sexual politics, and of music and politics. Several characters sing, for example: Clarissa sings on a boating trip as a young woman (*MD*, 53); a '"[p]oor old woman"' sings Richard Strauss (*MD*, 70);[41] Joseph Breitkopf sings Brahms; and Septimus Warren Smith imagines Evans and 'the dead' singing (*MD*, 59, 119 and 125). Similarly, there are several conversations about music at the party and Clarissa's 'impersonal' musical tastes in middle age are for Bach, whose music she praises to her guests (*MD*, 150). In contrast to Clarissa's mature disenchantment with Wagnerian emotionalism and her preference for the formal discipline of Bach, the men at the party are, like Peter, anything but impersonal in their musical interests, sharing bawdy stories about music hall singers which they refuse to tell the women (*MD*, 149). Peter decides to attend the party partly because he wants to be updated on London's music (*MD*, 136), and as he walks to it he hears music floating from open windows, reflecting that 'Beauty' includes 'a piano, a gramophone sounding', 'pleasure-making hidden' (*MD*, 138). Peter's sensitivity to music also links him to Septimus Warren Smith, the shell-shock victim who shares this trait. Septimus is powerfully moved by music; it terrifies him and repeatedly makes him weep (*MD*, 119). In his disturbed state he imagines music – including that of a 'shepherd boy's piping' – becoming visual (*MD*, 58).[42] The layered imagery of this hallucinatory passage recalls Shakespeare, Shelley and *The Waste Land*, but also – through its allusions to the shepherd boy and the sailor – *Tristan*. These details tell us that Septimus knows Wagner's opera, and thus that he has listened to live performances and possibly recordings of Wagner's music: Septimus and Rezia have a gramophone, which they discuss animatedly in a moment of affection and intimacy before Peter sets out for the party – like the Woolfs in the later 1920s, the Warren Smiths are presumably domestic Wagnerians.[43] When Peter walks from his hotel he hears a gramophone playing (*MD*, 138); his route from Bedford Place (*MD*, 138) is likely to have taken him straight past Septimus' lodgings 'off the Tottenham Court Road' (*MD*, 75). The overheard gramophone can't be the Warren Smiths', however, since Septimus is dead and Rezia sedated. Instead, the sound evokes Septimus' absence, the cessation of the domestic intimacy and contentment that the sound represents to Peter. Rather than hearing the Warren Smiths' gramophone, Peter hears instead the ambulance going to attend Septimus (*MD*, 128); rather than his recorded music floating from the window, Septimus himself has fallen to his death. Woolf underscores these painful associations between overheard music and the victims of war when Elizabeth hears the 'military music' near St Paul's:

> The noise was tremendous; and suddenly there were trumpets (the unemployed) blaring, rattling about in the uproar; military music; as if people were marching; yet they had been dying – had some woman breathed her last, and whoever was watching, opening the window of the room where she had just brought off that act of supreme dignity, looked down on Fleet Street, that uproar, that military music would have come triumphing up to him, consolatory, indifferent. (*MD*, 117)

In this grotesque echo of the shepherd boy's 'elegy' which Septimus had imagined in his hallucination about visible music (*MD*, 58), Elizabeth imagines 'military music' as 'consolatory, indifferent', the comforter of the bereaved. Anything less consolatory to the shell-shocked Septimus or the bereaved Rezia would be hard to imagine; Elizabeth's conclusion is as misjudged as Dr Holmes' repeated instruction that Septimus treat his depression by attending music halls (*MD*, 22 and 77). These parallel images of open windows, overheard music and gross misjudgements about the sources, politics and effects of music link Peter, the Dalloways and the Warren Smiths. Through these and other musical allusions, Woolf underlines the interdependence of the romantic and the political, gender and war, in *Tristan*, in her characters' histories and in *Mrs Dalloway*'s post-war political context.

The musical allusions in *Mrs Dalloway*, as in *The Voyage Out* and *Jacob's Room*, thus invite us to recognise the interdependence of music and politics – most obviously, the politics of nationalism and gender. Mark Hussey's observation that Woolf's work repeatedly explores the connections 'between the domestic and the civic effects of patriarchal society', 'between ethics and aesthetics' is as pertinent to these musical allusions as it is to her overt representations of war.[44] The musical allusions cumulatively contradict the view that music is a 'pure', apolitical art, a view exemplified by the complacent courtier Hugh Whitbread, to whom life appears 'musical, mysterious' during a lavish lunch consumed before composing eugenicist propaganda for Lady Bruton (*MD*, 89).[45] Woolf's depictions of Wagner's operas in these three novels repeatedly consider the cultural and political work of opera, the relationship between music and the politics of nationality, gender, class and empire. Her work shows a prescient awareness of music's function as a political discourse. Although Wagner is an over-determined example, a composer notorious for his nationalist and anti-Semitic writings, 'music', as Susan McClary observed, 'is always a political activity'.[46]

Notes

1. *Classical Music and Postmodern Knowledge*, 4.
2. Woolf refers to attending operas on 'Monday' and 'Wednesday', i.e. 6 and 8 May 1907; *Götterdämmerung* was performed on 6 May, and *Rheingold* on the 8th. These performances were part of a revived production of the *Ring* conducted by Hans Richter; Woolf probably attended all four parts as she was in London for the performances between 30 April and 15 May. Later that year she wrote, 'nothing will induce me to sacrifice my Richter' (*L*, I: 312).
3. Entry dated 2 February 1914, Leonard Woolf's Diary. University of Sussex, LWP II.R.6.
4. Entry dated 13 June 1924, Leonard Woolf's Diary, LWP II.R.18.
5. Entry dated 3 June 1926, Leonard Woolf's Diary, LWP II.R.20.
6. Entry dated 16 May 1930, Leonard Woolf's Diary, LWP II.R.24.
7. Stoddard Martin applies the term to the publication of *The Waste Land* (1922). *Wagner to 'The Waste Land'*, vii.
8. As Stuart N. Clarke has established, the novel alludes to events between 1907 and 1910; see 'Dating the Action of *The Voyage Out*'. I would like to thank Stuart N. Clarke for making an earlier version of this paper available to me before publication.
9. Cf. Mrs Ramsay's image of marriage as 'that solace which two different notes, one high, one low, struck together, seem to give each other as they combine' (*TL*, 34). Woolf frequently uses similar images of her own marriage, but in the fiction they seem more often to denote marital insincerity or complacency.
10. See, representatively, Vernon Lee's short story 'A Wicked Voice' (1890) and numerous essays on music, or Aubrey Beardsley's series of drawings for 'The Comedy of The Rhinegold' (1896). For further detail on similar constructions of eighteenth-century art, see Sutton, *Aubrey Beardsley*, 65–8 and Chapters 5 and 6.
11. For an introduction see Hughes and Stradling, *The English Musical Renaissance*.
12. *Music and Morals*, 573.
13. For more detail on this point, see Sutton, *Aubrey Beardsley*, especially 185–9.
14. Stanford and C. Forsyth, *A History of Music* (Macmillan) 1916, 305, cited in *The English Musical Renaissance*, 88. Hughes and Stradling note that Stanford's rejection of the Germanic tradition may have been due to the influence of his co-author, the nationalist Forsyth.
15. See Hughes and Stradling, *The English Musical Renaissance*, 87.
16. Hughes and Stradling, *The English Musical Renaissance*, 85. Staged performances of Wagner's work were also disrupted by Covent Garden's closure for the duration of the war.
17. 'A View without a Room' [1958], in Forster, *A Room with a View*, 231–3 (232).
18. Bechstein, for instance, closed its London showroom in 1916. See Ehrlich, *The Piano*, 160–3.
19. Peter reflects later: 'It was at Bourton that summer, early in the

'nineties, when he was so passionately in love with Clarissa' (*MD*, 50).

20. Peter uses the term about himself and calls the young Clarissa a 'Radical' (*MD*, 43 and 131).

21. For an introduction to Wagner's youthful politics, see Millington, *Wagner*, especially chapter 4.

22. A 'Colonial' who 'insulted the House of Windsor' starts 'a general shindy', for example (*MD*, 15). Did the insult relate to the German origins of the House of Windsor, renamed only six years before? See *MD*, 170, n.

23. Fräulein Daniels' surname suggests that she may be an Anglo-German or simply an English speaker of German; whichever is the case, the name is a further suggestion of Anglo-German intimacies before the war.

24. The publishers, founded c. 1719, quickly began to publish music, and became pre-eminent in German music publishing; by the nineteenth century the firm also manufactured pianos, one of which Wagner used. By this date the firm specialised in the publication of opera, and these editions were standard texts in Britain: they published Wagner's complete works. The firm was notoriously ungenerous to its composers – one reason why Breitkopf is invariably described as a 'poor old man'?

25. Other patriotic works include the *German Requiem* (1868); performances in 1871 established its enduring reputation as a patriotic work.

26. See *D*, II: 298. The Woolfs heard Gerhardt again on 28 May 1924; see Entry dated 28 May 1924, Leonard Woolf's Diary, LWP II.R.18.

27. Wagner, *Tristan and Isolda*, 14 and 13.

28. Wagner, *Tristan and Isolda*, 23.

29. In *To the Lighthouse*, too, Woolf's recollections of the Cornish landscape prefigure the war dead: the waves 'thundered hollow' to Mrs Ramsay and 'like a ghostly roll of drums remorselessly beat the measure of life, maki[ing] one think of the destruction of the island' (*TL*, 17).

30. Woolf was certainly familiar with Tennyson's *Idylls of the King*: his account of the legend of Tristan and the two Isoldes was first published as 'The Last Tournament' in *The Contemporary Review*, December 1871. See also Chapter 1, note 19, above.

31. My point here is simply that the literary source is open to appropriation by both nationalist and cosmopolitan narratives; more could be said about the triangulation of Germany, England and France in the novel.

32. Wagner, *Tristan and Isolda*, 50.

33. Woolf's letters and diaries include numerous satirical accounts of opera audiences and of their social exclusivity particularly. Cf. Jane Marcus' argument that Woolf perceived opera and Bayreuth specifically as a 'democratic' sublime, 'epic theatre for ordinary people'; such a reading is complicated by the social history of the festival that was, whatever Wagner's aspirations, dominated by the social elite: 'Thinking Back through Our Mothers', in Marcus (ed.), *New Feminist Essays on Virginia Woolf*, 10.

34. See Marcus, *Virginia Woolf and the Languages of Patriarchy*, 49, 50 and 58–60.

35. These are the only two uses of this self-referential verb in the novel. As David Bradshaw notes, these sounds are echoed in the account of the naval bombardment in the 'Time Passes' section of *To the Lighthouse*: 'there

came later in the summer ominous sounds like the measured blows of hammers dulled on felt' (*TL*, 109 and xxvi). This simile of a piano's action surely recalls the image of Mr Ramsay's mind as a keyboard, augmenting Woolf's association of the piano with (nineteenth-century) patriarchy and violence.

36. Iona Opie and Moira Tatem (eds), *A Dictionary of Superstitions* (London and New York: Oxford University Press, 1989), 164, cited in *MD*, xxi.
37. Cf. Woolf's story 'The Journal of Mistress Joan Martyn' (c. 1906) which similarly alludes to both Tristan and Isolde and Troy in its exploration of chivalric warfare and female disempowerment. The work is discussed by Louise A. DeSalvo in 'Shakespeare's *Other* Sister', in Marcus (ed.), *New Feminist Essays on Virginia Woolf*, 61–81.
38. This perception of Wagner and his work was (and remains) widespread, despite the fact that contradictory narratives about Wagner's own sexuality had circulated since the late nineteenth century. See Chapter 4, below.
39. The Rev. Edward Whittaker with whom Miss Kilman and Elisabeth have tea is presumably the same Edward Whittaker who appeared in *Jacob's Room*, following a miniature score of *Tristan* during the first opera scene – a further instance of the proximity of patriarchal gender roles and religion, Wagner's music and the institutionalised church. Nietzsche's attacks on the Christianity of *Parsifal* in works including *Nietzsche contra Wagner* may be pertinent here.
40. The parallels between Clarissa's 'renunciation' of Wagnerian emotionalism (presumably unsuccessful in the sense that her life in middle age is shadowy) and Woolf's incomplete rejection of Wagner invite us to reflect on Woolf's attitude towards Clarissa. *Der fliegende Holländer* is also a pertinent intertext here: see Sutton, 'Flying Dutchmen, Wandering Jews: Romantic Opera, Anti-Semitism and Jewish Mourning in *Mrs Dalloway*', in Adriana Varga (ed.), *Virginia Woolf and Music* (Bloomington: Indiana University Press, forthcoming).
41. See *MD*, 178, n.
42. See Vanessa Manhire's fine account of this passage, in which she suggests that music emphasises Septimus' disconnection, particularly – through the incongruous sounds of a car horn and a pastoral elegy – his inability to reconcile the pre- and post-war worlds. '"Not Regularly Musical"', Chapter 3.
43. Early recordings (between 1914 and 1925) were often incomplete in instrumentation as well as in length. Some early Wagner recordings (e.g. HMV's excerpts of the *Ring* and *Die Meistersinger*) had been released by the time of the novel's 1923 setting, and excerpts from *Tristan* were available by the time of the novel's completion: the instrumental *Liebestod* from *Tristan* conducted by Bruno Walter was released by HMV in 1924 and the Prelude to Act 1 of *Parsifal*, also conducted by Walter, in 1925. Columbia Records released an abridged *Tristan*, conducted by Karl Elmendorft, on mono in 1928.
44. 'Living in a War Zone: An Introduction to Virginia Woolf as a War Novelist', in Hussey (ed.), *Virginia Woolf and War*, 3.
45. For a discussion of eugenics in the novel, see *MD*, xxiv–xxvii.
46. *Feminine Endings*, 26.

Chapter 4

Fugues, Flights and Free Association

Loving Bach: shell shock and hysterical fugue

> She said she loved Bach. So did Hutton. That was the bond between them, and Hutton (a very bad poet) always felt that Mrs Dalloway was far the best of the great ladies who took an interest in art. It was odd how strict she was. About music she was purely impersonal. She was rather a prig. But how charming to look at! She made her house so nice, if it weren't for her Professors. Clarissa had half a mind to snatch him off and set him down at the piano in the back room. For he played divinely. (*MD*, 150)

This unobtrusive conversation from the final section of *Mrs Dalloway* takes place at the party, the event that concludes the day the novel traces. As the enthusiasm of hostess and guest suggests, Bach's fugues – the objects, as *Grove* puts it, of 'almost universal esteem' since at least the early nineteenth century – were enjoying a renewed vogue in the 1920s, partly due to the rise of musical neo-classicism.[1] Allusions to Bach are scattered throughout Woolf's letters and diaries of this period, and she attended several concerts at the Bach Festival in 1920 before starting work on the texts that became this novel;[2] the Woolfs' record collection eventually included eighty recordings of Bach's music. If we are tempted to pass over this passage of *Mrs Dalloway* as little more than social small talk, the evidence of Woolf's thorough knowledge of Bach should give us pause for thought. Why is Clarissa a 'lover' of Bach, and why might this matter for a reading of the novel?

A preliminary answer might suggest that Clarissa's 'impersonal' musical tastes hint at the intellectuality of Bach's music – or what was less sympathetically caricatured as a lack of emotional warmth. (Jacob makes just this assumption in *Jacob's Room* when he recalls Clara playing Bach and concludes that she will remain forever 'a virgin chained to a rock' [*JR*, 106–7], and the 'spinster' music teacher of 'Moments of Being: "Slater's Pins Have No Points"' 'lives, it seemed, in the cool, glassy world of Bach's fugues' [*CSF*, 209]).[3] Clarissa's musical tastes may be simply another indication of her repeatedly invoked 'cold spirit' (*MD*, 27) – a condition shared by the veteran Septimus Warren Smith, whose 'brain was perfect' though he 'could not feel' (*MD*, 75). Her musical tastes are certainly the opposite of the 'sentimental', 'morbid' emotionalism of Peter Walsh (*MD*, 128), quickly moved to tears by other people.[4] Clarissa's middle-aged enthusiasm for Bach thus denotes not only her dislike of emotional extremes but also, as the previous chapter proposed, represents a shift in musical tastes, a rejection of the emotionalism of Wagner's operas by which she and Peter were absorbed in their youth.[5] But the allusion to Bach is not only a matter of charac-terisation or a mimetic detail recording contemporary musical fashions: Bach's music seems to be central to the form and politics of this novel. More specifically, following Jocelyn Slovak's groundbreaking work, I will propose that fugue quite literally shapes *Mrs Dalloway*.[6] Though the word is never uttered in the novel, and Woolf does not provide any detail about the works that Clarissa and Jim Hutton admire, fugue is arguably the genre associated above all with Bach[7] (and in *The Voyage Out*, Rachel has an 'intense enthusiasm' for the composer, drawing 'figures in the thin white dust to explain how Bach wrote his fugues' [*VO*, 187 and 253]).

In addition to growing critical recognition that Woolf's formal experi-mentalism was indebted to musical genres or specific musical works (such as Beethoven's *Große Fuge*, Op. 133)[8] is the fact that 'fugue' was also a medical term current in the mental sciences and analyses of shell shock. As Ian Hacking and others have demonstrated, 'hysterical fugue' entered medical discourse in the late nineteenth century, primarily in the discipline of psychiatry.[9] The term was applied to individuals who suffered a form of amnesia or identity crisis: fugue was a 'flight from one's own identity, often involving travel to some unconsciously desired locality [. . .] during which all awareness of personal identity is lost though the person's outward behaviour may appear rational. On recov-ery, memory of events during the state is totally repressed'.[10] There was considerable popular as well as medical interest in individual fuguers in the late nineteenth and early twentieth centuries, and although the term was more widely debated in continental Europe than in Britain and America, William James discussed it in his 1896 Lowell Lectures and Charcot's lecture on the subject was 'widely reported' in Britain.[11] The condition was sufficiently well recognised for a psychiatric conference to be held in Nantes in 1909 on the subject of fugue and desertion from the army.[12] This section explores the significance of fugue to Woolf's work, offering a speculative reading of the role of fugue in the structure of the novel and its representation of shell shock. Fugue, I will suggest, is the method through which Woolf establishes connections between Septimus, his shell shock symptoms[13] and the other characters. Like Joyce's *Ulysses* (1922) and Huxley's *Point Counter Point* (1928), which are more conspicuously indebted to fugue, or Pound's *Cantos*, which he reportedly claimed would 'display a plot like a Bach fugue',[14] *Mrs Dalloway* is one of a number of contemporary experiments in using fugue to convey 'modern' experience.[15]

Woolf's own experience of mental illness and her reading in the mental sciences make it very likely that she would have known of hysterical fugue. Hysterical fugue and the closely related condition epileptic fugue were often described as symptoms or aspects of shell shock; the terms were applied to the dissociated wandering or identity crises experienced by soldiers and veterans. In his 1917 Chadwick lecture 'Mental Hygiene and Shell Shock During and After the War', for instance, Dr (later Sir) Frederick Walker Mott described soldiers who had 'absented' themselves from the trenches and 'were found in a dazed condition, unable to account for their actions or to recollect how they came there'. 'This condition,' he argued, 'is not unlike a fugue or automatic wandering of an epileptic'[16] (and here we might recall that one of Lady Bradshaw's 'interests' is the 'after-care of the epileptic' [*MD*, 80]). An article published in July 1918 in the *American Journal of Insanity* by the eminent French psychiatrist J. Rogues de Fursac also noted the similarities between hysterical fugue and shell shock.[17] Now Septimus is not, of course, a fuguer by any strict medical definition of the term: he doesn't make repeated journeys of which he has no recollection, nor is he (unlike Chris in Rebecca West's 1918 *The Return of the Soldier*, which Woolf read that year [*L*, II: 247]) suffering from extensive amnesia. He is, however, associated with fugue in several important ways. Firstly, fugue carried particular gender and class connotations, by which Woolf's representation of Septimus is informed. The great majority of fuguers were men; fugue was, as Hacking puts it, 'the body language of male powerlessness', a counterpart to the feminised condition of hysteria. Indeed fugue had become central to debates about the diagnosis of hysteria in the *fin de siècle*, shaping the gendered distinction between hysteria and epilepsy.[18] Fugue may have been a condition of men, but its proximity to hysteria lent it a 'feminine' colour. Fugue also carried specific class connotations: it was seen as a condition predominantly of artisans and labourers, 'humble, decent men' like the 'better sort' of clerk Septimus (*MD*, 71).[19] The most celebrated examples of fuguers were from these backgrounds, so fugue was a condition to which 'half-educated, self-educated' (*MD*, 71) soldiers like Septimus might be expected to be prone. And, as we shall see, Septimus is repeatedly associated with flight.

The medical and the musical terms share an etymological root: 'fugue', as Woolf would certainly have known, is related to both the Latin *fugere*, 'to flee', and *fugare*, 'to put to flight'.[20] A fundamental characteristic of musical fugue is that each voice enters separately and distinctly, so that thematic material is passed from one to another; as the 1879 edition of *Grove* observed, 'one part after another seems as it were to *chase* the subject or motive throughout the piece'.[21] The novel, too, repeatedly alludes to chasing and flight. Septimus' experiences mirror Mott's observation that the 'auditory or visual hallucinations' suffered by many shell shock victims often provoked 'a wild terrified look and attempt to escape by flight';[22] Septimus spends much of the novel trying to flee from hallucinations and from the attentions of other characters, most obviously his doctors. 'Holmes and Bradshaw were on him! The brute with the red nostrils was snuffling into every secret place!' (*MD*, 125), Septimus believes, as he reflects on his experience as a patient. It is striking how many other characters are compared to hunters: Peter Walsh's constant fingering of his knife is another obvious example, as is the episode in which he follows an anonymous young woman – he terms himself an 'adventurer' and a 'buccaneer' (*MD*, 45–6). But there are yet more, and more unexpected, allusions to chasing and hunting: Elizabeth Dalloway imagines an omnibus as a 'pirate', 'reckless, unscrupulous, bearing down ruthlessly' (*MD*, 115); the young Clarissa 'flung' herself on 'that great shaggy dog which ran after sheep' (*MD*, 51); and even Lucy imagines her mistress as a hunter – perhaps specifically as Diana, the virgin huntress – when she perceives Clarissa's umbrella as the 'sacred weapon' of a 'goddess' who has 'acquitted herself honourably in the field of battle' (*MD*, 25).

Images of aerial flight, and the word or its derivatives, also pepper the novel. The flight of the plane that prompts such widespread speculation from the observers is the most prominent example and it is even possible that the voices (one of which sounds 'like a mellow organ' [*MD*, 19]) deciphering the letters spelled by the plane playfully recall the various fugues that also spell words – Schumann and Liszt were among those who wrote fugues on the notes B-A-C-H.[23] In Septimus' hallucination about music becoming visible the sound 'cannoned' (*MD*, 58) – perhaps a hint at that other genre of imitative counterpoint, the canon? Septimus himself repeatedly feels airborne, even before his own 'flights' from Dr Holmes and from the window of his lodgings. It is in his most agonised moments that he feels weightless and airborne: in Regent's Park, he fears that without being 'weighted down' by Rezia's hand he would be 'mad'; later he feels 'he was falling' (*MD*, 19 and 74). As Mott noted, 'soldiers often complain of a falling or sinking feeling', augmenting the various manifestations of the terms 'flight' or 'fugue' in his lecture.[24] Is fugue, then, one reason why Septimus and Clarissa are both repeatedly represented as birds? Certainly, bird images are prominent throughout the novel: on the first page, Clarissa recalls the 'plunge' at Bourton as she stood watching the rooks 'rising, falling', and Scrope Purvis reflects she has 'a touch of the bird about her' (*MD*, 3); later, Peter sinks into the 'plumes and feathers' of sleep (*MD*, 48). Insofar as Septimus' flight from his own identity is a condition shared by the other characters, this suggests a less pathological understanding of fugue – that is, it suggests the widespread vulnerability of the (post-war) psyche.[25]

Fugue is, however, not only an etymological but also a formal matter in *Mrs Dalloway*. Although definitions of fugue have varied in its long history, the genre has always been recognised as one that is unusually tightly structured – 'a regular piece of music, developed from given subjects according to strict contrapuntal rules, involving the various artifices of imitation, canon, and double counterpoint, and constructed according to a certain fixed plan'.[26] *Mrs Dalloway* is also, like its protagonist, a conspicuously 'strict' text and its structure of two distinct but interrelated plots and subject matter is, as Slovak has suggested, modelled on the musical fugue. Its form imitates the principal characteristics of fugue – above all, the fact that it consists of and is worked up from two distinct units of musical material that remain separate but which are increasingly interwoven and elaborated as the work unfolds. Furthermore, the three principal characters fulfil equivalent structural roles to the fugal 'subject', its 'answer' and the 'countersubject'. Clarissa's party, her memories of Bourton and her Society acquaintances might be described as the subject – 'the theme, or chief melody, on which the whole fugue is based' and with which it begins. Peter Walsh's memories of Bourton, his love for Clarissa and life in India, serve as the answer – the 'correlative' of the subject, based on the same thematic material as the subject but transposed into the dominant key and, in consequence, frequently slightly modified following strict tonal rules. Septimus' memories of war, his mental illness and medical treatment function as the countersubject – initially an 'accompaniment' to the subject or its answer, but also their 'foil', used in 'alternation' with them.[27]

As she drafted the novel, Woolf repeatedly alluded to its double form and perspective – 'the world seen by the sane & the insane side by side' (*D*, II: 207) – and the novel's separation of these two principal protagonists and the two plots is its most obvious debt to the dualistic structure of fugue. Clarissa and Septimus never meet, and until the last section of

the novel when Clarissa hears of Septimus' suicide they have no awareness of each other: they exist contrapuntally. However, this is not simply
to equate Clarissa's indirect interior monologues with Society or the feminised domestic sphere (the subject) and Septimus' with war and the public
sphere (the countersubject). Rather, the subject and the countersubject
appear in the monologues of both protagonists and in those of the other
characters; as in a fugue, the subject, its answer and countersubject(s)
are passed from one voice to another. We see, for example, that Clarissa
is preoccupied not only with her party but also with the aftermath of
the war – indeed, as the party begins and she fears it is 'falling flat' she
reaches for an image of war:[28] 'any explosion, any horror was better
than people wandering aimlessly' (*MD*, 142–3). Woolf's 'discovery' that
she could 'dig out beautiful caves behind [her] characters' and that 'the
caves shall connect' (*D*, II: 263) allows the narrative to move from the
indirect interior monologue of one character to another, sometimes via
brief linking narratives by a third person narrator that serve as 'codettas'
('connecting notes' added to facilitate modulations and links between the
thematic material but not derived from the material of the subject, answer
or countersubject).[29] And the devices that connect these characters and
episodes are frequently forms of transport (the car and the plane) or
sounds (bells, songs) – things that (facilitate) travel or fly.[30] It seems more
than coincidence, then, that one of the most frequent of these devices
– the sound of Big Ben – mimics in miniature the formal relationship
between fugal subject, answer and countersubject: the four-note motif of
the 'Westminster chime' is answered by one or more four-note permuta-
tions before the contrasting strokes that mark the hour. Woolf's method
thus allows us to perceive parallels between the two plots, between the
protagonists and between the subject and countersubject – indeed, this
connectivity is central to Woolf's formal experiment.

Before we continue, some caveats are needed: *Mrs Dalloway* cannot,
of course, literally be a fugue. The importance of this metaphorical claim
(whether made by author or reader) lies rather in its invitation to attend
to the author's technique, their 'compositional virtuosity'. To compare
a literary work to fugue is to emphasise its formal qualities, and thus
to draw attention to the artifice of what are apparently 'natural'
conventions in tonal composition and realist narratives.[31] Unlike Joyce
or Huxley, however, Woolf does not make the analogy with fugue conspicuous; rather than directing the reader towards a particular approach
or interpretation she leaves the musical analogy implicit. Fugue's importance lies in its significance to Woolf's creative practice and conception
of her work; it doesn't privilege a 'fugal' reading of the novel over other
possible responses. Keeping these caveats in mind, I would suggest that

there are a number of specific as well as broad echoes of fugal form. *Mrs Dalloway* is divided by line breaks into nine sections, of which the second is subdivided by an ellipsis. As with the opening section (the 'exposition') of a fugue, the first section of the novel (*MD*, 3–12) is relatively brief yet contains all the thematic material that the fugue will repeat and develop. Clarissa's monologue begins with her reflections on the preparations for her party – buying the flowers, her servant Lucy and the fact that the doors will be removed for the party (the subject). But by the third paragraph Clarissa's thoughts have turned to her youth at Bourton and to Peter Walsh, due 'back from India one of these days' (*MD*, 3) (the answer). This and the following two paragraphs introduce topics including unfulfilled love, empire, foreboding, the passing of time, illness and London – material that recurs in Clarissa's and the other monologues throughout the novel. Paragraph six begins with reiterated statements about the war and its aftermath (the countersubject):

> For it was the middle of June. The War was over, except for some one like Mrs Foxcroft at the Embassy last night eating her heart out because that nice boy was killed and now the old Manor House must go to a cousin; or Lady Bexborough who opened a bazaar, they said, with the telegram in her hand, John, her favourite, killed; but it was over; thank Heaven – over. (*MD*, 4)

In sum, the first section follows the typical sequence in which subject, answer and countersubject enter. All the thematic and grammatical material of the novel (such as anaphoric sentences beginning 'For') is present in the work's exposition.

We might speculate too on the parallels between the structure of the novel and the tonal structure of fugue. If Clarissa's monologues serve the same structural role as the tonic ('home') key in which a fugue starts, it is at least worth considering whether the other characters' monologues might be heard as related keys.[32] Sections one and two of the novel move between four main focalisers (Clarissa, Peter, Septimus and Rezia), and Clarissa's perspective (the tonic) is heard frequently. Yet, as in fugue, as the novel unfolds it wanders further away from the tonic: there are no monologues from Clarissa's perspective in sections three, four or five, and Septimus and Rezia's monologues are the longest in section five, the central section (in the dominant, fifth, key?). Similarly, Clarissa's monologue in section six is one among numerous voices, and section seven is narrated predominantly from Peter's perspective. Therefore, like a fugue, the later parts of the novel involve increasingly intricate inter-weavings of subject, answer and countersubject, and increasing distance from the tonic while remaining in closely related keys. The novel's episodic structure also recalls the 'episodes' of a fugue, the large-scale, important passages in which fragments of the original thematic material provide the basis for 'new imitations'.[33] We may well wonder, then, whether one of the many associations suggested by Septimus' name is that of the 'leading note', the seventh note of the scale (a component of the dominant triad), which is dissonant and has to be 'resolved' into the tonic. In 1917, Woolf had read Rosalind Murray's novel, *The Leading Note*, in which the protagonist has composed a work ending on the leading note (*D*, I: 75); she defends her defiance of 'proper musical regulations' and describes the 'unfinished sound' as 'always asking something', 'calling for [. . .] something that doesn't come'.[34] When Clarissa eventually hears of Septimus' suicide, she echoes this idea: 'Death was an attempt to communicate' (*MD*, 156), she reflects.

In sections eight and nine, however, the tonic and subject return at more length with many reflections on and conversations about Clarissa. The novel ends with Peter's affirmations of her presence – 'It is Clarissa, he said. / For there she was' (*MD*, 165). As *Grove* explained:

[I]t is customary to bring the subject and answer nearer to one another as the fugue draws towards its conclusion. The way to effect this is to make the entries overlap; and this is called the Stretto (from stringere, 'to bind').[35]

Clarissa and Peter have certainly been brought 'nearer to one another' over the course of the day, and her party is itself a form of Stretto in which guests' voices are rapidly overlapped; Slovak suggests that Clarissa may even be heard as the deliberate 'composer' of this effect.[36] After all these suggestive parallels between fugal structure and that of the novel, can we hear Peter's repeated affirmations as a concluding return to the tonic, a restatement of the subject 'exalted' by chords?[37] Woolf's diary invites just such a reading. In September 1924, as she revised the final section, she wrote:

I find [present participles] very useful in my last lap of Mrs D. There I am now – at last at the party, which is to begin in the kitchen, & climb slowly upstairs. It is to be a most complicated spirited solid piece, knitting together everything & ending on three notes, at different stages of the staircase, each saying something to sum up Clarissa. Who shall say these things? Peter, Richard & Sally Seton perhaps: but I don't want to tie myself down to that yet. Now I do think this might be the best of my endings, & come off, perhaps. (*D*, II: 312)

The image of 'knitting together everything' is not an unfamiliar one for the end of a novel; what is perhaps more striking is Woolf's perception of the 'complicated' form of the final section, the 'three notes' reiterating statements about Clarissa, and the image of the staircase. The three notes certainly suggest a restatement of the principal theme of the novel, a return to the tonic key, and perhaps even a prose equivalent to a concluding tonic triad, or a prepared cadence, IV, V, I. And we might well wonder whether the image of the staircase recalls the most famous of all Western musical treatises – Fux's 1725 study of fugue, *Gradus ad Parnassum* (*Steps to Parnassus*). It was Fux's treatise, after all, that had expressed a preference for the fugue with two themes (i.e. the subject and countersubject) and popularised these terms; and the second part of the treatise, not unlike the novel, has a dual structure – a dialogue between Fux and Palestrina.[38] There are many routes through which Woolf could have known of Fux's work, even if she hadn't read it – not least through Hadow's work and Debussy's 'Doctor Gradus ad Parnassum', the first piece in his humorous piano suite *Children's Corner* (1908; orchestrated by André Caplet in 1911).[39]

Why, then, does Woolf appear to have found fugal form an appropriate structure for a novel about the individual and social legacy of war? Firstly, fugue's linking of the protagonists has political repercussions: it suggests a shared continuum of experiences of war and mental illness rather than separation of the public and the private spheres, male combatant and female domestic experience, 'insane' and merely 'nervous'. In consequence, it hints, for example, at parallels between the experiences of and patriarchal attitudes towards women and male veterans.[40] Counterpoint synthesises the often fractured, disjointed post-war experience of the characters. As Gillian Beer has observed, the 'activity of the novel' supports Clarissa's claim of connection to Septimus; furthermore, '[t]he reader becomes the medium of connection'.[41] And as any 'lover' of Bach will recognise, the aesthetic pleasure – and the emotional warmth that Clarissa's choice of verb suggests – comes partly from this gradual recognition of 'the bonds' between apparently unrelated components, the thematic and structural tightness of the text. Secondly, fugue (especially when applied to instrumental music such as Bach's keyboard works) has long carried connotations of 'learnedness', 'seriousness' and technical 'sophistication'. Fugues were often intended as compositional studies through which composers learned and displayed their mastery of 'intellectual' chamber music[42] and parodies such as Wagner's in *Meistersinger* confirm its connotations of learnedness. Woolf's use of a form associated above all with German composers and German 'pedantry' is thus, like Joseph Breitkopf's playing of Brahms, one aspect of the novel's cosmopolitanism;[43] the structure of the novel discreetly resists the anti-German prejudice experienced by individuals such as Miss Kilman. The fugal structure is one of a cluster of details intimating the difficulty of sustaining Anglo-German musical and social intimacies after the war.

But fugue, as a tightly ordered form, is also a means of providing an 'impersonal', orderly and literally balanced way of writing about this emotive subject-matter. In 1923, Woolf observed in her diary that the 'design is certainly original, & interests me hugely'; it is 'so queer & so masterful. I'm always having to wrench my substance to fit it' (*D*, II: 249). *Mrs Dalloway*'s contrapuntal structure allows Woolf to make a conspicuously measured contribution to public debate and fiction about the war, mental illness and nationalism, as well, perhaps, as providing a means that enabled her to draw on painfully personal experiences. The novel's structure sympathetically embodies the traumatised Septimus' preoccupation with order – apparent in his precise dressing of the hat, his '[d]iagrams' and 'designs' (*MD*, 125) and his desire to be 'above all scientific' (*MD*, 19) – and simultaneously ironises Sir William Bradshaw's diagnosis that he lacks a 'sense of proportion' (*MD*, 82). Septimus' problem is not that he has too little proportion but too much. Musical forms, especially fugues by Bach and his contemporaries, have been characterised as 'musical analogues to the notion of the centred Self'. If they can be understood to narrate a process of what Susan McClary calls '"subjective becoming"' 'in which heterogeneous elements of self come together as an autonomous whole', then Woolf's fugal fiction surely both yearns for and questions the possibility of a secure autonomous self in the aftermath of war. Fugal form can, as Nadya Zimmerman proposes, allow for 'a simultaneous reconciliation of various strands of the self in the moment', but it may also expose the irresolution of and tensions between these strands.[44]

Playing variations on the theme of sex

In *The Oxford History of Music*, Hadow described Beethoven's Op. 111, played by Lucy Honeychurch and Rachel Vinrace, as a 'magnificent example' of 'the fugal principle'.[45] The first movement is in sonata form, and its development section takes the form of a fugue based on the first subject of the sonata. Rather than having contrasting first and second subjects, however, as is more usual in a fugue, in this instance the second subject is based on the melodic shape of the first. For this reason, Charles Rosen has termed the movement a double-fugue, arguing that it is unusual because of the dominance of the first subject.[46] As the nineteenth-century music theorist A. B. Marx argued in his influential theories of sonata form, the first subject is conventionally identified as the masculine *Hauptsatz*, and the second as the subsidiary, feminine *Seitensatz*.[47] The apparent equality of the two subjects is, then, often a superficial equality: the forms encode gendered hierarchies. One effect of Beethoven's unusual use of sonata form is thus (to continue the argument of Chapter 2) to underline the masculinity of Op. 111's first movement. Following McClary's argument that (fugal) form is expressive of individual identity, I turn now to consider what parts gender and sexuality play in Woolf's uses of fugue and of music more widely.

Woolf alludes to Beethoven in *The Voyage Out* partly because he denotes hyper-masculinity, but she also frequently uses music to evoke gender liminality or ambiguity. In her fiction and writing on aesthetics, music is repeatedly associated with the disruption of polarised, inflexible gender roles, as the early essay 'Street Music' makes clear. As I have suggested elsewhere,[48] her celebration of musical rhythm, which she equates with literary and aesthetic value, encompasses both masculine and feminine properties:

> The whole of rhythm and harmony have been pressed, like dried flowers, into the neatly divided scales, the tones and semitones of the pianoforte. The safest and easiest attribute of music – its tune – is taught, but rhythm, which is its soul, is allowed to escape like the winged creature it is. (*E*, I: 30)

The essay characterises rhythm as a vigorous, corporeal 'masculine' property of music that eludes amateur music education (which is compared to the feminine accomplishments of flower pressing and piano playing) yet also feminises rhythm through the associations with ethereality and angels. She continues:

> The beat of rhythm in the mind is akin to the beat of the pulse in the body; and thus though many are deaf to tune hardly any one is so coarsely organised as not to hear the rhythm of its own heart in words and music and movement. (*E*, I: 30)

Despite her evocation of the body, Woolf resists limiting this image to either male or female, reaching instead for an androgynous term in the grammatically awkward phrase 'its own heart'. In 'Street Music', rhythm is simultaneously male and female (or neither) – analogous to the androgynous creative mind evoked in *A Room of One's Own* by the 'rhythmical order' of the 'ordinary sight' of a man and a woman getting into a cab (*ROTG*, 87). Musical rhythm, it seems, disrupts a dualistic understanding of gender based on the binary opposition of male and female. In *Orlando* too, music, androgyny and sexual ambiguity are often linked: flutes and trumpets herald the arrival of Sasha, whose sex Orlando struggles to identify, and the night Orlando falls into the sleep that marks his sex change, 'music of a rustic kind, such as shepherds play' is heard under his window (*O*, 26–7 and 93). Woolf's language suggests Pan, whose music was so frequently a metaphor for the sexual and, particularly, the homoerotic in *fin-de-siècle*, Edwardian and Georgian works from Aubrey Beardsley's drawings for *Le Morte Darthur* (1893–4) and Florence Farr's *The Dancing Faun* (1894) to Forster's 'The Story of the Siren' (1920). And Quentin Bell noted that one inspiration for *Orlando* itself was a party at which Jack Sheppard performed as a *prima donna* in drag.[49] As Woolf observed in the early 1920s, 'the future of Bloomsbury was to prove that many variations can be played on the theme of sex' (*MB*, 57).

If music allows a flight from inflexible or simplistic conceptions of gender and sexuality, this is in part the result of its prominent part in homoerotic discourse from the nineteenth century: sexual fugues are among many flights from societal norms in *Mrs Dalloway*. Presumably, Holmes would have been more cautious in recommending music as a 'cure' had he realised Septimus was a fan of *Tristan*: the opera's celebration of union through death amplifies the homoerotic dimension of Septimus' mourning for his friend and co-soldier Evans. The traces of *Tristan* in the Septimus–Rezia–Evans triangle suggest that Septimus' principal passion is for Evans rather than his wife. Rezia, echoing Isolde, repeatedly notes that marriage has made her an exile and Septimus, mimicking Tristan and Isolde's death wish, proposes joint suicide to her (*MD*, 56); however, Septimus' suggestion to Rezia lacks the emotional intensity of his imagined reunion with the dead Evans, ecstatically depicted as the singing of a duet – a true *Liebestod*, perhaps:

> He sang. Evans answered from behind the tree. The dead were in Thessaly, Evans sang, among the orchids [. . .] A man in grey was actually walking towards them. It was Evans! But no mud was on him; no wounds; he was not changed. (*MD*, 59)

The imagined reunion recurs in the intimate setting of Septimus and Rezia's flat: 'That man, his friend who was killed, Evans, had come, he said. He was singing behind the screen' (*MD*, 119). For all that Wagner and his music were often associated with insistent heteronormativity, they also had a prominent place in homosexual discourse: numerous nineteenth-century and Edwardian accounts intimated Wagner's own ambiguous sexuality, noted the popularity of his music with homosexuals, identified Bayreuth as a homosexual rendezvous, or characterised the plots and music of the operas as androgynous or homoerotic.[50] This cultural context allows Woolf to evoke antiphonal models of sexuality in the novel's erotic triangles. Woolf's discreet use of music to suggest homoeroticism in *Mrs Dalloway* follows more overt allusions in earlier works: 'Street Music' attributes English 'disfavour' towards musicians to a national perception of 'expression of any kind' as 'almost indecent' and 'unmanly' (*E*, I: 28), and in *The Voyage Out* Terence remarks of his failed musical education that '[m]y mother thought music wasn't manly for boys' (*VO*, 253) (a sentiment echoed in Lord Berners' account of his own childhood to Woolf [*D*, III: 63]). In the short fiction 'A Simple Melody' (c. 1925), the protagonist – a 'queer fish' whose 'affections' for his butler are the cause of speculation among his friends – is a lover of English song (*CSF*, 201) and a music lesson is the subject of Woolf's 'Sapphist story' (*L*, III: 431), 'Moments of Being: "Slater's Pins Have No Points"' (1928). *Jacob's Room*, too, repeatedly draws on British perceptions of music as effeminate: the sound of Beethoven's *Moonlight Sonata* fills the court of Trinity College, Cambridge at night (*JR*, 34), adding homoerotic overtones to Cambridge's homosocial world, much as Forster uses music to elucidate the inner lives of his gay Cambridge undergraduates in *Maurice* (drafted 1913–14).[51] And after they have attended *Tristan*, Bonamy (modelled on the flamboyantly homosexual Lytton Strachey and 'set a little apart from his fellows by the influence of the music' [*JR*, 58 and n]) bursts into Jacob's Cambridge room at midnight to discuss Wagner and Beethoven (*JR*, 58–60).[52] Most pointedly, at the Durrants' party, Mrs Durrant asks Jacob: 'Are you fond of music?' (*JR*, 75). Whether or not Mrs Durrant was aware of the numerous sexologists and artists from Havelock Ellis to Edward Carpenter and André Raffalovich who had remarked on 'music''s virtual synonymity with 'homosexuality' in Britain (Carpenter went so far as to propose that there 'are few in fact of this nature who have not some gift in the direction of music'),[53] Woolf surely knew that this question was, to the informed, a euphemistic enquiry about sexual orientation.[54] Woolf playfully permits the possibility that Mrs Durrant's question is not as naïve, nor as irrelevant, a one to ask her daughter's suitor as it might appear.

Music's association with same-sex desire also subtly informs the concert scene in *The Waves*, discreetly augmenting the representation of Rhoda's inner life.[55] To search for musical 'sources' behind this elliptically evocative and associative monologue may seem to miss the point and I certainly don't wish, in doing so, to suggest that one or more intertext provides a definitive or exhaustive reading of this rich passage. Nonetheless, Woolf's evocative, layered suggestions of several operas amplify ideas with which Rhoda and the novel as a whole are concerned:

> 'Swaying and opening programmes, with a few words of greeting to friends, we settle down, like walruses stranded on rocks, like heavy bodies incapable of waddling to the sea, hoping for a wave to lift us, but we are too heavy, and

too much dry shingle lies between us and the sea. We lie gorged with food, torpid in the heat. Then, swollen but contained in slippery satin, the sea-green woman comes to our rescue. She sucks in her lips, assumes an air of intensity, inflates herself and hurls herself precisely at the right moment as if she saw an apple and her voice was the arrow into the note, "Ah!"

'An axe has split a tree to the core; the core is warm; sound quivers within the bark. "Ah!" cried a woman to her lover, leaning from her window in Venice. "Ah, ah!" she cried, and again she cries "Ah!" She has provided us with a cry. But only a cry. And what is a cry? Then the beetle-shaped men come with their violins; wait; count; nod; down come their bows. And there is ripple and laughter like the dance of olive trees and their myriad-tongued grey leaves when a sea-farer, biting a twig between his lips where the many-backed steep hills come down, leaps on shore.

'"Like" and "like" and "like" – but what is the thing that lies behind the semblance of the thing? (*W*, 122–3)

We will return to 'things' and their 'semblance', but here I wish briefly to suggest a couple of the works – Rossini's *William Tell* (1829) and Offenbach's *Les Contes d'Hoffmann* (1881)[56] – brought into play by this passage and their implications for the novel's representation of gender and sexuality. William Tell, the Swiss folk figure who defends country and child through his bravura display of archery, is evoked conspicuously as the singer begins, but in Woolf's image his heroism is transferred from the master archer to the female performer. Rather than Tell's arrow splitting the apple on his son's head, ultimately saving the boy from execution by the Austrian tryant, here it is the singer's voice that is imagined as an arrow. This may be a feminist gesture, celebrating the singer (despite the satirical tone of 'assumes', 'inflates' and 'hurls'), and it is also a strikingly phallic image: in Rossini's opera, Tell's arrow splits the apple and the stake to which his son is tied, but here the voice enters the 'note'. At the first sound, the image expands from 'the note' to the 'warm' 'core' of 'the tree' in which sound 'quivers', suggestive not only of a tree or stake but also of homoerotic physical penetration of the female listener by the singer's voice.

These connotations are extended by the exclamation 'Ah!' that immediately follows, and by the allusions to the woman 'cr[ying]' to her 'lover' in Venice: the fourth Act of *Les Contes*, when the courtesan Giulietta sings the famous Barcarolle from a canal-side window or gondola, seems to me a resonant influence and the Woolfs had attended and heard recordings of the opera repeatedly.[57] Offenbach's opera, with its three uncanny, over-determined tales of female destruction, is surely a cautionary text for Rhoda despite her ecstatic response. (And, as Elicia Clements notes, Rhoda is repeatedly associated with singing, with a solitary voice, but has difficulty distinguishing her voice from others.)[58]

Act II deals with the automaton Olympia, a figure who appears real to the protagonist Hoffmann but who lacks any interiority or selfhood (a parallel, perhaps, to Rhoda's fragile identity); she is dismembered at the end of the Act by her creator, Coppélius. Act III presents the frail singer Antonia whose own exceptional voice is potentially fatal to her; the malevolent Dr Miracle animates a portrait of her dead mother so that it appears to sing to Antonia and, encouraged to emulate her mother's voice, Antonia sings. Far from effecting a reunion, or revivifying her longed-for mother, however, Antonia's performance kills her – an intimation of Rhoda's 'voicelessness' and another instance of Woolf's ambiguously elegiac and anxious representations of the maternal voice? In Act IV, Giulietta feigns affection for Hoffmann in order to steal his reflection from a mirror (recall Rhoda's fear of her own reflection): she insouciantly exits with a new lover but not before she 'loses her soul'.[59] Act V reveals that the three women are facets of the same character, Stella, the prima donna with whom the opera opened (and Offenbach intended the four roles to be sung by the same performer); Woolf, of course, famously observed that the six characters in the novel 'were supposed to be one' (*L*, IV: 397).[60]

The Barcarolle was a popular concert piece (Rachel plays an arrangement at the dance in *The Voyage Out* [*VO*, 161]) and the most celebrated part of the opera, slightly ironically given that it was recycled from Offenbach's failed Viennese opera *Die Rheinnixen* (1864) – an origin that Woolf's description of the singer as a 'sea-green woman' may recall. The sensuality of the Barcarolle's libretto, music and role in the opera's action is surely central to its popularity, and it is a plausible choice of repertoire for an afternoon concert at the Wigmore Hall.[61] It is scored for two female voices, Giulietta (usually sung by a dramatic soprano or mezzo-soprano) and an unidentified second voice (another mezzo), whose lilting, sensual melodic lines interweave through the duet. The song begins: 'Belle nuit, ô nuit d'amour / souris à nos ivresses! [. . .] Zéphyrs embrasés, versez-nous vos caresses, / donnez-nous vos baisers!' ('Fair night, o night of love, / smile upon our revels! [. . .] Burning zephyrs, / breathe over us your caresses! / Bestow on us your kisses!').[62] The singers' ecstasy is suggested by the abandonment of language in the refrain of the song – they simply repeat the 'cry' 'Ah!' Though Giulietta sings the Barcarolle to her new lover later in the Act, its sexual politics are ambiguous. The choice of two female voices with lower registers suggests mature female sexuality rather than, say, the girlish femininity of the coloratura; furthermore, the Barcarolle (a folk song sung by gondoliers) may be heard as a 'masculine' genre claimed by female voices but its text and lilting melody also suggest a lullaby and thus the maternal. Additionally, in the many productions that begin the Act with Giulietta offstage or singing on stage alone it isn't initially clear to what audience the song is addressed: the two female voices can be heard as addressing each other and intertwining.[63] It can be heard, that is, as a eulogy to same-sex female lovers as well as to heterosexual love. Kristeva and Garrett Stewart's observations on 'phonic language' are pertinent here. The song's abandonment of referential language and the 'musicalized' language of Woolf's novel are examples of what Stewart calls 'pulsional body language': 'Though the return of this nurturant and "maternal" phonic vibrancy in adult language [. . .] is not necessarily a gendered phenomenon, it is not sexless either.' And it 'satisfies its own desire', he suggests, 'by utterance itself, a vocal play ultimately devolved upon the alert, the *listening* reader'.[64]

Flights of the mind

Whether or not we accept that this passage is obliquely 'about' these operas, it is certainly about representation itself. '"Like" and "like" and "like" – but what is the thing that lies behind the semblance of the thing?' Rhoda asks, and again 'what is a cry?' 'Fugues' and 'flights' had their medical, diagnostic usages denoting trauma, as we saw in Septimus' hallucinations (and indeed in Freud's frequent use of 'flight'), but their colloquial usages as 'flights of fancy' or 'flights of the mind' have more positive connotations of creativity and inspiration for artists and their audiences alike. This chapter concludes with a brief discussion of music's association with rupture: not the disruption of mental health or gender binaries, but of meaning, of comprehension, of textual surface and of representation more widely. Such disruptions were of course creative principles and aesthetic tenets for writers including Pound, Eliot, Joyce and Stein, rather than (only) negative forces. Brad Bucknell suggests that music is not simply 'a metaphorical solution to the representation of consciousness, rather it becomes part of the larger question of the problem of representation in modernism itself'; many writers express 'a desire for congruence between work and expression' whilst registering the 'unattainability' of this wish.[65] This crisis of representation was fundamental to modernist understandings and uses of music – indeed, the concert scene's intertextuality with Katherine Mansfield's elliptical story 'The Wind Blows' (1920) exemplifies the centrality of these matters to experimental writing and to modernists' dialogues with each other.[66] The observations that follow are intended briefly to suggest their relevance to *Mrs Dalloway* and

Woolf's fiction of the 1920s, concluding this discussion of fugue and flights.

In contrast to the more familiar idea of music lending aesthetic or formal unity to a literary work (as through the use of 'fugal' form), music is also frequently a disruptive force in Woolf's writing, one that prompts moments of free association in writer, readers and listeners alike. The beggar woman's song in *Mrs Dalloway* famously confounds listeners and readers, appearing to lack recognisable formal shape or development, seeming ultimately senseless: 'bubbling up without direction, vigour, beginning or end, running weakly and shrilly and with an absence of all human meaning'. Language and semantics break down, the sounds rendered as 'ee um fah um so / foo swee too eem oo –' (*MD*, 68–9). The song is a form of Ur-language or Ur-music, a counterpart to similar originary models such as the tonic sol-fa singing method, which the sounds recall, or Wagner's accounts of the origins of music and language in *Oper und Drama* and elsewhere, or even his primeval Erda ('Earth') from the *Ring* (the voice is 'an ancient spring spouting from the earth' [*MD*, 69]). Whether or not we recognise the words of the Strauss song into which these phonemes morph,[67] or perceive echoes of 'Träume' from Wagner's 'Wesendonck-Lieder', a 'study' for *Tristan*, which eulogises the 'wondrous dreams / [that] hold my senses in thrall, [so] that they have not dissolved, / like empty bubbles, into nothingness',[68] is almost irrelevant: such 'recognitions' cannot fully explain the song to us or its fictional listeners. As Vanessa Manhire notes, the disruptive effects of the song are extensive and multiple, seeming to halt time and dissolve location (the woman sings 'through all ages' [*MD*, 69] and rural images are superimposed on the cityscape), and to suspend aesthetic and social hierarchies (the street woman sings a high art song), just as in Septimus' traumatised hallucinations sound becomes synaesthetic and often originates from concealed places (such as Evans behind the screen) so that sight and sound are not fully aligned, disrupting sensory perception.[69] This is Orphic, Dionysian sound, interrupting the surface of the text and the ontological certainties of its characters and readers. Rather than the order associated with and constructed through allusions to Bach, music here suggests something closer to the infamous effects of Stravinsky's neo-classicism and primitivism on contemporary audiences.[70] As long ago as 'Street Music' Woolf had celebrated 'the god of music who will breathe madness into our brains, [and] crack the walls of our temples' (*E*, I: 30), and love in *Orlando* is compared to the Orphic sounds of a 'horrid rout, [with] its shawms, its cymbals, and its heads with gory locks torn from the shoulders' (*O*, 57).[71] The description of the 'old blind woman' in *Jacob's Room* (*JR*, 56), who prefigures the beggar woman of *Mrs Dalloway*, also precipitates a crisis of narrative representation and empathy: the narrator's and Lady Charles' reflections on class division lead into the narrator's collapse into ellipses and silence as they attempt to describe the audience at Covent Garden.

Music thus interrupts and destabilises the surface of these texts, but it also enables characters and novelist to celebrate free association. Passages such as that describing Orlando and Shelmerdine's marriage in chapter 5 of *Orlando*, or that preceding the birth of Orlando's son, utilise 'sudden transpositions' and may be influenced specifically by De Quincey's 'Dream Fugue',[72] but 'The String Quartet' (1921) makes music's capacity to stimulate memory, association and speculation the subject of the story itself. The work to which the audience is listening is almost beside the point: even Woolf's inclusion of the remark '"That's an early Mozart, of course –"' is something of a tease (*CSF*, 133),[73] since we know that she attended a performance of a Schubert quintet to take notes for the story (*D*, II: 24), and indeed Schoenberg's Second String Quartet, Op. 10 (1908) is also a contender as a 'source'.[74] What is significant is music's capacity to stimulate multi-sensory experiences and highly subjective, layered memories. The narrator and audience members half-lament, as the story itself lauds, the almost intangible link between the music and the inspiration it stimulates, and the difficulty of apprehending and representing these experiences in language:

> 'But the tune, like all his tunes, makes one despair – I mean hope. What do I mean? That's the worst of music! I want to dance, laugh, eat pink cakes, yellow cakes, drink thin, sharp wine. Or an indecent story, now – I could relish that.' (*CSF*, 133)

Woolf celebrates the obliqueness of the relationship between the musical work and this flight of fancy: the effects of the music are rendered through colour and kinetic energy, movement and vision rather than sound. As Crapoulet notes, Woolf was fascinated by synaesthetic responses to music, from her early letter of 1906 in which she asks 'do you know that sound has shape and colour and texture as well?' (*L*, I: 264), to the eccentric Miss Marchmont in *Jacob's Room* whose philosophy is that 'colour is sound – or, perhaps, it has something to do with music' (*JR*, 91) to Septimus' 'discovery' 'that music should be visible' (*MD*, 58).[75] Even the passages that might be said to describe the music, do so in predominantly visual images (for all the prominence of assonance). The work is a bravura display of the processes of creativity and free association:

Flourish, spring, burgeon, burst! The pear tree on the top of the mountain. Fountains jet; drops descend. But the waters of the Rhone flow swift and deep, race under the arches, and sweep the trailing water leaves, washing shadows over the silver fish, the spotted fish rushed down by swift waters [. . .] the yellow pebbles are churned round and round, round and round – free now, rushing downwards, or even somehow ascending in exquisite spirals into the air. (*CSF*, 133)

The allusions to the Rhone and to other stock images from Romantic *Lieder* in this experimental prose suggest that Woolf is exuberantly displaying her own difference from earlier writing set to or about music – the ascent into 'exquisite spirals' is even a kind of flight. If 'The String Quartet' is a 'musical' work, this is not primarily because it adopts a specific musical form or because it describes and imitates sounds, but because 'it takes as its subject' – and relishes – 'the problem of finding complete meaning in sound'.[76]

Notes

1. Sadie, *New Grove Dictionary*, IX: 327 and 331.
2. See, for example, *D*, I: 5, n, 20, n, 33 and 206, and II: 31–2 and n; and *L*, II: 429 and III: 39. By 1925, Woolf had heard a variety of neoclassical repertoire though this 'influence' lies outside my immediate focus.
3. The image (which occurs as Jacob compares Fanny and Clara) is one of several in which music is used to differentiate the female characters' sexual knowledge: at Clara's party a singer performs Schubert's 1826 song 'Who is Sylvia' extolling female chastity (*JR*, 74); at a bohemian party a 'splendid Magdalen' sings sitting on the floor (*JR*, 95); and as Fanny reflects on 'the beauty of young men' at the Empire music hall she 'vibrat[es] like a fiddle-string' (*JR*, 102).
4. For more on Peter's 'susceptibility' and contemporary discourses about homosexuality, see Whitworth, *Virginia Woolf*, 138–40.
5. In *The Voyage Out*, a younger Clarissa expresses enthusiasm for both Bach and Wagner but also observes, prefiguring her musical tastes in the later novel, that music is not '"altogether good for people [. . .] [t]oo emotional, somehow"' (*VO*, 47).
6. Slovak's paper at the 2004 International Virginia Woolf Conference (subsequently published as 'Mrs Dalloway and Fugue') first alerted me to this topic and I am indebted to her fine readings; where she concentrates on fugue, canon and organic form, however, I have pursued the structural and political implications of fugue. Others have also considered the signifi-cance of fugue to Woolf's work: see Friedman, *Stream of Consciousness*; Clements, 'Transforming Musical Sounds into Words'; and Laurence, 'The Facts and Fugue of War'. Laurence's analysis, which says nothing about *Mrs Dalloway*, is unfortunately limited by her extremely imprecise use of musical terms.

7. See, representatively, Hewitt and Hill's *An Outline of Musical History*, I: 88: 'In considering Bach's compositions the first thing that leaps to our mind is the word "fugue".'

8. See Clements, 'Transforming Musical Sounds into Words'.

9. Hacking, 'Automatisme Ambulatoire' and *Mad Travellers.*

10. 'Fugue', *Oxford English Dictionary*, VI: 243.

11. Hacking, 'Automatisme Ambulatoire', 36.

12. Hacking, 'Automatisme Ambulatoire', 33.

13. This is not to say that this is the authoritative 'diagnosis' of Septimus' symptoms, only that this is the explanation proposed by his doctor: see Whitworth, *Virginia Woolf*, 169–76.

14. W. B. Yeats, 'A Packet for Ezra Pound', in *A Vision* (London: Macmillan; Papermac, 1989), 4, cited in Bucknell, *Literary Modernism*, 99.

15. A useful introduction to criticism on literature and fugue (particularly Joyce's work) can be found in Zimmerman, 'Musical Form as Narrator'. See also Shockley, *Music in the Words*.

16. Mott, 'Chadwick Lecture', 40.

17. de Fursac, 'Traumatic and Emotional Psychoses'.

18. Hacking, 'Automatisme Ambulatoire', 34.

19. Hacking, 'Automatisme Ambulatoire', 31.

20. Sadie, *New Grove Dictionary*, IX: 318 and Grove, *Dictionary*, I: 567. I use the 1879 edition below since it is one to which Woolf would have had access. The term 'fugue' can denote both a genre and a compositional technique; see Sadie, *New Grove Dictionary*, IX: 318.

21. Grove, *Dictionary*, I: 567. Emphasis in original.

22. Mott, 'Chadwick Lecture', 40.

23. 'H' is the German term for 'B natural'. As Gillian Beer notes, the plane is both 'bearer and breaker of signification': Beer, *Virginia Woolf*, 152 and see also 160–2.

24. Mott, 'Chadwick Lecture', 40.

25. Slovak, 'Mrs Dalloway and Fugue', 2.

26. Grove, *Dictionary*, I: 567.

27. Grove, *Dictionary*, I: 567.

28. Slovak, 'Mrs Dalloway and Fugue', 2.

29. Grove, *Dictionary*, I: 568.

30. Woolf never travelled by plane, but these images also register contemporary excitement and anxiety about new, modern forms of transport and embodiment.

31. Bucknell, *Literary Modernism*, 105 and 127.

32. My aim is only to draw attention to the formal relations between the parts of Woolf's text; for a discussion of the difficulty of identifying vocal registers and pitch in literary texts, see Bucknell, *Literary Modernism*, chapter 4.

33. Grove, *Dictionary*, I: 568.

34. Murray, *The Leading Note*, 18 and 17. The first line of Murray's novel – 'It was the afternoon of a June day' – and its Italian characters also suggest it is a relevant intertext for *Mrs Dalloway*.

35. Grove, *Dictionary*, I: 568.

36. Slovak, 'Mrs Dalloway and Fugue', 5.

37. Slovak, 'Mrs Dalloway and Fugue', 5.

38. Sadie, *New Grove Dictionary*, IX: 328.

39. Hadow, *The Oxford History of Music*, 278. Debussy's 'Gradus' parodies Clementi's series of piano studies, which shared Fux's title.

40. Whitworth, *Virginia Woolf*, 174.

41. Beer, *Virginia Woolf*, 55 and 53.

42. Sadie, *New Grove Dictionary*, IX: 322–3.

43. See, for example, Berlioz's parody of Germanic fugue in *La Damnation de Faust* (1854).

44. Zimmerman, 'Musical Form as Narrator', 109. The phrase 'subjective becoming' is McClary's: Susan McClary, 'The Impromptu that Trod on a Loaf: Or How Music Tells Stories', *Narrative*, V (January 1997), 21–34 (24), cited in Zimmerman, 109.

45. Hadow, *The Oxford History of Music*, 297.

46. Charles Rosen, *Sonata Forms* (New York: Norton, 1980), 98; and Rosen, *The Classical Style: Haydn, Mozart, Beethoven* (London: Faber, 1971), 441–8, cited in Zhou, 'Sublime Noise', 105–6.

47. Marx, *Musical Form in the Age of Beethoven: Selected from in the Age of Beethoven* [*sic*], ed. Scott Burnham (Cambridge: Cambridge University Press, 1997), cited in Zhou, 'Sublime Noise', 106. I am grateful to Mi Zhou for drawing this to my attention.

48. Sutton, '"Putting Words on the Backs of Rhythm"'.

49. Bell, *Virginia Woolf*, II: 132.

50. See Sutton, *Aubrey Beardsley*, chapter 1.

51. See Fillion's fine account in *Difficult Rhythm*, especially chapter 6.

52. In 'Old Bloomsbury', read to the Memoir Club in late 1921 or 1922 and thus contemporary with *Jacob's Room*, Woolf describes Strachey bursting into Thoby's room at Cambridge and crying '"Do you hear the music of the spheres?"' before fainting. The essay also recalls Thoby's homoerotic comparison of Walter Lamb to 'a Greek boy playing a flute' (*MB*, 49 and 53).

53. *The Intermediate Sex* (London: Allen and Unwin, 1908), 111, cited in Philip Brett and Elizabeth Wood, 'Lesbian and Gay Music', in Brett, Wood and Thomas (eds), *Queering the Pitch*, 351–89 (352).

54. For an introduction to this subject and criticism on it, see Brett, Wood and Thomas (eds), *Queering the Pitch*.

55. It also informs the novel's response to Wagner's *Parsifal*, characterised by numerous *fin-de-siècle* commentators as a homoerotic work; Bayreuth, the only venue at which staged performances of *Parsifal* were permitted until the twentieth century, was a recognised homosexual rendezvous. See Sutton, *Aubrey Beardsley*, 49, and Sherard, '"Parcival in the Forest of Gender"'.

56. More intertexts could no doubt be considered since some details in the passage are 'stock figures' of opera and operetta: see *The Waves*, ed. Herbert and Sellers, 343.

57. See, for example, entry dated 6 January 1912, Leonard Woolf's Diary, Sussex University, LWP II.R.4 and Leonard Woolf, 'Diary of Music Listened To', 1940–2, LWP II.R.64.

58. 'Transforming Musical Sounds into Words', 173.

59. Offenbach, *Les Contes d'Hoffmann*, CD notes, 153. The words are Dapartutto's and not necessarily authoritative, but other characters also vilify her.

60. Schumann may also be a pertinent figure to consider in relation to the novel's interlinked 'characters': after noting the exceptional influence of literature on his music (i.e. the intermediality of his work), *An Outline of Musical History* describes the group of imaginary friends representing sides of Schumann's character in whose personae he wrote his music criticism (II: 64–6). Hewitt and Hill's study was with Hogarth as Woolf worked on the novel.

61. See *The Waves*, ed. Herbert and Sellers, 343.

62. Offenbach, *Les Contes d'Hoffmann*, CD notes, 141.

63. Significantly different versions were performed during Offenbach's life and he died without approving a final text; the opera's performance history is complex and the sequence of the Acts was often altered or substantial cuts made. My synopsis follows what is now considered to reflect Offenbach's intended sequence. See Lamb, 'Les Contes d'Hoffmann' (accessed 4 December 2012).

64. Stewart, *Reading Voices*, 278, emphasis in original. Stewart is glossing Julia Kristeva, 'Phonetics, Phonology, and Impulsional Bases', trans. Caren Greenberg, *Diacritics* 4 (Fall 1974), 36.

65. Bucknell, *Literary Modernism*, 3 and 5.

66. The young female protagonist of Mansfield's story who is described preparing for and attending a piano lesson shares Rhoda's existential crisis: 'It is all over! What is? Oh, everything! And she begins to plait her hair with shaking fingers, not daring to look in the glass.' As she reaches her piano lesson, 'she can hear the sea sob: "Ah! . . . Ah! . . . Ah-h!"', and over the piano 'hangs "Solitude" – a dark tragic woman draped in white, sitting on a rock', an image possibly echoed in Woolf's association of Rhoda with Sappho and the rock from which she jumps to her death. 'The Wind Blows', in Mansfield, *The Collected Stories*, 106–10. Woolf admired the story and Hermione Lee suggests it may have shaped both *Jacob's Room* and *The Waves*. Lee, *Virginia Woolf*, 392. For more on Mansfield, Woolf and music see Manhire, '"The Queerest Sense of Echo"'.

67. See Hillis Miller, '*Mrs Dalloway*', especially 63–4.

68. Wagner, *Wesendonck-Lieder*, CD notes, 28. I would like to thank Tom Heacox for drawing this to my attention. 'Träume' shares with the passage about the beggar woman a stock of images and syntax and both celebrate female sensuality; furthermore, the 'Wesendonck-Lieder' are notoriously associated with a romantic triangle (that of Wagner, Mathilde and Otto Wesendonck) similar to those in *Mrs Dalloway* and were themselves an influence on Strauss' song.

69. Manhire discusses the disruptive effects of music in Woolf's work more widely in '"Not Regularly Musical"', chapter 3.

70. In the draft, Hugh Whitbread has 'heard of Freud & Stravinsky'. '*The Hours': The British Museum Manuscript of 'Mrs Dalloway'*, ed. Helen Wussow (New York: Pace University Press, 1997), 156–7, cited in Froula, 'Mrs Dalloway's Postwar Elegy', 154. Woolf had attended many performances by the Ballets Russes and would have been aware of perceptions

of the 'primitive emotional expression' of Russian music: Parry describes Tchaikovsky's work, for instance, as appealing to the 'musical masses' by the 'unrestrained abandonment to physical excitement which is natural to the less developed races': *Summary of the History*, 118–19.

71. Woolf's knowledge of classical writing on the Dionysian is certainly pertinent to these representations of music, and they may also be informed specifically by Nietzsche's work on this subject such as the account of (Wagner's) music, the Dionysian and Apollonian in *The Birth of Tragedy*.

72. Sandra Gilbert notes the echoes of De Quincey (*O*, 258). For a full account of the role of music in 'Dream Fugue', see Wolf, *Musicalization of Fiction*, 111–24.

73. In Werner Wolf's illuminating reading of this work he considers a number of possible 'musical pre-text[s]': *Musicalization of Fiction*, 148–63 (151). See also Clements, 'Transforming Musical Sounds into Words', 167–8, and Manhire, '"The Queerest Sense of Echo"'.

74. See de Mille, '"Turning the Earth Above a Buried Memory"'.

75. Crapoulet, *Virginia Woolf*, 29–30. On Woolf and synaesthesia see also Hussey, *The Singing of the Real World*, 61–5.

76. Bucknell makes this point of *Ulysses*' 'Sirens' (*Literary Modernism*, 137).

Chapter 5

What It Really Means to be English

Appropriately for a work that so thoroughly reinvents biography, even the exact starting point of *Orlando* is ambiguous: a painting of the hero(ine) precedes the title page, and the dedication is followed by a two-page 'Preface' in which Woolf declares her debts to 'dead' and 'illustrious' 'friends' from Thomas Browne to De Quincey to Pater. The living are also acknowledged in this playful meta-text and among them are several music scholars and amateurs. The preface records Woolf's thanks to Saxon Sydney-Turner's 'wide and peculiar erudition', to Edward Sackville-West and to Lord Berners, 'whose knowledge of Elizabethan music has proved invaluable' (*O*, 5). It would be a naïve reader who read *Orlando* literally, but this reference to Elizabethan music is less mischievous than some since it alerts readers to a subject that is indeed the focus of some attention in her fictional biography, as it was more extensively for many of her contemporaries. As we shall see, there was something of a Tudor craze in the 1920s and it was one that encompassed music; the 'discovery' of a history of English music was one facet of the English Musical Renaissance, a part closely allied to nationalism and to constructions of English identity. This chapter explores Woolf's responses to narratives about music and Englishness as manifested in three interrelated phenomena: the early music revival; the folk music movement; and anti- and philo-Semitic discourses about music.

'Merely a traditional tune': early music and the folk revival

The folk and early music revivals shared a number of aims and characteristics central to the English Musical Renaissance, a pertinent context for *Orlando*, *Between the Acts* and *The Years*. As Chapter 3 noted, the English Musical Renaissance, and the folk and early music movements more specifically, accommodated a spectrum of political sympathies: Fry and Dolmetsch's collaboration itself demonstrates the internationalist and pacifist rather than the nationalist and jingoistic aspects of revivalism. Nonetheless, nationalism was arguably the predominant ideology of both revivals and one explicitly promoted by their ideologues.[1] Cecil Sharp, founder of the Folk Song Society in 1898 and a leading if controversial figure in the movement for decades, complained in *English Folk Song: Some Conclusions* (1907) that, '[o]ur system of education is, at present, too cosmopolitan; it is calculated to produce citizens of the world rather than Englishmen'. He lauded folk song as 'a communal and racial product, the expression, in musical idiom, of aims and ideals that are primarily national in character'.[2] Parry gave the inaugural address to the Folk Song Society and in it championed folk music over commercialised contemporary popular music. Similarly, Vaughan Williams and other song-recorders omitted from their collections songs that showed the influence of popular urban music, promoting a history of folk music that ignored some aspects of working-class traditional music and eliding urban poverty, international influences and commercial factors in the celebration of (invented) English pastoral life.[3] Arguably, 'the folk revival was a constructed culture industry: the imaginary Englishness of its pastoral peasant classes was largely for the benefit of nostalgic city-dwellers'.[4] The folk song collector Dorothea Borlase in Forster's unfinished *Arctic Summer* (drafted 1911–12) expresses this prevalent ideology: '[a]ll that was beautiful and pure – and there was much – would be sifted out of the chaff, and resown'.[5] As Georgina Boyes observes in her fine study, '[a]ll the values projected on to rural life – simplicity, purity, directness, unaffected beauty – were suddenly given a focus and made available in the concrete forms of song and dance. A lyrical summation of the national character appeared in place of vulgar jingoism'.[6] Manhire persuasively proposes that Woolf was particularly suspicious of the revivalists' emphasis on the 'purity' of folk music in contrast to foreign art music and popular urban repertoire and her reservations may also have had a further cause: although the folk revival celebrated collective, anonymous music it did not rehabilitate women's voices as many might have expected. Woolf's representations of working-class women singers in *Mrs Dalloway* and the 'Time Passes' section of *To the Lighthouse* differ from the revivalists' concerns: they not only centralise women's voices, but also reflect the intersection of folk music with popular genres such as the music hall.[7] These details in Woolf's 'war novels' resist the folk revival's emphasis on aesthetic and national 'purity', and it is even possible she knew that folk dancing was an officially prescribed therapy for veterans, including amputees, during the war[8] – a 'cure' with which Septimus would have been threatened were he institutionalised?

In addition to the nationalism underpinning the folk revival's polemical works and critical practice, the movement's ideologues expounded a model of English (musical) identity strongly inflected by class politics, with an emphasis on social improvement. Informed by contemporary perceptions of the need to reform commercial popular culture, the revivalists identified folk culture as an alternative, 'a national art [. . .] produced by the race before the emergence of capitalism and class'.[9] Numerous writings by those associated with the English Musical Renaissance advocated leisure activities (such as folk dance) for the working-classes that were explicitly intended to divert workers from party political activity, from the urban, internationalist entertainment offered by music halls and from drinking culture. Folk dance and song 'offered', as Boyes puts it, 'pleasing prospects of a comprehensive remedy for vulgarity and a distraction from social agitation'.[10] Tellingly, presidency of English Folk Dance Society branches was 'almost invariably' awarded to a member of the local nobility: by 1931, thirty–seven of the forty branch presidents were titled, indicating the conservatism and value placed on (feudal) patronage by the Society.[11] Folk song's ideological appeal across the political spectrum was such that, by 1905, there was a move to centralise the teaching of national and folk songs in school curricula: English folk songs (not Scottish, Welsh or Irish) were, Sharp argued, 'ideal musical food' for young English children.[12]

Woolf's scathing assessments of the leading composers of the English Musical Renaissance throughout her life suggest her dislike of the movement's ideology, particularly its nationalism, and these critiques became overt by the 1930s. After hearing the National Anthem and work by Henry Wood at the Queen's Hall in 1915, Woolf concluded, 'I think patriotism is a base emotion' (*D*, I: 5). In 1918, she complained that her enjoyment of Bach's Suite no. 2 for flute and strings and his Concerto no. 3 for two violins and orchestra was spoiled by the 'usual vulgarity' of Wood's conducting: the works were merely 'ghosts of lovely things' (*D*, I: 206). In 1915, she heard a 'patriotic Revue' at the Coliseum, consisting of sea shanties, songs by Elgar and national anthems (*D*, I: 20); years later, she would congratulate Smyth for 'beat[ing]' Elgar in a joint programme (*L*, V: 47). In 1919, she described the 'amusing & instructive spectacle' of Morris dancing, and of naval songs, sea shanties and folk songs performed by a choir of five hundred, in Trafalgar Square for Life Boat Day (*D*, I: 270). (The performance included 'Tom Bowling', Charles Dibden's song set by Wood in the fourth movement of his *Fantasia on British Sea Songs*.) In the 1930s, Woolf also became reacquainted with Parry's daughter Gwen, who she had 'worshipped' as a child (*D*, III: 333 and *L*, IV: 254), and Woolf read a biography of Stanford, another figurehead of the English Musical Renaissance and vice-president of the English Folk Song Society, by Gwen's husband (*L*, V: 380). In a letter of 1933, she wrote to Smyth 'what a joy you snubbed Delius' (*L*, V: 178) and asked about her cousin by marriage, Vaughan Williams: 'is [he] a great composer? If so, why does he sound so dull?' (*L*, VI: 183)[13] Some of these remarks may spring as much from feminism, gossip and affection for Smyth, of course, but another letter points to a more specific cause: 'To my thinking [folk songs are] the ruin of all modern music – just as Synge and Yeats ruined themselves with keening Celtic dirges' (*L*, IV; 406). The allusions to the Celtic Revival suggest that it is the nationalist agenda that troubles Woolf. Robert Hull's *Delius*, published in 1928 as the twelfth in the second series of *Hogarth Essays*, similarly reflects the influence of folk on contemporary art music and tackles the question of nationalism head on: after admiringly acknowledging Delius' use of folk material, Hull describes the 'use and abuse of folk-tunes' as a 'leading characteristic in English music to-day'. Furthermore, he unequivocally refutes the nationalism underpinning many such uses and much discourse about English music: after observing that some of Delius' work 'is essentially English in character' he argues that 'part of the greatness of Delius is due to the fact that his breadth of conception ignores the limitations of country or continent'.[14] Hull's comments echo those in his *Contemporary Music* of the previous year in which he avoided a methodology based on the analysis of national schools, explaining that '[t]he term nationality, as applied to music, has no very precise significance. It is scarcely possible to tell exactly where internationality begins and nationality ends'.[15] Hull's works for the press, like Woolf's novels, celebrate the 'cosmopolitan' in music.[16]

During the 1920s and 1930s, Woolf had numerous opportunities to observe the activities of the folk and early music revivalists. At exactly the time the Woolfs were active members of the National Gramophonic Society, *Gramophone* published articles on English folk song and dance and on Shakespeare's songs by N. O. M. Cameron, first Squire of the Greensleeves Morris Men (South West London), and apparently editor of the *E. F. D. S.* [English Folk Dance Society] *News* in 1926.[17] (Shakespeare's songs were one point of intersection between the Tudor and folk revivals.)[18] Woolf attended a concert by Dolmetsch in March 1913,[19] and then Gluck's *Armide* in 1928 (*L*, III: 497), Purcell's *Faery Queen* in Cambridge in 1931 (it was 'to my taste' [*L*, IV: 286 and 292]), Purcell's *Dido and Aeneas* in 1932 ('absolutely and entirely satisfying'

[*L*, V: 135]), Gluck's *Orpheus* ('the loveliest opera ever written' [*L*, V: 259]) in 1933 and John Gay's *Beggar's Opera* (1728) at least three times.[20] The 'Elizabethan fever' was exemplified by the Byrd tercentenary festival of 1923 (the culmination of academic and public interest in madrigals), by Edmund Fellowes' work on Tudor madrigals and church music and by compositions such as Vaughan Williams' 'Fantasia on a Theme by Thomas Tallis' (1910) and 'Five Tudor Portraits' (1935).[21] Hewitt and Hill's *Outline of Musical History*, published by Hogarth a year after *Orlando*, touched on early music and its revival, noting with pride that Elizabethan English music was 'equal to anything written on the Continent'.[22] Francesca Allinson was immersed in folk song and early music, and in left-wing politics, during the 1920s and 1930s: whilst working on *A Childhood* for the Hogarth Press she produced a study of folk song, *The Irish Contribution to English Traditional Tunes*, edited Purcell's work, wrote a libretto for *Don Quixote* set to Purcell's music (c. 1937) and a score (1933) for Orlando Gibbons' *London Street Cries*.[23] By 1930 the Woolfs were acquainted with the great harpsichordist, friend of Dolmetsch and Smyth, Violet Gordon Woodhouse (*D*, III: 338). Bloomsbury homes too included decorative objects reflecting the early music revival, and several of these were objects Woolf saw almost daily: a fire screen at Monk's House was decorated with a mandolin; a log box at Charleston was painted by Duncan Grant with dancers and musicians, including a lutenist; the library included a book case decorated by Duncan Grant in about 1925 with mandolin players; and in 1936 Angelica Garnett painted a gramophone cabinet for the studio at Charleston one end of which depicts a nymph playing a lyre (Quentin Bell recalled that music – 'Haydn or Mozart, never Wagner' – played constantly in the studio). Furthermore, Duncan Grant's eighteenth-century English square piano was kept at Charleston.[24] The early music revival intersected with (high) modernism not only via Woolf's domestic life and work but also, for example, in Pound's numerous eulogies to Dolmetsch, including the essays 'Arnold Dolmetsch' and 'Vers Libre and Arnold Dolmetsch' (both 1918) and allusions to him in the *Cantos* (Pound owned a Dolmetsch clavichord). *Ulysses* also records this vogue, as Bloom reflects on 'the lutenist' Dowland and 'Mr Arnold Dolmetsch, whom Bloom did not quite recall, though the name certainly sounded familiar'.[25]

Orlando reflects this exposure to early music and instruments: the allusions to period music and instruments are one device through which Woolf represents her protagonist's expansive, kaleidoscopic memory, evoking different periods through their characteristic soundscapes. The Elizabethan poet Nick Greene plays 'half-a-dozen musical instruments'

(O, 64) and the novel refers in passing to period instruments including shawms (O, 57) and virginals (O, 23), as *Between the Acts* alludes to an early flute, the flageolet, during the mock Restoration comedy (*BTA*, 80). Orlando addresses one of his Elizabethan admirers as Euphrosyne – we are told she 'sang sweetly to the virginals; and was never dressed before mid-day owing to the extreme care she took of her person' (O, 23) – and the recycling of the ship's name from *The Voyage Out* may be one of *Orlando*'s numerous self-referential allusions, recalling Rachel's fondness for early music. Furthermore, during the frost, King James' courtiers dance to the 'fine music of flute and trumpet':

> Orlando, it is true, was none of those who tread lightly the corantoe and lavolta; he was clumsy and a little absent-minded. He much preferred the plain dances of his own country, which he had danced as a child to these fantastic foreign measures. He had indeed just brought his feet together about six in the evening of the seventh of January at the finish of some such qua-drille or minuet when he beheld, coming from the pavilion of the Muscovite Embassy [Sasha]' (O, 26)

All the dances performed here are of French or Italian origin: Orlando's dislike of 'fantastic foreign measures' and loyalty to his national dances are gently undercut, attributed as much to his physical awkwardness as to any ideological principle or national interest.

As these and numerous other details suggest, *Orlando* is certainly partly *about* English history, literature, landscape and identity but it is wary of nationalism and committed to cosmopolitanism. The novel's protagonist and narrator are persistently attentive to, and celebrate, other cultures and what we might anomalously call world or indigenous music. (Indeed, after Woolf's death, Leonard occasionally listened to examples of 'Indian music', 'Congo Music' and Sicilian folk songs).[26] The ostentation and triviality of the 'musical boxes' displayed at the Embassy party in Constantinople (O, 92) contrast, for example, with the mysterious energy of the music played by 'shepherds' the night Orlando falls into his second sleep (O, 93), and with the music of the gipsies in Turkey, 'singing or crooning contentedly at their work' (O, 103). And just before the birth of Orlando's son, the narrator welcomes the sound of 'one of these frail, reedy, fluty, jerky, old-fashioned barrel-organs which are still sometimes played by Italian organ-grinders in back streets' (O, 202). The narrator's invitation to the musician to 'fill this page with sound' (O, 202) celebrates working-class, non-British music, resisting the considerable xenophobic commentary on and legislation against barrel organs and street musicians more generally in the early twentieth century.[27] And in the section set in 1928, Orlando hears 'the loud speaker condensing on the terrace a dance tune that people were listening to in the red-velvet opera house at Vienna' (*O*, 220–3 [*sic*]), a detail suggesting the altered aural culture of modernity, certainly, but also Orlando's internationalist sympathies. Collectively, such details resist and critique the xenophobia and nationalism expressed by some exponents of the English Musical Renaissance, as the passage describing Orlando's departure from Turkey exemplifies.

Orlando's departure is precipitated by her growing sense of alienation from the gipsies, which is expressed through racist clichés – she compares her own 'ancient and civilised race' with the gipsies who were 'an ignorant people, not much better than savages' (*O*, 103). Her outbreak of racial and social pride and her perception of gipsy life as 'rude and barbarous' are remarked on by the narrator, who compares these attitudes to the 'desire to prevail' that propels national, religious and imperial conflicts: 'Towns have been sacked for less, and a million martyrs have suffered at the stake rather than yield an inch upon any of the points here debated' (*O*, 105). It is telling, then, that as Orlando's ship comes in sight of the English coast, the sailors 'began chanting, "So good-bye and adieu to you, Ladies of Spain"' (*O*, 116): Orlando's outbreak of xenophobia and nationalism is echoed by the patriotic contemporary appropriation of 'Spanish Ladies'. This late eighteenth-century naval song describes British sailors bidding farewell to their Spanish wives or lovers and the ships' efforts to locate the entrance to the English Channel in fog, the chorus beginning: '[w]e will rant and we'll roar like true British sailors'. Woolf may have known the song through one of the literary sources (including *Moby Dick* and *Ulysses*) in which it is (mis)quoted,[28] but it is also very likely that she was familiar with its prominence in the folk revival: it was one of the most frequently performed songs on English Folk Dance Society programmes.[29] Furthermore, Henry Wood had arranged the song in 1905 as part of his *Fantasia on British Sea Songs* to mark the centenary of the Battle of Trafalgar, and it became indispensable at the Last Night of the Proms (of which Wood was, of course, the founder). By the 1920s, when the Proms were held in the Queen's Hall, they invariably combined classical repertoire with a patriotic agenda (recall Woolf's revulsion in 1915 from the 'patriotic sentiment' expressed there [*L*, II: 57]). Wood's interest in sea songs was not unusual among composers of the English Musical Renaissance: Vaughan Williams also arranged three British examples for his short march 'Sea Songs', composed for military band and first performed in 1924 at Wembley during the British Empire Exhibition.[30] In addition to these songs' words and musical idioms, then, the genres of sea songs, naval songs and shanties were themselves strongly associated with nationalist and military contexts in the 1920s. The protagonist of 'A Simple Melody', who eulogises 'a perfectly quiet old English song' evoked by a landscape painting, has (like Woolf herself) attended the Exhibition, which he found 'very tiring'; 'he believed it was not being a success' (*CSF*, 195). Woolf's ambivalent portrait of him acknowledges the nationalism of the Exhibition's music (which is undercut by his comments) and his love for English song is further compromised by his belief in 'proportion' and his desire 'to be sure that all people were the same' and 'simple' (*CSF*, 199–200).

By the 1930s, Woolf's critique of nationalist (uses of) music and the folk revival had become much more explicit than was the case in her earlier fiction. Most obviously, *Between the Acts* (1941) takes as its subject and structure an event championed by the folk revivalists – the performance of a village pageant – but persistently undercuts the revivalists' aim of 'restoring pastoral ideals'.[31] (Woolf's subversion of the genre was not unique: the Communist Party pageants of 1936 described a history of radicalism and resistance, and Forster's 'Abinger Pageant' [1934] with folk song settings by Vaughan Williams is tentative about the definitions and legacy of the concept of Englishness. In 1940, the Women's Institute invited Woolf to write 'a play for the villagers to act' [*L*, VI: 391] and she expressed the wish to do so; it is intriguing to imagine how it might have compared to the novel.)[32] Much of the music played on the gramophone is resoundingly urban in its subject matter; the faltering, interrupted sounds suggest the difficulty or even absurdity of attempting to 'preserve' music through modern technology; and the effects of the disparate works and genres expose the limited, provisional sense of community. The first song played during the pageant on the gramophone is about a soldier, '*valiant Rhoderick*', and its 'pompous popular tune' is taken up by Mrs Manresa:

> My home is at Windsor, close to the Inn.
> Royal George is the name of the pub.
> And boys you'll believe me,
> I don't want no asking . . .

She was afloat on the stream of the melody. Radiating royalty, complacency, good humour, the wild child was queen of the festival (*BTA*, 49).

Woolf's account of the performance's effect on Mrs Manresa makes clear her suspicions of the affective powers of the 'melody' as well as the militaristic, royalist words. Both performance and song are portrayed as facile, visceral and self-aggrandising. Mrs Manresa's humming of a music hall song that mocks the royal family (*BTA*, 137, n) inadvertently undercuts the patriotic sentiments of the warriors and renders her own sense of 'royalty, complacency' ridiculous. And as the gramophone plays a 'drunk' song lauding Elizabethan explorers, sailors and imperialists, Mrs Manresa 'trolloped out the words of the song with an abandonment which, if vulgar, was a great help to the Elizabethan age' (*BTA*, 53). The folk and early music used in the pageant deals almost invariably with royalist, military and patriotic subjects and Woolf leaves us in no doubt of its capacity to amplify patriarchal aggression: William watches Giles approach, '[a]rmed and valiant, bold and blatant, firm, elatant – the popular march tune rang in his head. And the fingers of William's left hand closed firmly, surreptitiously, as the hero approached' (*BTA*, 67). Such moments recur throughout Woolf's representation of the pageant: the performance of 'Rule Britannia' during the Victorian picnic is an example (*BTA*, 101). The novel surely endorses anonymous, collective, folk culture, for all that it records her audience's unthinking privileging of canonical Austro-German art music over folk: 'was it Bach, Handel, Beethoven, Mozart or nobody famous, but merely a traditional tune?' (*BTA*, 112) and 'the tune – was it Bach, Handel, or no one in particular' (*BTA*, 119). Yet her celebration of 'Anon' and of community is very different from that of the ideologues of the English Musical Renaissance.[33]

Woolf further critiques the ideology of the English Musical Renaissance by juxtaposing allusions to folk music and popular idioms with allusions to historical and political events, contextualising the essentialising, atemporal construction of a national folk heritage in specific cultural and historical moments. Manhire observes of the folk music revival (to which I would add the early music movement) that 'Woolf shares the revivalists' interest in the past but not the ideology which accompanies their stress on authenticity. Where the rhetoric of the folk revival advocated the return to a simple and "natural" tradition, Woolf's deployment of folk music traces a more complicated sense of historical change.'[34] Stuart Christie too describes La Trobe's pageant as dramatising an 'aggressive model of engagement with history', rejecting the fiction of national culture as an imagined community.[35] Representatively, the sound of a 'merry little old tune' (*BTA*, 75) (suggesting 'Merrie England', perhaps) is preceded by the nursery rhyme 'Sing a Song of Sixpence' (*BTA*, 74) and by these anonymous speculations:

> 'I've a friend who's been to Russia. He says . . . And my daughter, just back from Rome, she says the common people, in the cafés, hate Dictators [. . .] And what about the Jews? The refugees . . . the Jews . . . People like ourselves, beginning life again. . . . But it's always been the same . . .' (*BTA*, 74)[36]

The scraps of conversation evoke Stalin, Mussolini and Hitler, and the persecution and displacement of Jews across Europe; they imply, too, parallels between these events in Continental Europe and the self-absorbed, wealthy British establishment, evoked through the image of the monarch in the English nursery rhyme. The spectator's expressions of affinity and empathy with Jews thus immediately expose the insularity and (ethnic) exclusivity articulated by the pageant's texts and by similar contemporary constructions of English history and identity.

The refugees . . . the Jews . . . people like ourselves

In *Orlando* and *Between the Acts* musical allusions critique the nationalism characteristic of much contemporary British music and discourses about music. In doing so, the allusions augment the cosmopolitan, internationalist sympathies of Woolf's fiction, apparent not only in these works but also, as we saw, in her representation of music in novels including *The Voyage Out*, *Jacob's Room* and *Mrs Dalloway*. The final part of this chapter considers one aspect of Woolf's responses to contemporary nationalist, ethnically exclusive, essentialist models of English identity and of music: her representation of Jews and music. The xenophobia of some formative polemics of the English Musical Renaissance shares with contemporary anti-Semitic discourse a desire to define and 'protect' the nature of English identity. Leena Kore Schröder has proposed, following Hannah Arendt and Zygmunt Bauman, that the 'threat' represented by Jews 'is not that of the foreigner or the outsider as the discrete Other but rather [. . .] the foreigner and the outsider as already *within*, implicated in the foundations of identity'.[37] These discourses about music and national identity intersect, then, through their policing of the English and the 'foreign'.

Woolf was undoubtedly familiar with the extensive contemporary philo- and anti-Semitic discourses about music and Jews, from popular clichés about the 'innate' musicality of Jews to *Trilby*'s anti-Semitic portrait of the musician Svengali to Eliot's sympathetic portraits of singers and other musicians in *Daniel Deronda*. She would certainly also have known (of) Wagner's notorious anti-Semitic essays *Das Judenthum in der Musik* (*Judaism in Music*, 1850) and *Was ist deutsch?* (*What is German?*, 1865), and of controversies about whether or not the dramas included anti-Semitic stereotypes of Jewish appearance, 'character' and voices.[38] More intimately and acutely, Woolf's responses to these debates were surely shaped by her marriage to Leonard and to her entrance into a Jewish family whose members included a number of accomplished amateur musicians; her adult family unit brought her, to a greater degree than most of her circle, into close relationships with those 'already *within*'. (And here, I will only note the multiple ironies of the fact that George Duckworth gave his teenage half-sister 'a Jews' harp [brooch] made of enamel with a pinkish blob of matter swinging in the centre' as an incentive for her to attend coming out parties with him [*MB*, 38].)[39] Leonard's and his relatives' musical knowledge and gifts were among the first characteristics that Woolf noted when describing Leonard to friends and she returned to them throughout her life: her diaries and letters include a number of observations on the musical interests of Leonard's family and other Jewish acquaintances in which admiration is tempered by distaste and unease. In 1915, for example, she lists singing among the accomplishments of Leonard's youngest sister Flora for whom 'there is something to be said' though she dislikes 'the Jewish voice' and 'the Jewish laugh' (*D*, I: 6); in 1916, she describes Leonard as 'a strict Jew as a small boy, and he can still sing in Hebrew' (*L*, II: 85); and in 1928, her mother-in-law's ignorance of *Scheherazade* and Marie Woolf's recollections of the Schubert songs she received as a wedding present inform a barbed account of her musicality (*L*, III: 524–5). After attending a rehearsal of Smyth's *The Prison* at Lady Lewis' in 1931, Woolf recorded what seemed to her 'the curiously sensitive, perceptive Jewish face of old Lady L.', concluding '[h]ow sensitised to music old Jewesses are – how pliable, how supple' (*D*, IV: 10). Whether we see these remarks as expressions of admiration, of difference or of both, they indicate Woolf's attention to Jewish singing and speaking voices and to Jews and musicality.

Throughout her adult life, Woolf was acquainted with a number of distinguished amateur and professional Jewish musicians, including Bruno Walter and Sydney J. Loeb. Woolf first met Loeb in London in 1909, describing him as 'the great Mr Loeb who has the finest collection of operatic photographs and autographs in Europe' (*L*, I: 398). As David Bradshaw has explained,[40] Loeb was indeed an exceptionally accomplished photographer and a serious collector of operatic ephemera; he was a 'consummate' Wagnerian, who married Hans Richter's daughter in 1912 and was highly regarded by the great Wagnerian conductor (of whom Woolf was a passionate admirer, writing in 1907 of his acclaimed *Ring* that 'nothing will induce me to sacrifice my Richter' [*L*, I: 312]). Loeb was an expert on Elgar and a connoisseur of London musical life, interested in suffrage and Fabianism as well as Wagner, which gave him considerable shared interests not only with Woolf but also with Shaw, whose conversation he recorded several times.[41] It is probable that Woolf encountered Loeb at Bayreuth and regularly at performances in London, though when she met him in 1925 she described him as 'that furtive Jew, Loeb, who dogs my life at intervals of 10 years' (*D*, III: 26). The hostility in this account can be explained in part by Woolf's dislike of being photographed and by Loeb's unexpected approach to her and Leonard in Hyde Park for this purpose, but it also of course deploys anti-Semitic images of Loeb (he is 'furtive' and essentialised – 'that [. . .] Jew'). Here, Woolf's response may also be informed by anti-Semitic discourse that associated Jews with the commercialisation and trivialisation of art: Loeb's wealth, his untroubled participation in the publicity industry that surrounded opera and opera stars, and his conspicuous 'consumption' of Society opera may have shaped Woolf's attitude towards him as they clearly did her accounts of his mother.[42]

In April 1933, she met the exiled German-Jewish conductor Bruno Walter, a 'refugee' from anti-Semitic persecution in Germany rather than, as Loeb's parents had been, voluntary emigrants. Woolf wrote in her diary:

> He is a swarthy, fattish, man; not at all smart. Not at all the 'great conductor'. He is a little Slav, a little semitic. He is very nearly mad; that is, he cant get 'the poison' as he called it of Hitler out of him. 'You must not think of the Jews' he kept on saying 'You must think of this awful reign of intolerance. You must think of the whole state of the world. It is terrible – terrible. That this meanness, that this pettiness, should be possible! Our Germany – which I loved – with our tradition – our culture – We are now a disgrace.' Then he told us how you cant talk above a whisper. There are spies everywhere. He had to sit in the window of his hotel in Leipzig? a whole day, telephoning. All the time soldiers were marching. They never stop marching. And on the wireless, between the turns, they play military music. Horrible horrible! He hopes for the monarchy as the only hope. He will never go back there. His orchestra had been in existence for 150 years: but it is the spirit of the whole that is awful. We must band together. We must refuse to meet any German. We must say that they are uncivilised. We will not trade with them or play with them – we must make them feel themselves outcasts – not by fighting them; by ignoring them. Then he swept off to music. He has the intensity – genius? – which makes him live everything he feels. Described conducting: must know every player. (*D*, IV: 153)

Woolf's 'record[ing]' (*D*, IV: 153) of Walter, conductor of the Leipzig Gewandhaus Orchestra from 1929 to 1933, took place just after he had fled Germany; he did not settle there again. Her account, I would suggest, mingles empathy and alienation. The attempts, with which this passage begins, to classify Walter ethnically are followed by an attentive and arguably more sympathetic record of his conversation. Despite the (dismissive? regretful?) assessment that Walter is 'very nearly mad' and her hesitancy about his 'genius', the distance between them collapses as she goes on, as the convergence of their diction illustrates. As Woolf's account unfolds, she abandons direct quotation: the sentence beginning 'His orchestra', for example, combines Walter's vocabulary with a third person pronoun. The diary entry details Walter's first-hand knowledge of the appropriation of music for propagandist purposes – the alterations to programming on the radio, for example, as well as the persecution of Jewish musicians – possibly recalling to Woolf her own scrutiny of the relationship between music and state in *The Voyage Out*, *Jacob's Room* and *Mrs Dalloway*. And Walter's non-violent response that advocated a policy not of 'fighting' but 'ignoring' surely chimed with the Woolfs' own pacifism. His account of course prefigured later political events too: many Jewish musicians were excluded from professional musical life in Germany and certain paradigmatically 'German' repertoire forbidden to them,[43] and on the day Hitler invaded Austria Woolf noted '[t]he Austrian national anthem was heard on the wireless for the last time. We got a snatch of dance music from Vienna' (*D*, V: 129). Despite the oscillating tone of the sketch, this dinner with Walter (arranged by Smyth) gave the Woolfs a detailed, informed account of the effects of anti-Semitism on German-Jewish musicians and musical life, and of persecution and the diaspora. This awareness was unquestionably augmented when the Woolfs visited Germany in 1935, where they witnessed anti-Semitic rallies and banners; collectively, these experiences shape her philo-Semitic use of music in *The Years*, which was 'in full flood' just weeks after she met Walter (*D*, IV: 162 and 168).

The Years (1937) contains Woolf's most explicit and extended exploration of the relationship between anti-Semitism and music. This subject isn't limited to her late fiction, however: Florinda's passing anti-Semitic reference to a 'Bechstein' (*JR*, 67) in *Jacob's Room*, for instance, conflates the name of the distinguished German piano makers with Jews, implying an intrinsic affinity between Jews and music. (And this is to say nothing of the opera-loving Jacob's forename, nor that of the pianist Rachel Vinrace.) Furthermore, I have suggested elsewhere that *Mrs Dalloway* may be read as an extended response to Wagner's anti-Semitism and as a philo-Semitic celebration of Jewish liturgy and liturgical music.[44] Specifically, I proposed that the novel draws extensively on Wagner's *The Flying Dutchman* (1843), the protagonist of which Wagner termed 'this Ahasuerus of the seas', the eternally damned Wandering Jew whose fate was an allegory of Jewish 'redemption'.[45] The novel's pervasive imagery of temporally displaced travellers (particularly Peter Walsh), Clarissa's absorption in a Dutch painting just before she re-encounters Peter and Septimus' jump to his death like Senta's at the end of the opera may all be read as critiques of Wagner's opera and of his anti-Semitism and sexual politics particularly. Peter shares something of the exiled, displaced position figuratively exemplified by the Flying Dutchman/Wandering Jew and by the actual experience of many (exiled) Jews in early twentieth-century Europe. Peter's marginalisation exposes the national, racial, gender and class prejudices dominating post-war English society and through which English identity is constructed and regulated. Furthermore, the personal histories and names of some of *Mrs Dalloway*'s minor characters – Joseph Breitkopf and Miss Kilman – suggest that they are Jewish or of Jewish descent. Through these characters, I suggest, Woolf evokes the Jewish diaspora, the various real, historical 'flights' of Jews during the late nineteenth and early twentieth centuries. Finally, I propose that the novel alludes to the Jewish mourning practice *shivah* (שבעה; 'seven'), using the rituals, imagery and sounds of *shivah* as counterparts to the Wagnerian model of self-sacrificing tragedy celebrated by the opera. The novel repeatedly draws on the customs and language of *shivah*, using the mourning protocols derived from biblical and rabbinical authority to depict literal and symbolic deaths in the text. These allusions cumulatively counter Wagner's attacks on what he called in *Das Judenthum in der Musik* the Jews' 'travesty' of religious music.[46] *Mrs Dalloway*, in other words, uses a Wagnerian intertext to embed philo-Semitic sympathies, as is the case more conspicuously in *The Years*.

The cosmopolitanism of London's musical life is stressed in the later novel (for which *Music* was a possible title [*Y*, xxix]), from the barrel organ playing 'Sur le pont d'Avignon' in 1891 (*Y*, 88), to Eugénie's 'indolent Southern manner' (*Y*, 118) and habitual music making, to the 'supple Italian face' of the organ player in 1914 (*Y*, 214), to the Russian ballet in 1914 and the 'present day' section (*Y*, 242 and 374). There are, additionally, numerous allusions to the Jewish population of the capital, emphasising London's ethnically diverse communities and history and recording, too, anti-Semitic prejudice against this population. In the 1880 section, for instance, Rose's casual anti-Semitic slur that '"Bertie Levy's got six toes on one foot"' (*Y*, 13)[47] is juxtaposed to Eleanor's care for the family and her 'great admiration for Mrs Levy, who was dying of cancer'; nonetheless, she feels obliged to 'say something to amuse her sister' so observes that '"They do love finery – Jews"' (*Y*, 30). And in the 'present day' section, North sees numerous East End houses chalked with British Union of Fascists' graffiti – the area was the site of extensive harassment of Jews by the BUF during the mid-1930s.[48] David Bradshaw has persuasively argued that the novel records contemporary anti-Semitic prejudice but also includes a number of philo-Semitic details 'stressing the rightful "place" of Jews in Britain'.[49] He proposes, further, that *The Years* draws 'a parallel between the anti-Semitism of [Woolf's] own class and the BUF'.[50] Similarly, I shall suggest that Woolf links the anti-Semitism of her upper-middle-class British characters in *The Years* with that of Fascist propaganda, specifically with Nazi appropriations of Wagner's work. The representation of the pre-war performance of *Siegfried* in *The Years* is informed by the contemporary political context of the 1930s, in particular by eugenics and by the conspicuous adoption of Wagner's work for Nazi rallies and Nazi ideology more generally. Hitler quoted *Meistersinger* in speeches as early as 1923[51] and supported Bayreuth financially during the war, for example; *Meistersinger* was staged at the Nuremberg party rallies from 1935; and during the war performances of this work at Bayreuth were opened to soldiers.[52] Hitler's 'cult of Wagner' was widely known by the time of the novel, reported, for example, in a 1936 biography of Hitler.[53] And Thomas Mann's essay 'Leiden und Größe Richard Wagners' ('The Suffering and Greatness of Richard Wagner'), in which he critiqued the central role of music in constructions of German identity, was published in the same year the Woolfs met Walter, a friend of Mann's; it was enormously controversial, prompting Mann's exile from Germany.[54] In 1935, Woolf reluctantly joined musicians including Donald Tovey on the committee of an anti-Fascist art exhibition (*L*, V: 367–8); music was, she wrote in 1936, 'our one resource against politics' (*L*, VI: 19). Despite *The Years*' pervasive allusions to popular genres, dance music, nursery rhymes, street musicians and jazz, the longest diegetic account of any single piece of music is of Kitty Lasswade's attendance at *Siegfried* in 1910. This is an exceptional section of the novel: although it describes only one Act of the third part of Wagner's tetralogy it is one of the longest uninterrupted passages and a unique depiction of art music, to which this novel (like *Between the Acts*) gives little overt attention. And it is a scene that draws together *The Years*' attention to music, Jews and anti-Semitism.

Kitty hears *Siegfried* – 'her favourite opera' (*Y*, 173) – at Covent Garden and is joined in her box by her cousin Edward and by a handsome young man who works at the Foreign Office. As Chapter 3 suggested, her reflections as the orchestra tune up reveal the royalist and imperialist sentiments of this listener, sentiments amplified by the 'overture': 'The music made her think of herself and her own life as she seldom did. It exalted her; it cast a flattering light over herself, her past' (*Y*, 174–5). The first Act of the opera concerns the young Siegfried, product of Siegmund and Sieglinde's sibling incest, who has been raised by the dwarf Mime in the hope that Siegfried will be able to forge the magic sword Nothung, allowing Mime to obtain the ring and the omnipotence it confers. The curtain rises on Mime's ineffectual attempts to forge the sword:

> The dwarf was hammering at the sword. Hammer, hammer, hammer, he went with little short, sharp strokes. She listened. The music had changed. *He*, she thought, looking at the handsome boy, knows exactly what the music means. He was already completely possessed by the music. She liked the look of complete absorption that had swum up on top of his immaculate respectability, making him seem almost stern . . . But here was Siegfried. She leant forward. Dressed in leopard-skins, very fat, with nut-brown thighs, leading a bear – here he was. She liked the fat bouncing young man in his flaxen wig: his voice was magnificent. Hammer, hammer, hammer he went. (*Y*, 175)

Kitty's language reflects the opera's juxtaposition of the two characters. Siegfried is identified and his appearance recorded, the details about his costume, physique and leading of the bear revealing Kitty's admiration for his vitality. Her approving observation of his 'fat' physique, 'bouncing' demeanour and 'flaxen wig' evokes the spectre of eugenics: his body, the wig (that emphasises, as was customary in mimetic period productions, his Aryan appearance) and his 'magnificent' voice all elicit her approval. Siegfried's physical robustness is reiterated as the passage unfolds: when Kitty lifts her opera glasses she sees his 'fat brown arms glistening with paint' (*Y*, 175). Mime, on the other hand, is unnamed (simply 'the dwarf') and undescribed except through the noise he makes, the aggressive sound of his hammering amplified by the alliteration of 'short, sharp strokes'. Omission, silencing, textual effacement: these sound like the strategies of anti-Semitism and some may read this passage as such. Kitty's observations certainly reflect the scene's opposition of the two characters, but Woolf's lack of detail about Mime's appearance and voice may be read not as prejudice but rather as a philo-Semitic strategy. Unlike Wagner's insistence on Mime's grotesque body and speech, which many have recognised as reiterating anti-Semitic stereotypes about 'Jewish' physique, physiognomy and voices,[55] Woolf does not reiterate these stereotypes. Furthermore, the cursory attention to Mime foregrounds Kitty's admiration for Siegfried's appearance, making clear his appeal to Kitty's hyper-masculine, bellicose sentiments. The heroism of the *Heldentenor* and Kitty's admiration for him are, consequently, problematised, particularly as the passage places Siegfried and Wagner in the novel's matrix of references to 'dictators; Napoleon; the psychology of great men' (*Y*, 267, 293 and 299). These allusions suggest a continuum between music and politics, between opera encountered in an élite social context and the mass appeal of contemporary and historical dictators, between the qualities Kitty admires in Siegfried and contemporary eugenicist and Fascist ideology.

As the opera unfolds, Kitty recalls her youth in Oxford until Wotan, disguised as the Wanderer, enters. The substance of Wotan's address to Mime isn't recorded by Woolf; instead, we are told, 'On and on he went; on and on. [Kitty's] attention flagged' (*Y*, 176). Then:

At last the Wanderer had gone. And now? she asked herself, leaning forward. Siegfried burst in. Dressed in his leopard-skins, laughing and singing, here he was again. The music excited her. It was magnificent. Siegfried took the broken pieces of the sword and blew on the fire and hammered, hammered, hammered. The singing, the hammering and the fire leaping all went on at the same time. Quicker and quicker, more and more rhythmically, more and more triumphantly he hammered, until at last up he swung the sword high above his head and brought it down – crack! The anvil burst asunder. And then he brandished the sword over his head and shouted and sang; and the music rushed higher and higher; and the curtain fell. (*Y*, 176)

Again, it is Siegfried's energy and the music's that are emphasised: he 'burst[s]' on stage, is described in present participles, the 'excit[ing]' effects of the music are noted and the 'magnificen[ce]' (of the music rather than the singer's voice this time) is reasserted. The increasing length of the sentences and the increasingly prominent repetition (especially of 'hammering') arguably mimic the 'rush' of the music itself, evoking the dynamism and violence of this climactic scene. The operatic episode is certainly triumphalist and phallic in its imagery and its uniform impact on the entire audience is stressed as Woolf describes the 'clapping and waving', the repeated curtain calls, the extended standing ovation that continues even after the musicians have left the stage, and the repeated cries of 'Bravo!' by the young man in her box, who 'had forgotten her. He had forgotten himself' (*Y*, 177). In the context of the novel's allusions to dictators, such a homogeneous visceral response, in which the individual audience members lose their sense of self(-control), takes on disturbing connotations rather than simply indicating an exceptional performance of an exceptional work. Woolf's account describes the genteel aesthetic audience in terms more usually associated with the troublingly undifferentiated unit of the mass, the crowd or the rabble. The apparent political indifference and social exclusivity implicit in the idea of 'the audience' are overlaid here with the values attributed to the lower-class 'mass': potential violence and political volatility.[56] The *effect* of this performance may even be intended to evoke mass political rallies, and perhaps specifically Nazi uses of Wagner's music and the aestheticisation of political events more generally under the Third Reich – recall Bayreuth full of soldiers, a paradigmatically homogeneous audience.

The passage is, in several ways, a return to the Covent Garden

episodes in *Jacob's Room*. The attention to the audience, the suggestions of homosexuality in the musical absorption of the beautiful young
man, and the attention to imperialism are shared by both novels. Here,
however, the homogeneity of the audience is stressed even more than in
Jacob's Room: the audience's unvaried affluence and conservatism are
emphasised, partly because we see the scene from Kitty's perspective
and lack the spatial mobility of the narrator in the earlier novel. Woolf's
intention here is surely to underscore the conservatism of (this) operatic
performance. The fact that *Siegfried* is Kitty's favourite opera is in this
sense ironic: she may be drawn to the opera's iconoclastic protagonist
and its subject of the over-throwing of one era by another (the rule of
the gods ends, and that of man begins), but she herself has clearly lost
her childhood subversive zeal. (Indeed, as an old woman she appears to
Nicholas to '"come into a room as if the whole world belonged to her"'
[Y, 373] and strikes North as 'dictatorial' [Y, 374]). Here, we should
consider that Woolf's critique may be as much of Kitty as of Wagner
and the tetralogy. Kitty's intermittent attention and her perception that,
unlike the young man, she doesn't know 'exactly what the music means',
may suggest that her response is that of an insufficiently alert and
informed Wagnerian – if she'd paid more attention, she might have critiqued Siegfried's hyper-virile character and aggression, as many would
argue the tetralogy itself does. There is thus the possibility, at least, that
Woolf found a more palatable political narrative in Wagner's magnum
opus than first appears, and that her critique is directed as much at the
reception and misreadings of Wagner's work as at the composer himself.
And it is possible too, as Jane Marcus plausibly suggests, that Woolf
believed 'the Wagnerian ideas, with their own superman hero and anti-
Semitism [. . .] betray the theme of freedom the music itself expresses'.[57]

The novel's representation of Wagnerian heroism also invites attention in relation to contemporary eugenics. Kitty's admiration for the
'handsome Roman head' of the young man accompanying Edward
and for the tenor's physique echoes (however causally or knowledge-
ably) eugenics' valorisation of the classical world and obsession with
individual and ethnic 'purity'. Certainly, the topics of racial and familial
purity recur in the novel, as in the opera and Nazi appropriations of it.
This Act of the opera in particular celebrates the aggressive 'hero', but
Siegfried as a whole also deals with the subject of illicit family relations
(and Siegmund and Sieglinde's incest is echoed in Kitty's repeated reflections, as she listens, on her cousin Edward: 'It wouldn't have done,' she
observes three times during the performance, suggesting her unresolved
feelings for him [Y, 174 and 176]). Kitty's attraction to Edward is one
of the novel's numerous discreet allusions to taboo family relations,

evoked from the very start of the novel by Abel Pargiters' forename with its echo of the original biblical fratricide and paralleled in this Act of the opera by Wotan's allusion to the giant Fafner's murder of his brother Fasolt.[58] In the 1914 section, Maggie even asks Martin '"Are we brother and sister?"' (*Y*, 235). The questions of fatherhood and racial purity are central to Mime's arguments with Siegfried in Act I, scene i, as they are in Wotan's long conversation with Mime in scene ii. Mime tells Siegfried, 'I'm your father / and mother in one', for example, to which Siegfried responds by noting the difference in their appearance, 'as like to a toad / were a glittering fish.'[59] In scene ii, Mime asks Wotan three questions about the 'races' who live in different parts of the world, and describes Wotan's love for the 'favoured race' the Walsungs and for Siegfried, off-spring of 'a wildly desperate / pair of twins'.[60] The novel neither quotes nor describes either of these exchanges, though – indeed, Kitty is bored by the Wanderer. As in her representation of Mime, Woolf, I would suggest, relies on her readers' knowledge of the opera's themes of racial purity and inheritance without reiterating these sentiments in her work.

This episode in *The Years* thus evokes familial and dynastic change, notably through Wagner's opera but also through the precise historical context of the *Siegfried* performance. In *Jacob's Room*, the opera scenes suggested the imminent war and the end of a pre-war 'idyll': here, Edward VII's imminent death is discussed by Kitty and her companions and the scene again evokes both endurance and a passing regime.[61] The (waning) influence of patriarchs – social and familial – is a central theme of the opera and the novel. The works explore the parallels between state and familial politics, as in Woolf's attacks on the patriarchs in *Three Guineas*. In the opera, Mime and Wotan are rival father figures for Siegfried, who shows himself far more unhesitating in throwing off any parental guidance than the characters watching the opera; in broad terms, the novel suggests that the patriarchs are not so easily rejected or relinquished and the Wagnerian intertext thus throws into relief patriarchy's enduring pernicious influence in the 1910s and 1930s. As in *Jacob's Room*, Woolf suggests that the audience fail to recognise the ideology and pertinence of the work they are attending. Yet, the opera's theme of a passing era is echoed in the allusions to the imminent death of the British monarch: the characters look at the royal box, wondering if *Siegfried* has been cancelled, and the young man remarks that '"[t]he doctors have given him up"' (*Y*, 174). Woolf and Leonard had, we remember, attended this opera in May 1911 during their courtship and Woolf's precise setting of this performance in 1910 places the opera in a matrix of historical allusions to the ailing monarch who died on 6 May 1910. As several of Edward VII's biographers noted in the 1930s, the king had many Jewish friends and was known for his philo-Semitism.[62] His death marked the end, then, of a period of prominent, socially authoritative, philo-Semitism. Combined with the allusions to *Siegfried* and its central themes of racial identity, the monarch's death foreshadows the rising anti-Semitic sentiment in Britain, which the latter parts of the novel document.

Woolf concludes this cluster of details about philo-Semitism, anti-Semitism and music by juxtaposing the opera with a parallel episode: Maggie and Sara's conversation at Hyams Place after dinner. As Bradshaw has argued, the fictional location Hyams Place, and Sara's name, may be placed among a number of philo-Semitic details in the novel. Although Sara makes a series of virulently anti-Semitic slurs about Abrahamson's bath later in the novel, her name associates her with the biblical Abraham's wife and, by extension, symbolically with Jews.[63] The effect is to render her bigotry more shocking, and to emphasise the social marginalisation she shares with the very figure she vilifies. It is, therefore, suggestive that Sara's music making immediately follows the Covent Garden scene and is juxtaposed to the operatic performance:

> Sara sat hunched on the music stool, but she was not playing.
> 'Sing something,' said Maggie suddenly. Sara turned and struck the notes.
>   'Brandishing, flourishing my sword in my hand . . .' she sang. The words were the words of some pompous eighteenth-century march, but her voice was reedy and thin. Her voice broke. She stopped singing.
>   She sat silent with her hands on the notes. 'What's the good of singing if one hasn't any voice?' she murmured. (*Y*, 177–8)

For all the differences between the two locations, performers, audience and musical works, the words of Sara's song immediately recall the forging of Nothung in *Siegfried*. The powerful voice of the professional emphasises the vulnerability of Sara's: echoing the phrase repeatedly applied to Joseph Breitkopf, Woolf notes that Sara '"hasn't any voice"'. The contrast between Siegfried and Sara could hardly be more pointed:[64] Jews, women, the poor and the disabled are easily silenced and their voices falter, whilst those of the 'bouncing young m[e]n' ring out even to the point of 'shout[ing]'.[65] Sara's striking of the piano keys is a gentler echo of Mime's and Siegfried's hammering; it places her in opposition to the patriarchs, especially as the words of the song also recall her father in the 1907 section and anticipate her singing at the dinner set in 1917. In 1907, Sara hears her father bullying her mother and bitterly observes, '"Pirouetting up and down with his sword between his legs; with his opera hat under his arm and his sword between his legs"' (*Y*, 138).

Patriarchal aggression and Society opera are conflated in this phallic image. And at the wartime dinner Sara plays 'God save the King' on her cutlery, holding 'her knife and fork as if they were weapons' (*Y*, 272). (The phrase recalls that of an early draft of *The Voyage Out*: 'Music is a tiny tin sword which was clasped into their hands to fight the world with, if other weapons failed.')[66] Dinner table playing and grand opera, national anthems and Wagner, form a continuum of musical allusions exploring Englishness, national 'purity' and patriarchy. In *The Years*, as in *The Waves* to which the last chapter turns, familial and societal politics are inextricably linked.

Notes

1. Katharine Ellis similarly observes of the parallel French early music revival that it was propelled by 'questions of national pride (or inferiority) and national identity, education and the democratization of musical experience, decadence and regeneration (whether religious or moral), and perceptions of musical style as embodying (value-laden) stereotypes of gender'. *Interpreting the Musical Past*, xvi.
2. Sharp, *English Folk Song: Some Conclusions*, 3rd edn (London: Faber, 1954), 135–6 and xx, cited in Manhire, '"The Lady's Gone A-Roving"', 237.
3. Manhire, '"The Lady's Gone A-Roving"', 238. On the musical and textual bowdlerisation of folk song, see also Hughes and Stradling, *The English Musical Renaissance*, 210–11.
4. Manhire, '"The Lady's Gone A-Roving"', 237 and 238. Landscape was, of course, central to many politically diverse contemporary constructions of Englishness, including those by Woolf. See Briggs, *Reading Virginia Woolf*, 190–207.
5. *'Artic Summer' and Other Fiction*, 183.
6. *The Imagined Village*, 71.
7. Manhire, '"The Lady's Gone A-Roving"', 239.
8. Hughes and Stradling, *The English Musical Renaissance*, 180.
9. Boyes, *The Imagined Village*, 63.
10. Boyes, *The Imagined Village*, 74.
11. Boyes, *The Imagined Village*, 106.
12. Sharp, no source cited, in Boyes, *The Imagined Village*, 67.
13. Her criticism of Vaughan Williams' dullness is followed, more warmly, by the remark that he is a 'very adorable man I gather' (*L*, VI: 183–4). See also *L*, VI: 391. Woolf had heard the *Ring* with Vaughan Williams in 1898, and she also attended several performances of his music before the war: see, for example, *L*, I: 216 and *PA*, 249. I am unconvinced, however, that Woolf's description of him as '[t]he great Ralph' (*L*, I: 150) is as unambiguous as Crapoulet suggests (*Virginia Woolf*, 18).
14. 38 and 8–9.
15. 5–6.
16. *Delius*, 8.

17. See Cameron, 'Shakespeare's Songs', 'English Folk Songs' and 'English Folk Dances'.
18. Boyes, *The Imagined Village*, 70.
19. Entry dated 6 March 1913, Leonard Woolf's Diary, Sussex University, LWP II.R.5.
20. See *D*, II: 72 and 212, and entry dated 10 July 1922, Leonard Woolf's Diary, LWP II.R.16.
21. See Hughes and Stradling, *The English Musical Renaissance*, 211–12.
22. I: 41.
23. See Southworth, 'Perfect Strangers?', 19–20. I am grateful to Helen Southworth for additional information on Allinson.
24. For accounts and reproductions of these objects, see Bell and Nicholson, *Charleston: A Bloomsbury House and Garden*, 49, 95, 69 and 41. Angelica Garnett recalls Grant's piano in *Deceived with Kindness*, 128.
25. Joyce, *Ulysses*, 615. I would like to thank Charlotte de Mille for drawing Pound's and Joyce's interest in Dolmetsch to my attention.
26. See Leonard Woolf, 'Diary of Music Listened To', Sussex University, LWP II.R.64.
27. See Anna Snaith's plenary lecture, '*The Years*, Street Music and Acoustic Space', at the International Virginia Woolf conference, Fordham University, New York, June 2009. I am grateful to Anna Snaith for making a copy of this lecture available to me.
28. Woolf was re-reading *Moby Dick* in September 1928, though it is not clear at what date she started: *D*, III: 195 and see Silver, *Virginia Woolf's Reading Notebooks*, 85 and Marcus, 'Brittania Rules *The Waves*', 144. Joyce, *Ulysses*, 606.
29. Boyes, *The Imagined Village*, 100.
30. Kennedy, *The Works of Ralph Vaughan Williams*, 493–5.
31. Manhire, '"The Lady's Gone A-Roving"', 241.
32. See Briggs, *Reading Virginia Woolf*, 200.
33. For further discussion of *Between the Acts* and the essay 'Anon', see Eisenberg, 'Virginia Woolf's Last Words on Words', in Marcus (ed.), *New Feminist Essays on Virginia Woolf*, 253–66.
34. '"The Lady's Gone A-Roving"', 236. Manhire proposes, for instance, that Woolf's work of the 1930s resists the model of 'static authenticity', whether of language or music, valued by Parry and Sharp (240).
35. 'Willing Epigone', 165.
36. The clipped language of these speakers associates cosmopolitanism and internationalism with a social and cultural élite; there may well be an element of snobbery in Woolf's depictions of effusions of patriotism, such as her representation of Mrs Manresa's 'vulgarity' or the jingoistic London public recorded in the opening pages of *Mrs Dalloway*.
37. Schröder, 'Tales of Abjection and Miscegenation', 300. Emphasis in original.
38. For an introduction to these questions, see Weiner, *Richard Wagner and the Anti-Semitic Imagination*.
39. The episode is part of Woolf's long account of George's bullying of her and Vanessa, ending with the revelation that he was their 'lover'. It is worth noting that (other than etymologically) the instrument appears not to have

a particular association with Jews; nonetheless, it seems an extraordinary choice of gift and of subject for a brooch – chosen, or described, in error because of its visual resemblance to a lyre? The social, racial and sexual insensitivities of the gift are excruciating.

40. For more details on Loeb, and a balanced assessment of Woolf's behaviour towards him to which my summary is indebted, see Bradshaw's notes on 'Jews', in *'Carlyle's House'*, 38–45.

41. Woolf recorded with pleasure Shaw's conversation on music and would certainly have known some of his prolific writing on music, which included a Marxist analysis of the *Ring, The Perfect Wagnerite* (1898). See, for example, *D*, IV: 106–7.

42. In the sketch 'Jews' she describes attending Mrs Loeb's for dinner and the 1909 letter quoted above (*L*, I: 398) probably refers to her.

43. For further details see: Kater, *The Twisted Muse*, especially chapter 3; Potter, *Most German of the Arts*; Potter, 'Music in the Third Reich'; and Kater and Reithmüller (eds), *Music and Nazism*.

44. 'Flying Dutchmen, Wandering Jews: Romantic Opera, Anti-Semitism and Jewish Mourning in *Mrs Dalloway*', in Varga (ed.), *Virginia Woolf and Music*. There has, for good reasons, been extensive critical attention to Woolf's anti-Semitism and that of her contemporaries but one effect of this has been to occlude the possibility that these prejudices co-existed with respectful, informed, engaged responses to Jews and Jewish culture. In particular, there has been almost no extended consideration of the possibility that Woolf had a serious, knowledgeable interest in Jewish history, writing or liturgy and of the implications of this for readings of her work. Despite some subtle and nuanced accounts of particular examples of her 'Jewish' writing and representations of Jews there is more work to be done on this topic.

45. Wagner, *Prose Works*, I: 17.

46. Wagner, *Prose Works*, III: 91.

47. Abnormal feet were a staple ingredient of anti-Semitic stereotype; see Weiner, *Richard Wagner and the Anti-Semitic Imagination*, chapter 4.

48. Further references to Jews include: the 'clever little Jew-Boy from Birmingham' who is Edward's rival in the Oxford exam (*Y*, 48 and 61); and, at Kitty's party in 1914, Mrs Treyer, an 'Oriental looking woman, with a feather floating back from her head in harmony with her nose, which was Jewish' (*Y*, 245); the 'Russian, Polish, Jewish?' guest at Maggie and Renny's dinner during the war (*Y*, 269); and, of course, Abrahamson, whose bath is discussed by Sara and North (*Y*, 322–4). A substantial deleted passage concerning Miriam Parrsh is reproduced in *Y*, 421–2. For further detail on BUF activity in the East End, see Bradshaw, 'Hyams Place', 182–4.

49. Bradshaw, 'Hyams Place', 179.

50. Bradshaw, 'Hyams Place', 186.

51. Hans Rudolf Vaget, 'Hitler's Wagner: Musical Discourse as Cultural Space', in Kater and Reithmüller (eds), *Music and Nazism*, 27.

52. For more detail on Hitler and Wagner see: Potter, 'Music in the Third Reich'; Kater and Reithmüller (eds), *Music and Nazism*; and Spotts, *Bayreuth*, 163–88 and 189–204.

53. See Vaget, in Kater and Reithmüller (eds), *Music and Nazism*, 15.
54. See Vaget, in Kater and Reithmüller (eds), *Music and Nazism*, 22.
55. See Weiner, *Richard Wagner and the Anti-Semitic Imagination*.
56. For further accounts of these terms, see: Sutton, *Aubrey Beardsley*, chapter 3; Carey, *The Intellectuals and the Masses*; and Weliver, *The Musical Crowd*.
57. *Virginia Woolf and the Languages of Patriarchy*, 50.
58. *Wagner's 'Ring of the Nibelung'*, 211.
59. *Wagner's 'Ring of the Nibelung'*, 202 and 203.
60. *Wagner's 'Ring of the Nibelung'*, 213.
61. See also the 'present day' section: "'I thought we were on the verge of a smash," said Kitty. "Not that it looked much like it at Covent Garden tonight"' (*Y*, 379).
62. See Bradshaw, 'Hyams Place', 187.
63. Bradshaw, 'Hyams Place', 185 and 187.
64. We should note that Sara shares with Siegfried a willingness to overthrow convention though her liberalism certainly doesn't extend to her attitudes towards Jews.
65. In 'A Society', Woolf links women's oppression to that of Jews. See Marcus, 'Thinking Back through Our Mothers', in Marcus (ed.), *New Feminist Essays on Virginia Woolf*, 2.
66. *Melymbrosia*, no page cited, quoted in Marcus, *Virginia Woolf and the Languages of Patriarchy*, 111.

Chapter 6

Only Suggest

The Waves (1931) has long been perceived as Woolf's most 'musical' – and most Wagnerian – novel. Studies of Wagner's literary influence from the 1960s onwards recognised the novel's thematic and structural affinities to the *Ring* and explored (albeit briefly) Woolf's use of the leitmotiv. William Blissett termed the novel 'pervasively leitmotivistic in its structure and symbolism', John DiGaetani characterised Wagner's influence as 'pervasive, despite the fact that his name never appears' and Raymond Furness described the work's 'symbols and motifs' as 'derived incontrovertibly from Wagner'.[1] More recently, Woolf scholars have explored the novel's debts to *Parsifal*[2] and its intermediality with Beethoven's late string quartets.[3] Numerous contemporary reviewers and more recent critics have compared the novel to a poem or to music, describing it, for instance, as 'a kind of symphonic poem [. . .] in prose' and 'a poetic novel'.[4] Without diminishing these recognitions of the novel's formal experimentalism or forgetting that Woolf herself described the work as a hybrid genre, Linden Peach rightly notes that in these comparisons 'music' and 'poetry' often denote the ineffable, suggesting that the novel is essentially apolitical.[5] Yet Woolf herself was dissatisfied with this reception, stating that *The Waves* 'is solid & means something' (*D*, IV: 45).[6] Public school, the established church, imperialism and social class are among the 'solid' things critiqued in the novel.

These subjects inform the novel's representation of heroism, critiqued most obviously through the figure of Percival, but also through allusions to numerous heroes of literature, history and myth, including the heroic innovators of nineteenth-century music, Beethoven and Wagner. *The Waves* reworks aspects of Wagner's two most complex mythological works, the *Ring* and *Parsifal*, repeatedly undercutting totalising mythologies whilst acknowledging the pull they exert on Woolf's characters and their society. The novel includes a number of explicit criticisms of grandiose myth making, even by the arch 'phrase-maker' Bernard himself; he unequivocally states 'I am no mystic' (*W*, 216) and, beginning his final monologue, observes 'there are so many' 'stories' 'and none of them are true' (*W*, 183). Woolf's conceptions of mythology and symbols were arguably influenced by Wagner's music and ideas about music more generally, as her response to *The Waste Land* suggests. When Woolf first heard the poem in 1922, she made no comment on its quotation of Wagner's dramas or of Verlaine's 'Parsifal' but noted the musicality of Eliot's delivery:

> Eliot dined last Sunday & read his poem. He sang & chanted it rhythmed it. It has great beauty & force of phrase: symmetry & tensity. What connects it together, I'm not so sure [. . .] One was left, however, with some strong emotion. (*D*, II: 178)

Discussing the poem with Yeats in 1930, however, the writers reflect on Eliot's use of mythology and on the work's connectivity: Yeats 'said that Tom very cleverly made use of mythologies, for instance the Fisher King in the Waste Land; & mythologies are necessary. Ezra Pound writes beautifully when he uses them' (*D*, III: 330). Such reading and conversations surely shaped Woolf's ideas about her own uses of mythology and symbolism, and of her difference from those of her contemporaries. Although, like Eliot, she draws on Verlaine,[7] her use of allusions, symbols and myth is far more discreet – it would be an obtuse reader who failed to notice the presence of Wagnerian and other allusions in Joyce, Eliot or Pound, but it is perfectly possible to read Woolf in this way, as many have.

Writing on De Quincey in 1932, Woolf praised his prose which 'does not wish to argue or to convert or even to tell a story'; 'we shall find that we are worked upon as if by music – the senses are stirred rather than the brain' (*E*, V: 453). She suggests here that the 'musicality' of De Quincey's prose is intrinsically related to the absence of 'story' and to a positive aesthetic experience in which the reader retains their autonomy, ideas that she had considered from another perspective much earlier in her career. Despite the notorious affectivity of Wagner's music, which Woolf warily acknowledges in works including *Jacob's Room* and *The Years*, 'Impressions at Bayreuth' had outlined a conception of music in the abstract as inclusive, as accommodating the diverse autonomous subjectivities of its listeners, a capacity that Woolf attributes to music's 'lack of definite articulation': '[p]erhaps music owes something of its astonishing power over us to this lack of definite articulation; its statements have all the majesty of a generalisation, and yet contain our private emotions' (*E*, I: 291). Music seems to appeal here because of what we might anomalously call its incomplete signification: as Prieto notes, the model of music as 'associative syntax' dependent on 'music's inability to denote efficiently' is shared by many twentieth-century novelists.[8]

In 1909, Woolf had also, however, objected to the 'gross symbolism' at Bayreuth: 'I can never quite get over the florid Teuton spirit, with its gross symbolism – and its flaxen tresses. Imagine a heroine in a nightgown, with a pig tail on each shoulder, and watery eyes ogling heaven' (*L*, I: 407). Woolf doesn't expand on the unpalatable nature of this 'symbolism' other than to suggest that it is somehow crude, simplistic or overbearing, but later letters are more suggestive. Writing to Roger Fry in 1927 about *To the Lighthouse*, she observed that she meant '*nothing*' by the lighthouse, but that others 'would make it the deposit for their own emotions', and continued: 'I can't manage Symbolism except in this vague, generalised way. Whether its right or wrong I don't know, but directly I'm told what a thing means, it becomes hateful to me' (*L*, III: 385, emphasis in original). The year before, Woolf had noted with relish that she was discussing '19th Century music and rhetoric' with Edward Sackville-West and Smyth (*L*, III: 254). It seems probable, given the mention of 'musical rhetoric', that the Wagnerian leitmotiv or 'symbol' was part of these discussions in the period preceding *The Waves*' composition since, as I suggested in Chapter 1, the leitmotiv was fundamental to perceptions of the narrative capacity of the music dramas. For all the sophistication of Wagner's usage and Woolf's formal debts to the leitmotiv, it was readily caricatured as mechanistic, heavy-handed or 'gross' and reception conditions may have augmented this, as the practice of labelling leitmotivs – often with abstract nouns – in critical guides and programme notes was common practice when Woolf first encountered Wagner's work. Her 1931 observations on *The Waves* suggest her difference from such schematic approaches: 'my imagination picked up used & tossed aside all the images & symbols which I had prepared. I am sure that this is the right way of using them – not in set pieces, as I had tried at first, but simply as images; never making them work out; only suggest' (*D*, IV: 10–11).

The importance of music to Woolf's aesthetics and her creative practice especially is further suggested by the fact that she repeatedly measured others' writing in these terms, comparing contemporaries' – notably Lawrence's – work to strident, simplistic music. She was reading Lawrence's letters in 1932 with 'the usual sense of frustration [. . .] I dont like strumming with two fingers – & the arrogance [. . .] Art is being rid of all preaching' (*D*, IV: 126). She wrote to Stephen Spender in 1935:

living writers are to me like people singing in the next room – too loud, too near; and for some reason I am so exacerbated by their being flat or sharp; as if I were singing my own song and they put me out. Hence my unfairness to Lawrence; but how can you put him with the very great? How can you call him a great psychologist? (*L*, V: 408)

Similarly, she described Huxley's conspicuously 'musicalized' novel *Point Counter Point* as 'raw, uncooked, protesting' (*D*, IV: 276) and alluded dryly in a review of Viola Meynell's fiction to contemporary literary 'experiment[s] with phrases which recur like the motive in a Wagner opera' (*E*, II: 238).

The Waves is suffused with symbols found in the *Ring* (and, as others have explained, in *Parsifal*) but they are often used in incongruous, parodic contexts (the ring which confers omnipotence becomes, for instance, a cupboard handle [*W*, 220 and 224]). The *Ring*'s symbols are domesticated, historically located, particularised; they are also used un-systematically, as Woolf's characters are associated with various Wagnerian protagonists at different moments. The inconsistent, intermittent use of images from the *Ring* is one strategy by which she undercuts Wagner's project, adopting his leitmotivic technique for profoundly anti-Wagnerian purposes (as she had done in *The Voyage Out* too). Woolf's 'symbols' are not intended cumulatively to construct an increasingly rich and complex mythology offering one authoritative narrative of society's and individuals' origins and decline, but rather bathetically to qualify each other, to undercut myth. They invite us to relish the pluralist rather than the homogenising effects of myth and symbolism. In the first draft of the novel (initially conceived, like the *Ring*, in four parts),[9] Bernard describes his narrative in near-Wagnerian terms: 'I am telling myself the story of the world from the beginning'.[10] (Wagner famously wrote to Liszt in 1853, '[m]ark well my new poem – it contains the world's beginning and its end').[11] Bernard's emphasis here, like Wagner's, is on the singular – the single, authoritative story; the single author and listener. The completed novel, in contrast, celebrates pluralist narratives: 'I have made up thousands of stories; I have filled innumerable notebooks with phrases to be used when I have found the true story, the one story to which all these phrases refer. But I have never yet found that story. And I begin to ask, Are there stories?' (*Y*, 143). There is, Woolf suggests, no one story; her Wagnerian 'symbols' contradict each other, are interleaved with numerous other allusions, and require us to recognise their partial, limited signification. Woolf uses Wagner's leitmotivic technique to undercut the political work and rhetorical allure of myth, to question the interests served by particular mythologies and the generalising tendency inherent in myth itself.

Beginnings

The first scene of *Das Rheingold* is a vital intertext for the 'interlude'[12] with which *The Waves* begins.[13] Woolf may diverge from and critique Wagner later in the novel but the beginning of her work closely resembles his, drawing on Wagner's libretto, music and stage directions. Both begin with relatively brief 'preludes' portraying the waves: Wagner's cycle opens with the rippling sound of the waves of the Rhine before the curtain rises, and Woolf's brief italicised interlude (*W*, 3–4) describes the natural world before the monologues commence. Evocations of the elements and nature therefore precede the appearance of increasingly anthropomorphised figures: in the opera, the Rhinemaidens and Nibelung dwarf of scene i are followed by the gods Wotan and Fricka in scene ii; in the novel, the allusions to the birds late in the interlude precede the appearance of the children in the monologues. Both works begin at dawn on the water's edge (the Rhine and the sea shore) and in darkness: Wagner's innovative practice of dimming the lights ensured that the opera audience sat in semi-darkness as the music began to unfold (the curtain rises only from bar 126), whilst Woolf writes that the '*sun had not yet risen*' and the '*sea was indistinguishable from the sky*'. Her allusion to the '*indistinguishable*' elements recalls the music and theatrical effect of the opening bars of *Das Rheingold* which begins with a low E flat marked *pianissimo* on the double-basses: the volume and pitch of the note (towards the bottom of the register audible to humans) and the concealment of the musicians in the darkened theatre make it difficult to identify precisely the moment when the music begins. The novel's opening, I would suggest, echoes the deliberate indeterminacy of Wagner's. These characteristics might appear generic to origin myths rather than specifically Wagnerian,[14] but we should remember that the Woolfs' library included a copy of the libretto of *Das Rheingold*[15] and the extensive parallels between the two works' plots, imagery and characters confirm that the *Ring* is an important intertext for the novel as a whole.

There are further echoes of the opening of the cycle in Woolf's first interlude. The bands of '[g]*reenish twilight, lighter above, darker below*'[16] specified in Wagner's stage directions anticipate Woolf's: '*Gradually the dark bar on the horizon became clear*', Woolf writes, and '*flat bars of white, green and yellow spread across the sky*'. As sunlight falls on the Rhinegold the contrast between light and dark becomes more distinct: '[a]*n increasingly bright glow penetrates the floodwaters from above [. . .] gradually becoming a blinding and brightly beaming gleam of gold*'.[17] Compare Woolf's final sentence of the second paragraph: '*Slowly the arm that held the lamp raised it higher and then higher until a broad flame became visible; an arc of fire burnt on the rim of the horizon, and all round it the sea blazed gold.*' The colours (green, gold, red) and the images of light and flame recur in both texts: the Rhinemaidens observe the river '"glow[ing]"' and the '"flood"' '"aflame"'[18] whilst Woolf describes the '*incandescence*' of the '*burning bonfire*', the '*broad flame*' and '*arc of fire*'. Woolf's precise use of colour in this scene and in the novel as a whole may be indebted not only to the libretto but also to her theatrical experience of Wagner's works, particularly his innovative, symbolic use of colour and lighting.[19] It is even possible that Woolf's late decision to italicise the interludes was prompted by her familiarity with a text of Wagner's work, mimicking the typographic conventions of stage directions in printed scores and libretti.[20] Woolf repeatedly noted the novel's affinity to drama (*D*, III: 128 and 139) and this detail may be another of the novel's theatrical debts.

Furthermore, the first interlude, like scene i, represents the waves aurally as well as visually. The first 'speech' (by the Rhinemaidens) is addressed to the waves and imitative of them: '"Weia! Waga! / Woge, du Welle, / walle zur Wiege! / Wagalaweia! / Wallala weiala weia!"'.[21] Woglinde's opening words ('"Weia! Waga!"') continue the orchestral representation of the waves, the rippling string quavers and (from bar 81) semi-quavers in 6/8 time which began the cycle. Additionally, the first representational words of the opera – '"Woge, du Welle"' ('Welter, you wave') – are onomatapoeiac. The Rhinemaidens thus (aurally) personify the river: they playfully chase each other through the water '*like fish*' (and Alberich in turn '*pursu[es]*' them),[22] not dissimilarly to the waves '*following each other, pursuing each other, perpetually*' in the interlude. Woolf's allusions to the birds also imitate the sounds and movements of the Rhinemaidens. Both begin by making non-signifying noises: the birds sing a '*blank melody*' (in later interludes their songs are expressive),[23] just as the first sound we hear of the Rhinemaidens is lyrical but non-referential. These natural creatures make similar spatial movements: Woglinde begins the opera guarding the gold '"alone"' and sings first; Wellgunde calls to her '*from above*' before '*div[ing] down through the waves*'.[24] '*One bird chirped high up;*' Woolf writes, '*there was a pause; another chirped lower down.*' The birds, the waves and the Rhinemaidens (sisters of Woolf's 'nymph of the fountain' [*W*, 87 and 199]), suggest the amoral beauty of nature and appear at the start and end of Wagner's and Woolf's texts, when the parallels between opera and novel are clearest. Woolf's instruction, in notes for the first monologues, that the 'rhythm of the waves must be kept going all the time'[25] indicates that the interlude was intended to represent the waves aurally; the repetitive syntax and diction, characterised by anaphoras and present participles, are appropriately cyclical. Woolf's predominantly monosyllabic opening sentence is followed by sentences of increasing clausal complexity and repetitive polysyllabic vocabulary[26] – a prose equivalent, perhaps, to the expansiveness of Wagner's music in scene i, which gradually crescendos towards Alberich's entrance and, eventually, his theft of the gold? The rippling string quavers and semi-quavers in which the waves are evoked throughout *Das Rheingold* may be, then, one possible source for the novel's idiosyncratic prose. Garrett Stewart identifies a 'slowed phonic pulse' as distinctive of Woolf's 'explicitly antipatriarchal style' that subverts received diction and syntax through 'an intrusion of the phonic into the scriptive'.[27] Crucially, Woolf's intense attention to Wagner's formal techniques may have shaped this feminist style which challenges so much the composer represents.

Both works, then, begin by telling multiple origin narratives – of a single day, of creation, of humans' or gods' presence in the natural world, of the senses and of the emergence of language and music from apparently inchoate sound. Furthermore, both gender the sun as female and allude to human birth: Woglinde describes the gold sleeping in its '"cradle"' and, in a draft of the interlude, Woolf compared the waves to women in labour.[28] Both emphasise the cyclical as well as the originatory: Woolf's waves move '*perpetually*' and their movement, like that of the Rhine, implicitly predates audience observation. The cyclical, embodied in the shape of the ring itself, is vital to Wagner's tetralogy as it is to Woolf's novel: the subjects of temporality and repetition, ephemerality and permanence, are prominent in both works. Just as the opening of the operatic cycle anticipates, through its images of golden light, the conflagration with which it concludes, Woolf's first interlude evokes destruction, an ending as well as a beginning. The '*incandescence*', the '*arc of fire*' and the '*red and yellow fibres like the smoky fire that roars from a bonfire*' recall the burning pyre with which *Götterdämmerung* ends, signalling the end of the reign of the gods and the start of the era of man. The first interlude, like the opening of *Das Rheingold*, is elegiac as well as celebratory.

The shift from this interlude to the first monologues also mimics the relationship between *Das Rheingold*'s first and second scenes. Both works move from the water's edge to domesticity and less sublime natural scenes; in both, the second episodes are again set at dawn depicting awakening consciousness. The monologues begin early in the morning (an unspecified time before 'breakfast' [*W*, 7]); the characters' initial attention to sunlight and visual differentiation (the repeated 'I see' [*W*, 5]) suggests that they are describing daybreak. The early references to the 'tassel', the 'balcony' and the 'window' (*W*, 5) hint that the children are in a nursery; they then explore the garden, observing the domestic activities of the servants, Mrs Constable and Biddy (*W*, 6). Woolf's monologues thus begin in domesticity, in the presence of maternal nurturing figures, and in a flower-filled garden. Wagner's second scene also begins in the '*dawning light*' of the mountains as Fricka and Wotan sleep on a '*flowery bank*'.[29] Despite their natural setting, the domesticity of the gods' relationship is immediately emphasised: Fricka repeatedly addresses Wotan as '"husband"'[30] before praising the '"domestic bliss"' intended to '"bind"' Wotan to her.[31] Although Woolf's representations of women later diverge from Wagner's, in these second daybreak scenes both works evoke the security and restrictions represented by domesticity.

Brass handles and snake belts

The first words thought or spoken by Woolf's 'characters'[32] – Bernard's 'I see a ring' (*W*, 5) – were a late alteration to the text: even in the second draft Bernard makes no early reference to a ring and instead describes a 'pale, purple ball'.[33] As we will see, Woolf typically excised the more overt parallels to the *Ring* during her revisions so it is notable that her alteration to the very start of the monologues foregrounds this Wagnerian image. Bernard's words are the first of numerous allusions to a ring; the words 'ring', 'rings' or 'ringed' occur more than thirty times in the published text and there are, additionally, numerous other cyclical or circular images. In contrast to the frequency of this image in the monologues, there are only two references to rings in the interludes (*W*, 55 and 112), though references to gold are frequent. Like Wagner, Woolf associates rings with the human rather than the natural world; it is, after all, Alberich who forges the ring from the Rhinegold and it is only with the first appearance of an individualised human voice that the ring appears in the novel. The first interlude makes no reference to a ring and 'gold' appears as a colour rather than as a metal or synonym for wealth; it recalls, therefore, the Rhinemaidens' aesthetic rather than materialistic appreciation of the gold. Furthermore, in the first monologue, Bernard's immediate observation of the ring hints at his affinities with the composer himself:[34] Bernard and Louis, the novel's principal story-teller and poet, repeatedly associate rings with verbal fluency and literary creativity – with composition and artistry. '[I]f I find myself in company with other people, words at once make smoke rings' (*W*, 49), Bernard reflects, the smoke rings suggesting a benevolent desire to communicate but also anticipating the lasso image of his conversation on the train: 'A smoke ring issues from my lips (about crops) and circles him, bringing him into contact' (*W*, 50). Louis' use of ring images is also ambiguous, especially as he is associated with forged, metallic rings: he repeatedly imagines poetic composition as an attempt 'to fix in words, to forge in a ring of steel' (*W*, 28). Louis' 'forging' evokes Alberich's forging of the ring[35] and Siegfried's forging of the shattered sword Nothung – two objects that, in the *Ring*, allow their possessors to dominate others. In the first draft of the novel, Louis imagines a church service 'welding him together into a formidable weapon', 'a single blade',[36] and he recognises the desire for power implicit in word-smithing: successful poetry has a 'binding power' and the forged ring suggests Louis' desire to control, to 'reduce you to order' through art (*W*, 70). The ring and forging are two of the most protean, recurrent images in the *Ring* and they are central to the novel, but Bernard and Louis' images persistently expose the totalising aspirations of Wagner's text.

In *The Waves*, as in the cycle, rings are also associated with sexuality and patriarchal gender roles. The references to jewellery (numerous rings and the necklace that Jinny imagines as a 'cold ring round our throats' [*W*, 94], for example) evoke the wedding band and its pivotal part in the *Ring*'s plot and ideology. In *Götterdämmerung*, Siegfried gives the ring to Brünnhilde as a love token and the action marks Brünnhilde's joyous acceptance of human rather than divine status; it also marks the start of her increasingly conventional (sexual) morality. In the first Act of *Götterdämmerung*, Brünnhilde's sister begs her to return the ring to the Rhinemaidens but it is only at the very conclusion of the cycle that Brünnhilde releases it, ending human and divine control of the ring: after Brünnhilde's death, the Rhine bursts its banks and the Rhinemaidens reclaim the ring. Woolf echoes Wagner's association of the wedding ring with constriction and loss as well as intimacy and joy when Susan describes Bernard's engagement in an image of a ring thrown into a river:[37] '[s]omething irrevocable has happened. A circle has been cast on the waters; a chain is imposed. We shall never flow freely again' (*W*, 107). Bernard's 'irrevocable' step echoes, perhaps, Brünnhilde's acceptance of mortality, the necessary prelude to her human love, and it also recalls Woolf's satirical associations of wedding rings with social convention in her earlier fiction: *Orlando*, in a lighter register, echoes Brünnhilde through the servant Bartholomew who fetishises her wedding ring.

The novel's pervasive allusions to gold are also surely drawn from the *Ring*; like the ring itself in Wagner's tetralogy, gold is a protean symbol, associated with beauty, and with the power of illusion and imagination via the *Tarnhelm* (magic helmet), recalling Wagner the myth-maker. Elvedon, for instance, the location of childhood imagination and storytelling, is golden: Bernard observes 'the stable clock with its gilt hands shining' (W, 11); later Susan recalls 'the gilt hands of the clock sparkling among the trees' (W, 164). Rhoda, too, associates her flights of imagination about the other school girls with gold: 'If they should say, or I should see from a label on their boxes, that they were in Scarborough last holidays, the whole town runs gold, the whole pavement is illuminated' (W, 31, cf. 157). Gold here evokes the pleasures of imagination and narrative but it is also used conventionally to evoke money. Entering the adult world of employment, Louis reflects: 'I go vaguely, to make money vaguely. Therefore a poignant shadow, a keen accent, falls on these golden bristles [. . .] this flowing corn' (W, 48) and he anticipates financial success and ownership of a 'gold-headed cane' (W, 155). Gold is also repeatedly associated with sexuality, most obviously in the representation of Jinny, with whom the colour is conspicuously linked: 'O come, I say to this one, rippling gold from head to heels' (W, 78, cf. 76, 105, 106 and 134); 'my gold signal is like a dragon-fly flying taut' (W, 135). She sits on a 'gilt chair' at the dance (W, 76, 77 and 105) and compares herself to flame: 'I am volatile for one, rigid for another, angular as an icicle in silver, or voluptuous as a candle flame in gold' (W, 170, cf. 30). Jinny's 'rippling' temperament associates her with fire and with water: Woolf's vocabulary suggests the Rhinemaidens (the flirtatious, inconstant objects of male desire) and the fire god Loge, the amoral trickster who liaises between Wotan, the giants and the Nibelung dwarfs. Jinny is thus associated with two elemental forces in the *Ring*, and her 'rippling' recalls the rapid chromatic semi-quavers of Loge's leitmotiv as well as the rippling watery sounds of the Rhinemaidens ('I stream like a plant in the river,' she reflects [W, 76]). In the first draft of the novel, the Wagnerian affinities had been more overt: Jinny was (like the Rhinemaidens) 'some sprite, something of water' and (like Loge) 'something that had burnt a million years'.[38]

There are numerous other echoes of the *Ring*'s protagonists in the novel. The birds, whose songs are initially '*blank*' but seem to convey meaning in the later interludes, recall the Woodbird of *Siegfried* whose song gradually enlightens Wagner's belligerent, ignorant hero Siegfried (that archetypal 'boasting boy'). The repeated references to trees, canes and walking sticks recall the World Ash Tree from which Wotan, king of the gods, makes his staff. The price of this power-giving staff is partial blindness: like the figure in Bernard's 'story of the man with one eye' (W, 27), Wotan has lost one eye and in *Siegfried* travels the world incognito as the Wanderer, carrying his staff and dressed in a cloak. In adulthood, Bernard sports a 'cloak' and 'cane' (*W*, 65) and recalls '[s]winging his stick' outside St Paul's (*W*, 216). (And in *Ulysses* Stephen taps with the 'ash sword' that 'hangs at my side.')[39] In middle age Bernard reflects: 'I walked unshadowed; I came unheralded. From me had dropped the old cloak' (*W*, 220). These references, and those to the apple tree, evoke Wotan's and Bernard's mortality: Neville refers to 'the immitigable tree; the implacable tree with its greaved silver bark [. . .] we are doomed, all of us, by the apple trees, by the immitigable tree which we cannot pass' (*W*, 17). The apple tree's association with a man's suicide and Percival's death hints at Wotan's metaphorical death when he gains the ash branch; it also evokes the near loss, in *Das Rheingold*, of Freia's apples on which the gods depend for eternal youth. Bernard is thus associated in middle age with Wotan; he has taken on something of the dignity of the disenfranchised, displaced god ('I walked alone in a new world, never trodden' [*W*, 220]) who has accepted death and relinquished his attempts to prevent the collapse of the gods' reign and the rise of men.

Louis, in contrast, is frequently associated with mining, metals and the subterranean, linking him to Nibelheim, the mines of the materialistic Nibelung dwarfs. He reiterates: 'My roots go down to the depths of the world, through earth dry with brick, and damp earth, through veins of lead and silver' (*W*, 7, cf. 8, 24–5 and 71). Louis' experience early in the novel temporarily evokes the Nibelung Alberich: he is 'alone' (*W*, 7), until 'struck on the nape of the neck' (*W*, 8) by Jinny's kiss; Jinny, the Rhinemaiden, interrupts his isolation and 'All is shattered' (*W*, 8). Like Alberich, who must renounce love after the Rhinemaidens' flirtation in order to forge the ring, Louis has made 'denials' (*W*, 101): 'I, who desire above all things to be taken to the arms with love, am alien, external' (*W*, 70); 'I have an immeasurable desire that women should sigh in sympathy' (*W*, 95–6). Louis is further (parodically) associated with Alberich through his wealth and the 'brass snake' on the belt that supports his knickerbockers (*W*, 7, 13 and 184): Alberich transforms himself into a snake in order to demonstrate the power of the *Tarnhelm* forged from the gold. The magic helmet may also be recalled in Bernard's description of William III as 'a little figure with a golden teapot on his head. Soon one recovers belief in figures: but not at once in what they put on their heads' (*W*, 174). Even had Woolf not known Shaw, whose Marxist study of the *Ring*, *The Perfect Wagnerite* (1898), argued that Nibelheim was an indictment of nineteenth-century capitalism, she would surely have recognised the anti-materialism of Wagner's Nibelheim; arguably, Woolf's representation of London (particularly the Underground) as mechanical and industrialised, a 'churning of the great engines'

(*W*, 148), bears traces of Wagner's subterranean city (as it does of Eliot's waste land).

There are further examples of the intermittent parallels between Wagner's characters and Woolf's. Susan's love for her father and her association with horses align her with Brünnhilde, Wotan's daughter and the leader of the Valkyrie warrior maidens who collect the bodies of dead heroes from the battlefield and transport them on horseback to Valhalla: anticipating the summer holidays, Susan reflects, 'The great horses of the phantom riders will thunder behind me and stop suddenly' (*W*, 39).[40] Susan's affinities with Brünnhilde are even more extensive in the drafts: Brünnhilde's defiance of Wotan in rescuing Sieglinde, pregnant with Siegfried as a result of sibling incest, is evoked in Susan's reflection, 'Brother & sister lie together in those cottages. Why not? What does it matter?' and in her perception that 'Now I am terrible; eager; awake; a huntress; a woman grown; with my desire fixed on a man.'[41] Through the echoes of Brünnhilde, Woolf critiques the Oedipal plot of the *Ring*. Like Brünnhilde, Susan is initially fiercely desirous of her father: 'And there is my father, with his back turned, talking to a farmer. I tremble. I cry. There is my father in gaiters. There is my father' (*W*, 46). Woolf's scepticism about the sexual politics of this father–daughter relationship emerges in her account of a performance of *Die Walküre* in 1925:

> Walküre completely triumphed, I thought; except for some boredom – I can't ever enjoy those long arguments in music – when it is obviously mere conversation upon business matters between Wotan and Brunhilde: however, the rest was superb. (*L*, III: 186)

As Brünnhilde is feminised through her relationship with Siegfried and loses her intimacy with Wotan, Susan becomes exclusively domesticated, interested only in nurturing her numerous children. The association with Brünnhilde suggests the fierce, protective qualities of Susan's maternity and the limitations of her conventional domestic role; however, the novel has no equivalent to Brünnhilde's resounding celebration of heterosexual love, suggesting Woolf's reservations about Wagner's sexual politics. Yet it is at the very end that Brünnhilde is evoked most conspicuously, as Woolf's novel reworks the conclusion of the *Ring*.

In its final part, Woolf's work, like Wagner's, privileges the narrative of one figure: Elicia Clements compellingly demonstrates the influence of Beethoven's string quartets at this point,[42] but Act III, scene iii of *Götterdämmerung* is also a vital intertext here. Bernard's last monologue places him in the position of Brünnhilde – after her long aria celebrating human love and her resolution to return the ring to the Rhinemaidens, Brünnhilde springs into Siegfried's funeral pyre on her horse Grane; the scene is then engulfed by the Rhine. Compare Bernard:

> And in me too the wave rises. It swells; it arches its back. I am aware once more of a new desire, something rising beneath me like the proud horse whose rider first spurs and then pulls him back. What enemy do we now perceive advancing against us, you whom I ride now, as we stand pawing this stretch of pavement? It is death. Death is the enemy. It is death against whom I ride with my spear couched and my hair flying back like a young man's, like Percival's, when he galloped in India. I strike spurs into my horse. Against you I will fling myself, un-vanquished and unyielding, O Death! (*W*, 228)

Woolf, we might recall, heard *Die Walküre* in 1925 (*L*, III: 186), *Götterdämmerung* in 1926[43] and *Siegfried* in 1931 (*L*, IV: 303–5), and alluded several times in this period to the *Ring*'s final conflagration: she wrote to Vita Sackville-West that burning gorse in Cornwall was 'exactly like the death of Siegfried: a crimson gauze rising over crags' (*L*, III: 309) and to Smyth during revisions that *The Waves*, 'a very flickering flame at the moment, starts to draw' (*L*, IV: 159).[44] Bernard's final speech shares *Götterdämmerung*'s combination of destruction and renewal: the 'canopy of civilisation is burnt out', Bernard believes, yet in this destruction (as in that of the reign of the gods) is a 'kindling', the 'eternal renewal' of the waves (*W*, 228). The references to the destruction of one era, the 'redness' of the landscape, the waves and the renewal all suggest, even before Bernard's challenge to Death, that Wagner's cycle is a resonant intertext at this point. And, just as both novel and opera cycle had begun with the waves, so both end: '*The waves broke on the shore*' and the Rhine floods the stage. Woolf had parodied the conclusion of the *Ring* earlier in the novel when the burst pipe floods Bernard's bookcase – 'We shout with laughter at the sight of ruin. Let solidity be destroyed. Let us have no possessions' (*W*, 163) – and in the first draft of the novel Bernard twice refers to a 'river in spate' as his death approaches.[45] Yet for all that the novel persistently undermines the totalising aspirations of the *Ring*, the conclusion – like the opening – of Woolf's novel draws heavily, and surely admiringly, on Wagner's work.

Coda

In Bernard's final monologue he recalls that he went:

> into a shop, and bought – not that I love music – a picture of Beethoven in a silver frame. Not that I love music, but because the whole of life, its masters, its adventurers, then appeared in long ranks of magnificent human beings

behind me; and I was the inheritor; I, the continuer; I, the person miracu-
lously appointed to carry it on. So, swinging my stick, with my eyes filmed,
not with pride, but with humility rather, I walked down the street. (*W*, 195)

This passage, voiced by a writer, encapsulates many of Woolf's enduring
attitudes towards the classical canon discussed in this study. The insistence of 'I' here – 'I, I, I; not Byron, Shelley, Dostoevsky, but I, Bernard' –
and in the preceding lines critiques patriarchy, as elsewhere in her fiction
and essays. The male lineage of 'masters' and 'adventurers', Beethoven
as heroic and commemorated in a silver frame, and the military 'ranks'
of which Bernard is a chosen 'inheritor' all point towards the exclusion
of women from conventional histories and aesthetic traditions, from
totalising, male-authored narratives about the 'whole of life'. (And in
An Outline of Musical History, published by Hogarth in 1929, Hewitt
described Schutz as 'the first of a long line of famous German composers'.)[46] As in *The Voyage Out*, Woolf uses this commonplace image
ambiguously: in her first novel, Gibbon's prose (exemplary of the 'man's
sentence' [*ROTG*, 69]) evokes for Hirst 'a whole procession of splendid
sentences' that 'went marching through his brain in order' (*VO*, 116),
whereas when Rachel plays Bach after the dance the 'ennobling' effects
of the music conjure images of 'the whole of human life advancing very
nobly' (*VO*, 187). In *The Waves*, too, this image suggests both patriarchal authority and Bernard's 'humility'; the passage oscillates between
modesty and Brünnhilde-like exultation. Bernard's monologue reflects,
I would suggest, Woolf's own ambivalence towards the canonising
of the figures of (musical) history: it is informed by her own 'love' of
Beethoven's music but also by her wariness, here and elsewhere in her
fiction, of the narratives told about him and his work – paradigmatically, in Wagner's *Eine Pilgerfahrt zu Beethoven*.[47] The repetition of
'not that I love music' emphasises Bernard's attraction to the heroic
composer rather than to his music, to which Woolf was listening during
the completion of the novel.[48] Beethoven is the only composer named in
The Waves and is present diegetically in the form of his portrait rather
than his work – his music, in contrast to *The Voyage Out*, is silent.

Yet this last monologue also suggests what the writer – Bernard, and
Woolf herself – has learned from music, and acknowledges affinity to it.
As Bernard reflects on the impossibility of recording life in its fullness,
the 'million' fish that 'slip through my fingers', he exclaims:

Faces recur, faces and faces – they press their beauty to the walls of my
bubble – Neville, Susan, Louis, Jinny, Rhoda and a thousand others. How
impossible to order them rightly; to detach one separately, or to give the
effect of the whole – again like music. What a symphony with its concord and

its discord, and its tunes on top and its complicated bass beneath, then grew up! Each played his own tune, fiddle, flute, trumpet, drum or whatever the instrument might be. (W, 197)

Following Bernard's purchase of the picture of Beethoven, the passage evokes his nine symphonies of which Woolf had written with such admiration and authority early in her literary career.[49] The passing simile exemplifies Woolf's lifelong engagement with musical form and with the politics of music. By hinting at Beethoven's symphonies, Woolf again critiques myth-making and hyper-virile heroism: four of the symphonies are highly programmatic (i.e. have a narrative element to them), recounting respectively the combat, triumph and death of the ideal hero (the 'Eroica', no. 3), the spirit of man overcoming the trials of Fate (no. 5), the artist's responses to nature (the 'Pastoral', no. 6) and human joy, heroism and redemption through love (the 'Choral', no. 9). The 'subjects' of some of the symphonies, particularly the third and the fifth, champion ideologies that Woolf explores and challenges throughout this novel and elsewhere in her fiction. Yet even here Beethoven may have been a force not only to resist but also to draw on: the 'Eroica', despite the part it has frequently played in the reception of Beethoven's work, suggests an ambivalent attitude towards heroism, as Hewitt and Hill's *Outline of Musical History* explained. Ralph Hill noted Beethoven's republicanism and his disgust at Napoleon's adoption of the title 'Emperor'; the symphony's title was altered from 'Buonoparte' to 'Eroica' to reflect Beethoven's disenchantment with the individual if not with the ideal of heroism. And the symphony's dedication to 'the memory of a great man' (the phrase reiterated in *The Years*) made Beethoven's turn from Napoleon more pointed.[50] Furthermore, the symphonies' programmatic qualities, and particularly the 'Choral''s incorporation of voices into its conclusion, also parallel Woolf's own intermedial formal experimentation and her lifelong exploration of the relationship between music, writing and narrative, between sounds and words. And Beethoven's late style, by which the novel is arguably shaped, is itself indebted to operatic genres and to vocal writing more generally.[51] Bernard's simile expresses admiration for and affinity to music, even as he registers the difference of the mediums, the artifice of the comparison. The pleasure, the ambivalence and the indebtedness expressed by the passage are surely Woolf's own.

Notes

1. Blissett, 'Wagnerian Fiction in English', 259; DiGaetani, *Richard Wagner and the Modern British Novel*, 118; and Furness, *Wagner and Literature*, 20.

2. See, for example, Phillips, 'Re(de)composing in the Novel' and Sherard, '"Parcival in the Forest of Gender"'.

3. Clements, 'Transforming Musical Sounds into Words'. Gerald Levin has also proposed that the novel is influenced by J. W. N. Sullivan's *Beethoven: His Spiritual Development* (New York: Knopf, 1927) and by serial music. See 'The Musical Style of *The Waves*'.

4. See Peach, 'No Longer a View', 196. For further examples of similar reviews, see *The Waves*, ed. Herbert and Sellers, lxxx–lxxxiii.

5. For a helpful summary of Woolf's writing on the relations between poetry and prose during the novel's composition, see *The Waves*, ed. Herbert and Sellers, xl-xli.

6. Peach, 'No Longer a View', 195–6.

7. Bernard's 'the boy's voice soars in the dome' (W, 217) echoes Verlaine's line 'Et, O ces voix d'enfants, chantant dans la coupole!' quoted in 'The Fire Sermon': Eliot, 'The Waste Land', 31. For more information on Eliot's and the poem's place in the novel, see *The Waves*, ed. Herbert and Sellers, 247 and the Explanatory Notes.

8. *Listening In*, 56.

9. Woolf, '*The Waves*', ed. Graham, Draft I: 1, 14v, 58v.

10. Woolf, '*The Waves*', ed. Graham, Draft I: 6. Cf. pp. 9 and 42.

11. Cited in *Wagner's 'Ring of the Nibelung': A Companion*, 2.

12. Woolf, '*The Waves*', ed. Graham, Draft II: 744.

13. Cf. Emma Sutton, 'Woolf Rewriting Wagner: *The Waves* and *Der Ring des Nibelungen*', in Katherine O'Callaghan (ed.), *Musical Modernism: Essays on Language and Music in Modernist Texts* (Aldershot: Ashgate, forthcoming). I would like to thank Katherine O'Callaghan and Ashgate Press for permission to draw on this material.

14. Furness, *Wagner and Literature*, 21.

15. The text was *Vorspiel zu der Trilogie Der Ring des Nibelungen* (Mainz: Schott's Söhne, n.d.); see King and Miletic-Vejzovic (eds), *The Library of Leonard and Virginia Woolf*. For accessibility, I have used a modern translation.

16. *Wagner's 'Ring of the Nibelung'*, 57.

17. *Wagner's 'Ring of the Nibelung'*, 65.

18. *Wagner's 'Ring of the Nibelung'*, 66.

19. See Carnegy, *Wagner and the Art of the Theatre*, chapter 3.

20. It appears that this decision was made after the typescript had been sent to the printers. See *The Waves*, ed. Herbert and Sellers, lx.

21 *Wagner's 'Ring of the Nibelung'*, 57.

22. *Wagner's 'Ring of the Nibelung'*, 58 and 65.

23. E.g.: '*passionate songs*', 112.

24. *Wagner's 'Ring of the Nibelung'*, 57.

25. Woolf, '*The Waves*', ed. Graham, 749.

26. The last sentence of the novel also consists of six words, all monosyllabic, underlining, as Wagner does, the cyclical qualities of the work.

27. *Reading Voices*, 261.

28. *Wagner's 'Ring of the Nibelung'*, 57, and, Woolf, '*The Waves*', ed. Graham, Draft I: 7, 9, 62 and 63.

29. *Wagner's 'Ring of the Nibelung'*, 69.

30. *Wagner's 'Ring of the Nibelung'*, 70.
31. *Wagner's 'Ring of the Nibelung'*, 71.
32. The term is, as many have noted, anomalous but convenient.
33 Woolf, *'The Waves'*, ed. Graham, Draft II: 402.
34. Clements proposes another musical counterpart to Bernard: she suggests that his habit of classifying 'phrases' 'in his notebook under A or B' may allude to the sonata form of Beethoven's Op. 130. Clements, 'Transforming Musical Sounds into Words', 169.
35. Again, there are echoes of the libretto of *Das Rheingold*, scene i, in which the word 'forge' is repeated, most conspicuously at the moment when Alberich manages to wrench the gold from the rock: '"[I'll] forge the avenging ring / [. . .] / thus I lay a curse on love!"' (*Wagner's 'Ring of the Nibelung'*, 69).
36 Woolf, *'The Waves'*, ed. Graham, Draft I: 102. The fantasy collapses when Louis recalls his Australian accent: a critique, perhaps, of Wagner's attempts to 'forge' national identity?
37. The ring is also associated with unity of the individual and between friends as well as lovers; most ring images occur before Percival's death.
38. Woolf, *'The Waves'*, ed. Graham, Draft I: 12.
39. Joyce, *Ulysses*, 37.
40. Cf. Rhoda 'It is to ['life'] we are attached; it is to this we are bound, as bodies to wild horses' (*W*, 47).
41. Woolf, *'The Waves'*, ed. Graham, Draft II: 502.
42. Clements, 'Transforming Musical Sounds into Words', 163.
43. Entry dated 3 June 1926, Leonard Woolf's Diary, University of Sussex, LWP II.R.20.
44. In September 1930, whilst working on the second draft of the novel, Woolf was reading a volume of Smyth's autobiography with the apocalyptic title *A Final Burning of Boats* (1929) (*L*, IV: 213).
45. Woolf, *'The Waves'*, ed. Graham, Draft I: 362 and 364.
46. I: 68.
47. Cf. Clements, who reads Bernard's and Woolf's rejection of Beethoven's heroism as unequivocal: 'Transforming Musical Sounds into Words', 164. Arianne Burford proposes Woolf is 'reconceptualizing' Dorothy Richardson's use of Beethoven in *Pilgrimage*, and also sees Woolf's rejection of 'patriarchal male composition' as unequivocal: 'Communities of Silence and Music', 273.
48. For more detail, see Clements, 'Transforming Musical Sounds into Words'.
49. i.e. in her 1905 review of Hadow's *The Oxford History of Music*.
50. Hill was the author of the second volume. II: 29 and 32–3.
51. Clements, 'Transforming Musical Sounds into Words', 172.

Bibliography

Abbate, Carolyn, *Unsung Voices: Opera and Musical Narrative in the Nineteenth Century* (Princeton: Princeton University Press, 1991).

—, *In Search of Opera* (Princeton: Princeton University Press, 2001).

Applegate, Celia and Pamela Potter, eds, *Music and German National Identity* (Chicago: University of Chicago Press, 2002).

Adorno, Theodor W., *Essays on Music*, trans. Susan H. Gillespie (Berkeley and Los Angeles: University of California Press, 2002).

—, *Philosophy of Modern Music*, trans. Anne G. Mitchell and Wesley V. Blomster (London: Continuum, 2007).

Albright, Daniel, *Untwisting the Serpent: Modernism in Music, Literature, and Other Arts* (Chicago: University of Chicago Press, 2000).

—, ed., *Modernism and Music: An Anthology of Sources* (Chicago and London: University of Chicago Press, 2004).

Aronson, Alex, *Music and the Novel: A Study in Twentieth-Century Fiction* (Totowa, NJ: Rowman & Littlefield, 1980).

Attali, Jacques, *Noise: The Political Economy of Music*, trans. Brian Massumi, foreword by Fredric Jameson, afterword by Susan McClary, *Theory and History of Literature*, vol. XVI (Minneapolis and London: University of Minnesota Press, 1985).

Barthes, Roland, *Image Music Text*, trans. Stephen Heath (London: Fontana, 1977).

Beer, Gillian, *Virginia Woolf: The Common Ground* (Edinburgh: Edinburgh University Press, 1996).

—, Malcolm Bowie and Beate Perry, eds, *In(ter)discipline: New Languages for Criticism* (London: Legenda, 2007).

Bell, Quentin, *Virginia Woolf: A Biography* (New York: Harcourt Brace Jovanovich, 1972).

—, and Virginia Nicholson, *Charleston: A Bloomsbury House and Garden* (London: Frances Lincoln, 1997; repr. 2004).

Bell, Vanessa, *Selected Letters of Vanessa Bell*, ed. Regina Marler (London: Bloomsbury, 1993).

Benson, Stephen, *Literary Music: Writing Music in Contemporary Fiction* (Aldershot: Ashgate, 2006).

Bishop, Edward, *A Virginia Woolf Chronology* (London: Macmillan, 1989).

Blissett, William, 'Wagnerian Fiction in English', *Criticism* 5.3 (1963), 239–60.

Borchmeyer, Dieter, 'The Question of Anti-Semitism', in Ulrich Müller and Peter Wapnewski, eds, *Wagner Handbook* (Cambridge, MA: Harvard University Press, 1992), 166–85.

Bowlby, Rachel, *Virginia Woolf: Feminist Destinations* (Oxford: Basil Blackwell, 1988).

—, ed., *Virginia Woolf. Longman Critical Readers* (London and New York: Longman, 2002).

Boyes, Georgina, *The Imagined Village: Culture, Ideology and the English Folk Revival* (Manchester and New York: Manchester University Press, 1993).

Bradshaw, David, 'Hyams Place: *The Years*, the Jews and the British Union of Fascists', in Maroula Joannou, ed., *Women Writers of the 1930s: Gender, Politics and History* (Edinburgh: Edinburgh University Press, 1999), 179–91.

Brett, Philip, Elizabeth Wood and Gary C. Thomas, eds, *Queering the Pitch: The New Gay and Lesbian Musicology*, 2nd edn (New York and Abingdon: Routledge, 2006).

Briggs, Julia, *Reading Virginia Woolf* (Edinburgh: Edinburgh University Press, 2006).

Bronfen, Elisabeth, *Over her Dead Body: Death, Femininity and the Aesthetic* (Manchester: Manchester University Press, 1992).

Bucknell, Brad, *Literary Modernism and Musical Aesthetics: Pater, Pound, Joyce and Stein* (Cambridge: Cambridge University Press, 2010).

Burford, Arianne, 'Communities of Silence and Music in Virginia Woolf's *The Waves* and Dorothy Richardson's *Pilgrimage*', in Jeanette McVicker and Laura Davis, eds, *Virginia Woolf and Communities: Selected Papers from the Eighth Annual Conference on Virginia Woolf* (New York: Pace University Press, 1999), 269–75.

Burgan, Mary, 'Heroines at the Piano: Women and Music in Nineteenth-Century Fiction', *Victorian Studies*, 30 (1986), 51–76.

Cameron, N. O. M., 'Shakespeare's Songs', *Gramophone*, 2.10 (March 1925), 368–70.

—, 'English Folk Songs', *Gramophone*, 3.4 (September 1925), 177–8.

—, 'English Folk Dances', *Gramophone*, 3.8 (January 1926), 372–4.

Carey, John, *The Intellectuals and the Masses: Pride and Prejudice Among the Literary Intelligentsia, 1880–1939* (London: Faber & Faber, 1992).

Carnegy, Patrick, 'The Staging of *Tristan and Isolde*: Landmarks along the Appian Way', in *Tristan & Isolde: Opera Guide* (New York: Riverrun and London: Calder/English National Opera, 1981; repr. 1993).

—, *Wagner and the Art of the Theatre* (New Haven, CT and London: Yale University Press, 2006).

Christie, Stuart, 'Willing Epigone: Virginia Woolf's *Between the Acts* as Nietzschean Historiography', *Woolf Studies Annual*, 8 (2002), 157–74.

Clarke, Stuart N., 'Dating the Action of *The Voyage Out*', *Virginia Woolf Bulletin*, 31 (May 2009), 17–21.

Clément, Catherine, *Opera, or the Undoing of Women*, trans. Betsy Wing (London: Virago, 1989).

Clements, Elicia, 'A Different Hearing: Voicing *Night and Day*', *Virginia Woolf Bulletin*, 11 (September 2002), 32–9.

—, 'Transforming Musical Sounds into Words: Narrative Method in Virginia Woolf's *The Waves*', *Narrative*, 13.2 (May 2005), 160–81.

—, 'Virginia Woolf, Ethel Smyth, and Music: Listening as a Productive Mode of Social Interaction', *College Literature*, 32.3 (Summer 2005), 51–71.

Cone, Edward T., *The Composer's Voice* (Berkeley: University of California Press, 1974).

Conrad, Peter, *Romantic Opera and Literary Form* (Berkeley and London: University of California Press, 1977).

—, *Verdi and/or Wagner: Two Men, Two Worlds, Two Centuries* (London: Thames & Hudson, 2011).

Correa, Delia da Sousa, *George Eliot, Music, and Victorian Culture* (Basingstoke and New York: Palgrave Macmillan, 2003).

—, ed., *Phrase and Subject: Studies in Literature and Music* (London: Legenda, 2006).

—, 'Performativity in Words: Musical Performance in Katherine Mansfield's Stories', *Katherine Mansfield Studies* 3 (2011), 21–34.

Crapoulet, Emilie, 'Voicing the Music in Literature: "Musicality as a Travelling Concept"', *European Journal of English Studies*, 13.1 (April 2009), 79–91.

—, *Virginia Woolf: A Musical Life. Bloomsbury Heritage* 50 (London: Cecil Woolf, 2009).

Cuddy-Keane, Melba, 'Virginia Woolf, Sound Technologies, and the New Aurality', in Pamela L. Caughie, ed., *Virginia Woolf in the Age of Mechanical Reproduction* (New York: Garland, 2000), 69–96.

—, *Virginia Woolf, the Intellectual, & the Public Sphere* (Cambridge: Cambridge University Press, 2003).

Dalhaus, Carl, *Richard Wagner's Music Dramas* (Cambridge: Cambridge University Press, 1979).

—, 'What is a musical drama?', trans. Mary Whittall, *Cambridge Opera Journal*, 1.2 (1989), 95–111.

Dayan, Peter, *Music Writing Literature, from Sand via Debussy to Derrida* (Aldershot: Ashgate, 2006).

de Mille, Charlotte, '"Turning the Earth Above a Buried Memory": Dismembering and Remembering Kandinsky', in de Mille, ed., *Music and Modernism, c. 1849–1950* (Newcastle upon Tyne: Cambridge Scholars, 2011), 182–203.

Denisoff, Dennis, 'The Forest Beyond the Frame: Picturing Women's Desires in Vernon Lee and Virginia Woolf', in Talia Schaffer and Kathy Alexis Psomiades, eds, *Women and British Aestheticism* (Charlottesville, VA and London: University Press of Virginia, 1999), 251–69.

DeSalvo, Louise A., 'A Textual Variant in *The Voyage Out*', *Virginia Woolf Miscellany*, 3 (Spring 1975), 9–10.

—, '*The Voyage Out*: Two More Notes on a Textual Variant', *Virginia Woolf Miscellany*, 5 (Spring/Summer 1976), 3–4.

—, *Virginia Woolf's First Voyage: A Novel in the Making* (London: Macmillan, 1980).

—, 'Shakespeare's *Other* Sister', in Jane Marcus, ed., *New Feminist Essays on Virginia Woolf* (London and Basingstoke: Macmillan, 1981), 61–81.

DiGaetani, John Louis, *Richard Wagner and the Modern British Novel* (Rutherford, NJ: Fairleigh Dickinson University Press and London: Associated University Press, 1978).

Dunn, Jane, *Virginia Woolf and Vanessa Bell: A Very Close Conspiracy* (London: Virago, 2000; repr. 2007).

Ehrlich, Cyril, *The Piano: A History* (London: J. M. Dent & Sons, 1976).

—, *The Music Profession in Britain Since the Eighteenth Century: A Social History* (Oxford: Clarendon, 1985).

Eisenberg, Nora, 'Virginia Woolf's Last Words on Words: *Between the Acts* and "Anon"', in Jane Marcus, ed., *New Feminist Essays on Virginia Woolf* (London and Basingstoke: Macmillan, 1981), 253–66.

Eliot, T. S., *'The Waste Land' and Other Poems* (London: Faber & Faber, 1999).

Ellis, Katharine, *Interpreting the Musical Past: Early Music in Nineteenth-century France* (Oxford: Oxford University Press, 2005).

Ellis, Steve, *Virginia Woolf and the Victorians* (Cambridge: Cambridge University Press, 2007).

Fewster, Anna, 'Bloomsbury Books: Materiality, Domesticity, and the Politics of the Marked Page', PhD Thesis, University of Sussex, 2009.

Fillion, Michelle, 'Edwardian perspectives on Nineteenth-century Music in E. M. Forster's *A Room with a View*', *Nineteenth-century Music*, 25. 2–3 (Fall/Spring 2001–2), 266–95.

—, *Difficult Rhythm: Music & the Word in E. M. Forster* (Champaign: University of Illinois Press, 2010).

Forster, E. M., *Two Cheers for Democracy. The Abinger Edition of E. M. Forster*, vol. XI, ed. Oliver Stallybrass (London: Edward Arnold, 1972).

—, *'Artic Summer' and Other Fiction. The Abinger Edition of E. M. Forster*, vol. IX, ed. Elizabeth Heine and Oliver Stallybrass (London: Edward Arnold, 1980).

—, *A Room with a View*, ed. Oliver Stallybrass (London: Penguin, 1978; repr. 1988).

Frattarola, Angela, 'Listening for "Found Sound" Samples in the Novels of Virginia Woolf', *Woolf Studies Annual*, 11 (2005), 133–59.

Friedman, Melvin, *Stream of Consciousness: A Study in Literary Method* (New Haven, CT: Yale University Press, 1955).

Froula, Christine, 'Mrs. Dalloway's Postwar Elegy: Women, War, and the Art of Mourning', *Modernism/Modernity*, 9.1 (January 2002), 125–63.

Fuller, Sophie, and Nicky Losseff, eds, *The Idea of Music in Victorian Fiction* (Aldershot: Ashgate, 2004).

Furness, Raymond, *Wagner and Literature* (Manchester: Manchester University Press, 1982).

Fursac, J. Rogues de, 'Traumatic and Emotional Psychoses: So-called Shell Shock', trans. Aaron J. Rosanoff, *American Journal of Insanity*, 75 (1918), 19–51.

Garnett, Angelica, *Deceived with Kindness: A Bloomsbury Childhood* (London: Pimlico, 1995).

Glendinning, Victoria, *Leonard Woolf: A Biography* (New York: Free Press, 2006).

Gillett, Paula, *Musical Women in England, 1870–1914: 'Encroaching on all Man's Privileges'* (Basingstoke: Macmillan, 2000).

Goldman, Jane, *The Feminist Aesthetics of Virginia Woolf: Modernism, Post-Impressionism and the Politics of the Visual* (Cambridge: Cambridge University Press, 1998).

Grand, Sarah, *The Beth Book: Being a Study of the Life of Elizabeth Caldwell Maclure, a Woman of Genius* (New York: Appleton, 1897).

Grove, George, ed., *A Dictionary of Music and Musicians*, 2 vols (London: Macmillan, 1879).

Gruber, Ruth, *Virginia Woolf: The Will to Create as a Woman* (New York: Carroll & Graf, 2005).

Hacking, Ian, 'Automatisme Ambulatoire: Fugue, Hysteria, and Gender at the Turn of the Century', *Modernism/Modernity* 3.2 (April 1996), 31–43.

—, *Mad Travellers: Reflections on the Reality of Transient Mental Illnesses* (Charlottesville, VA: Virginia University Press, 1998).

Hadow, W. H., *The Oxford History of Music, Vol. V: The Viennese Period* (Oxford: Clarendon, 1904).

Hafley, James, 'Another Note on Rachel and Beethoven in *The Voyage Out*', *Virginia Woolf Miscellany*, 4 (Fall 1975), 4.

Halliwell, Michael, 'Intrusive narrators: The representation of narration and narrators in the operatic adaptations of *The Great Gatsby* and *Sophie's Choice*', in Emma Sutton and Michael Downes, eds, *Opera and the Novel*, Special Issue of *Forum for Modern Language Studies*, 48.2 (April 2012), 222–35.

—, *Opera and the Novel: The Case of Henry James. Word and Music Studies 6* (Amsterdam and New York: Rodopi, 2005).

Haweis, H. R., *Music and Morals* (London: Strahan, 1871).

Heine, Elizabeth, 'Virginia Woolf's Revisions of *The Voyage Out*', in Virginia Woolf, *The Voyage Out: The Definitive Edition*, ed. Elizabeth Heine (London: Vintage, 1992), 399–452.

Hewitt, Thos. J. and Ralph Hill, *An Outline of Musical History*, 2 vols (London: Hogarth, 1929).

Hillis Miller, J., '*Mrs Dalloway*: Repetition as the Raising of the Dead', in Morris Beja, ed., *Critical Essays on Virginia Woolf* (Boston, MA: G. K. Hall, 1985), 53–72.

Hughes, Meirion and Robert Stradling, *The English Musical Renaissance 1840–1940: Constructing a National Music*, 2nd edn (Manchester: Manchester University Press, 2001).

Hull, Robert H., *Contemporary Music. Hogarth Essays Second Series no. 10* (London: Hogarth, 1927).

—, *Delius. Hogarth Essays Second Series no. 12* (London: Hogarth, 1928).

Humm, Maggie, *Modernist Women and Visual Cultures: Virginia Woolf, Vanessa Bell, Photography and Cinema* (Edinburgh: Edinburgh University Press, 2002).

—, *Snapshots of Bloomsbury: The Private Lives of Virginia Woolf and Vanessa Bell* (New Brunswick, NJ: Rutgers University Press, 2006).

Hussey, Mark, *The Singing of the Real World: The Philosophy of Virginia Woolf's Fiction* (Columbus, OH: Ohio State University Press, 1986).

—, 'Living in a War Zone: An Introduction to Virginia Woolf as a War Novelist', in Mark Hussey, ed., *Virginia Woolf and War: Fiction, Reality, and Myth* (Syracuse, NY: Syracuse University Press, 1991), 1–13.

—, *Virginia Woolf A to Z: A Comprehensive Reference for Students, Teachers and Common Readers to Her Life, Work and Critical Reception* (London: Cecil Woolf, 2011).

Huxley, Aldous, *Point Counter Point* (London: Vintage, 2004).

Hyde, Derek, *New-Found Voices: Women in Nineteenth-century English Music*, new edn (Ash: Tritone, 1991).

Jacobs, Peter, '"The second violin tuning in the ante-room": Virginia Woolf and Music', in Diane F. Gillespie, ed., *The Multiple Muses of Virginia Woolf* (Columbia, MO and London: Missouri University Press, 1993), 227–60.

Joyce, James, *Ulysses*, ed. Jeri Johnson (Oxford: Oxford University Press, 1993).

Kelley, Joyce E., 'Virginia Woolf and Music', in Maggie Humm, ed., *The Edinburgh Companion to Virginia Woolf and the Arts* (Edinburgh: Edinburgh University Press, 2010), 417–36.

Kater, Michael H., *The Twisted Muse: Musicians and their Music in the Third Reich* (New York and Oxford: Oxford University Press, 1997).

—, and Albrecht Reithmüller, eds, *Music and Nazism: Art Under Tyranny, 1933–1945* (Laaber: Laaber-Verlag, 2003).

King, Julia and Laila Miletic-Vejzovic, eds, *The Library of Leonard and Virginia Woolf: A Short-title Catalog* (Pullman, WA: Washington State University Press, 2003).

Kennedy, Michael, *The Works of Ralph Vaughan Williams* (London: Oxford University Press, 1964).

Koulouris, Theodore, *Hellenism and Loss in the Work of Virginia Woolf* (Farnham: Ashgate, 2011).

Kramer, Lawrence, *Classical Music and Postmodern Knowledge* (Berkeley and London: California University Press, 1995).

Lamb, Andrew, 'Les Contes d'Hoffmann', *The New Grove Dictionary of Opera. Grove Music Online. Oxford Music Online.* Oxford University Press, http://www.oxfordmusiconline.com/subscriber/article/grove/music/O008963 [accessed 4 December 2012]

Laurence, Patricia, 'The Facts and Fugue of War: From *Three Guineas* to *Between the Acts*', in Mark Hussey, ed., *Virginia Woolf and War: Fiction, Reality, and Myth* (Syracuse, NY: Syracuse University Press, 1991), 225–45.

—, 'Virginia Woolf and Music', *Virginia Woolf Miscellany*, 38 (Spring 1992), 4–5.

Large, David C. and William Weber, eds, *Wagnerism in European Culture and Politics* (Ithaca, NY: Cornell University Press, 1984).

Lawrence, D. H., *The Trespasser*, ed. Elizabeth Mansfield (Harmondsworth: Penguin, 1994).

Lee, Hermione, *Virginia Woolf* (London: Vintage, 1997).

Leighton, Angela, 'Pater's Music', *The Journal of Pre-Raphaelite Studies*, 14.2 (Fall 2005), 67–79.

—, *On Form: Poetry, Aestheticism, and the Legacy of a Word* (Oxford: Oxford University Press, 2007).

Levenback, Karen L., *Virginia Woolf and the Great War* (Syracuse, NY: Syracuse University Press, 1999).

Levin, Gerald, 'The Musical Style of *The Waves*', *Journal of Narrative Technique*, 13.3 (1986), 164–71.

Loesser, Arthur, *Men, Women and Pianos: A Social History* (London: Victor Gollancz, 1955).

Loewenberg, Alfred, *Annals of Opera 1597–1940*, 3rd edn (London: John Calder, 1978).

MacLachlan, Christopher, *Tolkien and Wagner: The Ring and 'Der Ring'* (Zurich and Zena: Walking Tree, 2012).

Majumdar, Robin and Allen McLaurin, eds, *Virginia Woolf: The Critical Heritage* (London: Routledge & Kegan Paul, 1975).

Manhire, Vanessa, '"The Lady's Gone A-Roving": Woolf and the English Folk Revival', in Jessica Berman and Jane Goldman, eds, *Virginia Woolf Out of Bounds: Selected Papers from the Tenth Annual Conference on Virginia Woolf* (New York: Pace University Press, 2001), 236–42.

—, '"Not regularly musical": Music in the Work of Virginia Woolf', PhD Thesis, Rutgers University, 2010.

—, 'Mansfield, Woolf and Music: "The queerest sense of echo"', *Katherine Mansfield Studies*, 3 (2011), 51–66.

Mansfield, Katherine, *The Collected Stories of Katherine Mansfield* (London: Penguin, 1981; repr. 2001).

Marcus, Jane, '*The Years* as Greek Drama, Domestic Novel, and Götterdämmerung [*sic*]', *Bulletin of the New York Public Library*, 80.2 (Winter 1977), 276–301.

—, 'Enchanted Organs, Magic Bells: *Night and Day* as Comic Opera', in Ralph Freedman, ed., *Virginia Woolf: Revaluation and Continuity* (Berkeley: University of California Press, 1979), 97–122.

—, *Virginia Woolf and the Languages of Patriarchy* (Bloomington and Indianapolis: Indiana University Press, 1987).

—, 'Brittania Rules *The Waves*', in Karen R. Lawrence, ed., *Decolonizing Tradition: New Views of Twentieth-Century 'British' Literary Canons* (Urbana and Chicago: University of Illinois Press, 1992), 136–62.

—, 'Thinking Back through Our Mothers', in Jane Marcus, ed., *New Feminist Essays on Virginia Woolf* (London and Basingstoke: Macmillan, 1981), 1–30.

Marcus, Laura, *Virginia Woolf. Writers and their Work*, 2nd edn (Tavistock: Northcote House, 2004).

Martin, Stoddard, *Wagner to 'The Waste Land': A Study of the Relationship of Wagner to English Literature* (London: Macmillan, 1982).

Martin, Timothy, *Joyce and Wagner: A Study of Influence* (Cambridge: Cambridge University Press, 1991).

Maurier, George du, *Trilby*, ed. Elaine Showalter (Oxford: Oxford University Press, 1995).

McClary, Susan, *Feminine Endings: Music, Gender, and Sexuality* (Minneapolis: Minnesota University Press, 1991).

McCluskey, Kathleen, *Reverberations: Sound and Structure in the Novels of Virginia Woolf* (Ann Arbor: UMI Research Press, 1983).

Meisel, Perry, *The Absent Father: Virginia Woolf and Walter Pater* (New Haven, CT: Yale University Press, 1980).

Meyer, Michael J., *Literature and Music. Rodopi Perspectives on Modern Literature* 25 (Amsterdam and New York: 2002).

Millington, Barry, *Wagner* (London: J. M. Dent and Sons, 1984; repr. 1992).

Mott, F. W., 'The Chadwick Lecture on Mental Hygiene and Shell Shock During and After the War', *British Medical Journal* 2.2950 (14 July 1917), 39–42.

Murray, Rosalind, *The Leading Note* (London: Sidgwick & Jackson, 1910).

Nancy, Jean-Luc, *Listening*, trans. Charlotte Mandell (New York: Fordham University Press, 2007).

Nicolson, Nigel, *Virginia Woolf* (Harmondsworth: Penguin, 2000).

Nietzsche, Friedrich, *'The Birth of Tragedy' and 'The Case of Wagner'*, trans. Walter Kaufmann (New York: Vintage, 1967).

Offenbach, Jacques, *Les Contes d'Hoffmann*, Nicolai Gedda, Victoria de los Angeles, Elisabeth Schwarzkopf, Gianna d'Angelo, Jean-Christophe Benoit, Ernest Blanc, Nicola Ghiuselev and George London, cond. André Cluytens (EMI Classics: Great Recordings of the Century, 1965; remastered, 2003). [sound recording]

Oxford English Dictionary, 2nd edn, 20 vols (Oxford: Clarendon, 1989).

Parry, C. Hubert, *Summary of the History and Development of Medieval and Modern European Music*, new edn (London: Novello, 1905).

Peach, Linden, 'No Longer a View: Virginia Woolf in the 1930s and the 1930s in Virginia Woolf', in Maroula Joannou, ed., *Women Writers of the 1930s: Gender, Politics and History* (Edinburgh: Edinburgh University Press, 1999), 192–204.

Pendle, Karin, ed., *Women and Music: A History* (Bloomington: Indiana University Press, 1991).

Phillips, Gyllian, 'Re(de)composing in the novel: *The Waves*, Wagnerian Opera and Percival/Parsifal', *Genre: Forms of Discourse and Culture*, 28.1–2 (Spring-Summer 1995), 119–44.

Potter, Pamela M., *Most German of the Arts: Musicology and Society from the Weimar Republic to the End of Hitler's Reich* (New Haven, CT: Yale University Press, 1998).

—, 'Music in the Third Reich: The Complex Task of "Germanization"', in Jonathan Huener and Francis R. Nicosia, eds, *The Arts in Nazi Germany: Continuity, Conformity, Change* (New York and Oxford: Berghahn, 2006), 85–110.

Pridmore-Brown, Michele, '1939–40: Of Virginia Woolf, Gramophones, and Fascism', *PMLA* 113.3 (May 1998), 408–21.

Prieto, Eric, *Listening In: Music, Mind and the Modernist Narrative* (Lincoln, NE: University of Nebraska Press, 2002).

Raitt, Suzanne, 'Virginia Woolf's Early Novels: Finding a Voice', in Susan Sellers, ed., *The Cambridge Companion to Virginia Woolf*, 2nd edn (Cambridge: Cambridge University Press, 2010), 29–48.

Reed, Christopher, *Bloomsbury Rooms: Modernism, Subculture, and Domesticity* (New Haven, CT and London: Yale University Press, 2004).

Riley, Matthew, ed., *British Music and Modernism, 1895–1960* (Farnham: Ashgate, 2010).

Rosen, Charles, *Sonata Forms* (New York and London: W. W. Norton, 1980).

Rosenbaum, S. P., '*Voyage Out* Variant No. 2', *Virginia Woolf Miscellany*, 5 (Spring/Summer 1976), 4.

Sadie, Stanley, ed., *The New Grove Dictionary of Music and Musicians*, 2nd edn, 29 vols (London: Macmillan, 2001).

Sarker, Sonita, 'An Unharmonious Trio? Georg Lukás, Music, and Virginia Woolf's *Between the Acts*', in Diane F. Gillespie and Leslie K. Hankins, eds, *Virginia Woolf and the Arts: Selected Papers from the Sixth Annual Conference on Virginia Woolf* (New York: Pace University Press, 1997).

Schröder, Leena Kore, 'Tales of Abjection and Miscegenation: Virginia Woolf's and Leonard Woolf's "Jewish" Stories', *Twentieth-Century Literature*, 49.3 (Autumn 2003), 298–327.

Schulze, Robin Gail, 'Design in Motion: Words, Music, and the Search for Coherence in the Works of Virginia Woolf and Arnold Schoenberg,' *Studies in the Literary Imagination*, 25.2 (Fall 1992), 5–22.

Sherard, Tracey, '"Parcival in the forest of gender": Wagner, Homosexuality, and *The Waves*', in Ann Ardis and Bonnie Kime Scott, eds, *Virginia Woolf: Turning the Centuries: Selected Papers from the Ninth Annual Conference on Virginia Woolf* (New York: Pace University Press, 2000), 62–9.

Shockley, Alan, *Music in the Words: Musical Form and Counterpoint in the Twentieth-century Novel* (Farnham: Ashgate, 2009).

Shone, Richard, *Bloomsbury Portraits: Vanessa Bell, Duncan Grant and their Circle* (London: Phaidon, 1976; repr. 1993).

Silver, Brenda R., *Virginia Woolf's Reading Notebooks* (Princeton: Princeton University Press, 1983).

Slovak, Jocelyn, 'Mrs Dalloway and Fugue: "Songs without Words, Always the Best . . ."' http://www.unsaidmagazine.com/magazine/issue2/Slovak.html [accessed 15 February 2010].

Solie, Ruth A., *Music in Other Words: Victorian Conversations* (Berkeley and Los Angeles: University of California Press, 2004).

—, 'No "Land without Music" After All', *Victorian Literature and Culture*, 32 (2004), 261–76.

Southworth, Helen, 'Perfect Strangers? Virginia Woolf and Francesca Allinson', *Virginia Woolf Bulletin*, 39 (January 2012), 16–23.

Spalding, Frances, *Roger Fry: Art and Life* (St Albans and London: Granada, 1980).

Spotts, Frederic, *Bayreuth: A History of the Wagner Festival* (New Haven, CT: Yale University Press, 1994).

Stewart, Garrett, *Reading Voices: Literature and the Phonotext* (Berkeley and Los Angeles: California University Press, 1990).

Sutton, Denys, ed., *Letters of Roger Fry*, 2 vols (London: Chatto & Windus, 1972).

Sutton, Emma, *Aubrey Beardsley and British Wagnerism in the 1890s* (Oxford: Oxford University Press, 2002).

—, '"Putting Words on the Backs of Rhythm": Woolf, 'Street Music', and *The Voyage Out*', in Peter Dayan and David Evans, eds, *Rhythm in Literature after the Crisis in Verse*, Special Issue of *Paragraph: A Journal of Modern Critical Theory*, 33.2 (July 2010), 176–96.

—, 'Shell shock and hysterical fugue, or why Mrs Dalloway likes Bach', in Trudi Tate and Kate Kennedy, eds, *Literature and Music of the First World War*, Special Issue of *First World War Studies*, 2.1 (2011), 17–26.

—, 'Wagner in the Visual Arts', in Nicholas Vazsonyi, ed., *The Cambridge Wagner Encyclopedia* (Cambridge: Cambridge University Press, forthcoming).

—, 'Flying Dutchmen, Wandering Jews: Romantic Opera, Anti-Semitism and Jewish Mourning in *Mrs Dalloway*', in Adriana Varga, ed., *Virginia Woolf and Music* (Bloomington: Indiana University Press, forthcoming).

Trubowitz, Lara, 'Concealing Leonard's Nose: Virginia Woolf, Modernist Antisemitism, and "The Duchess and the Jeweller"', *Twentieth-century Literature*, 54.3 (Fall 2008), 273–306.

Vaget, Hans Rudolf, 'Hitler's Wagner: Musical Discourse as Cultural Space', in Michael H. Kater and Albrecht Reithmüller, eds, *Music and Nazism: Art Under Tyranny, 1933–1945* (Laaber: Laaber-Verlag, 2003), 15–31.

Verga, Ines, *Virginia Woolf's Novels and their Analogy to Music. English Pamphlet Series* 11 (Beunos Aires, 1945)

Wagner, Richard, *Tristan and Isolda. Lyric Drama in 3 Acts by Richard Wagner. Rendered into English in exact accordance with the original*, trans. H. and F. Corder (London and Leipzig: Breitkopf & Härtel, [1882]).

—, *Wagner's 'Ring of the Nibelung': A Companion*, trans. Stewart Spencer with commentaries by Barry Millington, Elizabeth Magee, Roger Hollinrake and Warren Darcy (London: Thames and Hudson, 1993).

—, *The Prose Works of Richard Wagner*, trans. William Ashton Ellis, 8 vols (London: Kegan Paul, Trench, Trübner, 1893–9; repr. Lincoln, NE and London: Nebraska University Press, 1993–5).

—, *Selections from 'Tristan und Isolde', 'Tannhäuser', [and] 'Götterdämmerung' [and the] Wesendonck-Lieder*, Eileen Farrell, New York Philharmonic, cond. Leonard Bernstein (Sony Classical, The Royal Edition, 100: 1962, 1968 and 1971; remastered 1993). [sound recording]

Wearing, J. P., *The London Stage 1890–1899: A Calendar of Plays and Players*, 2 vols (Metuchen, NJ and London: Scarecrow, 1976).

—, *The London Stage 1900–1909: A Calendar of Plays and Players*, 2 vols (Metuchen, NJ and London: Scarecrow, 1981).

—, *The London Stage 1910–1919: A Calendar of Plays and Players*, 2 vols (Metuchen, NJ and London: Scarecrow, 1982).

—, *The London Stage 1920–1929: A Calendar of Plays and Players*, 3 vols (Metuchen, NJ and London: Scarecrow, 1984).

—, *The London Stage 1930–1939: A Calendar of Plays and Players*, 3 vols (Metuchen, NJ and London: Scarecrow, 1991).

Weiner, Marc A., *Richard Wagner and the Anti-Semitic Imagination* (Lincoln, NE and London: Nebraska University Press, 1995).

Weliver, Phyllis, *Women Musicians in Victorian Fiction, 1860–1900: Representations of Music, Science and Gender in the Leisured Home* (Aldershot: Ashgate, 2000).

—, *The Musical Crowd in English Fiction, 1840–1910: Class, Culture and Nation. Palgrave Studies in Nineteenth-Century Writing and Culture* (Basingstoke: Palgrave Macmillan, 2006).

—, 'A Score of Change: Twenty Years of Critical Musicology and Victorian Literature,' *Literature Compass*, 8.10 (2011), 776–94.

Whitworth, Michael H., *Virginia Woolf: Authors in Context* (Oxford: Oxford University Press, 2005).

Wiley, Christopher, '"When a Woman Speaks the Truth About her Body": Ethel Smyth, Virginia Woolf, and the Challenges of Lesbian Auto/Biography', *Music & Letters*, 85.3 (August 2004), 388–414.

Wolf, Werner, *The Musicalization of Fiction: A Study in the Theory and History of Intermediality* (Amsterdam and Atlanta, GA: Rodopi, 1999).

Woolf, Leonard, *Sowing: An Autobiography of the Years 1880 to 1904* (Orlando: Harvest/ Harcourt Brace Jovanovich, 1960).

—, *Growing: An Autobiography of the Years 1904–1911* (Orlando: Harvest/ Harcourt Brace Jovanovich, 1961).

—, *Beginning Again: An Autobiography of the Years 1911 to 1918* (Orlando: Harvest/ Harcourt Brace Jovanovich, 1975).

—, *Downhill all the Way: An Autobiography of the Years 1919–1939* (London: Hogarth, 1968).

—, *The Journey Not the Arrival Matters: An Autobiography of the Years 1939–1969* (Orlando: Harvest/ Harcourt Brace Jovanovich, 1969).

—, *Letters of Leonard Woolf*, ed. Frederic Spotts (London: Bloomsbury, 1992).

—, *The Wise Virgins: A Story of Words, Opinions and a few Emotions* (London: Persephone, 2003).

—, *The Village in the Jungle* (London: Eland, 2005).

Woolf, Virginia, *Melymbrosia: An Early Version of 'The Voyage Out'*, ed. Louise A. DeSalvo (New York: The New York Public Library, 1982).

—, *The Voyage Out*, ed. Lorna Sage (Oxford: Oxford University Press, 2001).

—, *The Voyage Out: The Definitive Edition*, ed. Elizabeth Heine (London: Vintage, 1992).

—, *Night and Day*, ed. Suzanne Raitt (Oxford: Oxford University Press, 1999).

—, *Jacob's Room*, ed. Sue Roe (London: Penguin, 1992).

—, *Mrs Dalloway*, ed. David Bradshaw (Oxford: Oxford University Press, 2000).

—, *To the Lighthouse*, ed. David Bradshaw (Oxford: Oxford University Press, 2006).

—, *Orlando: A Biography*, ed. Brenda Lyons (London: Penguin, 1993).

—, *The Waves*, ed. Kate Flint (London: Penguin, 2000).

—, *The Waves. The Cambridge Edition of the Works of Virginia Woolf*, ed. Michael Herbert and Susan Sellers, with research by Ian Blyth (Cambridge: Cambridge University Press, 2011).

—, *'The Waves': The Two Holograph Drafts*, ed. J. W. Graham (Toronto and Buffalo: Toronto University Press in association with the University of Western Ontario, 1976).

—, *Flush: A Biography* (London: Vintage, 1991).

—, *The Years*, ed. Hermione Lee (Oxford: Oxford University Press, 1999).

—, *Between the Acts*, ed. Gillian Beer (London: Penguin, 2000).

—, *'A Room of One's Own' / 'Three Guineas'*, ed. Michèle Barrett (Harmondsworth: Penguin, 1993).

—, *Roger Fry: A Biography* (London: Vintage, 2003).

—, *A Haunted House: The Complete Shorter Fiction*, ed. Susan Dick (London: Vintage, 2003).

—, *'The Mark on the Wall' and Other Short Fiction*, ed. David Bradshaw (Oxford: Oxford University Press, 2001).

—, *'Carlyle's House' and Other Sketches*, ed. David Bradshaw (London: Hesperus, 2003).

—, *Moments of Being: Autobiographical Writings*, 2nd edn, ed. Jeanne Schulkind (London: Pimlico, 2002).

—, *The Platform of Time: Memoirs of Family and Friends*, ed. S. P. Rosenbaum (London: Hesperus, 2007).

—, *The Common Reader*, ed. Andrew McNeillie, 2 vols (London: Vintage, 1984–6).

—, *The Essays of Virginia Woolf*, ed. Andrew McNeillie (vols I–IV) and Stuart N. Clarke (vols V–VI), 6 vols (London: Hogarth, 1986–2011).

—, *A Passionate Apprentice: The Early Journals 1897–1909*, ed. Mitchell A. Leaska (Orlando: Harcourt Brace Jovanovich, 1990).

—, *The Diary of Virginia Woolf*, ed. Anne Olivier Bell assisted by Andrew McNeillie, 5 vols (Harmondsworth: Penguin, 1977–84).

—, *The Letters of Virginia Woolf*, ed. Nigel Nicolson and Joanne Trautmann, 6 vols (New York: Harcourt Brace Jovanovich, 1975–1980).

—, and Vanessa Bell with Thoby Stephen, *Hyde Park Gate News: The Stephen Family Newspaper*, ed. Gill Lowe (London: Hesperus, 2005).

Zhou, Mi, 'Sublime Noise: Reading E. M. Forster Musically', PhD thesis, University of Cambridge, 2009.

Zimmerman, Nadya, 'Musical Form as Narrator: The Fugue of the Sirens in James Joyce's *Ulysses*', *Journal of Modern Literature* 26.1 (2002), 108–18.

Zimring, Rishona, 'Suggestions of Other Worlds: The Art of Sound in *The Years*', *Woolf Studies Annual*, 8 (2002), 125–56.

Zuckerman, Elliott, *The First Hundred Years of Wagner's 'Tristan'* (New York and London: Columbia University Press, 1964).

Zwerdling, Alex, *Virginia Woolf and the Real World* (Berkeley and Los Angeles: University of California Press, 1986).

Index